# The Three Faces of Leadership

# The Three Faces of Leadership

## Manager, Artist, Priest

MARY JO HATCH
MONIKA KOSTERA
ANDRZEJ K. KOŹMIŃSKI

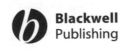

Blackwell
Publishing

© 2005 by Mary Jo Hatch, Monika Kostera, and Andrzej K. Koźmiński

BLACKWELL PUBLISHING
350 Main Street, Malden, MA 02148-5020, USA
108 Cowley Road, Oxford OX4 1JF, UK
550 Swanston Street, Carlton, Victoria 3053, Australia

The right of Mary Jo Hatch, Monika Kostera, and Andrzej K. Koźmiński
to be identified as the Authors of this Work has been asserted in accordance
with the UK Copyright, Designs, and Patents Act 1988.

First published 2005 by Blackwell Publishing Ltd

*Library of Congress Cataloging-in-Publication Data*

Hatch, Mary Jo.
The three faces of leadership : manager, artist, priest / Mary Jo Hatch,
Monika Kostera, Andrzej K. Koźmiński.
p. cm.
Includes bibliographical references and index.
ISBN 1-4051-2259-5 (hardcover : alk. paper) – ISBN 1-4051-2260-9 (pbk. : alk.
paper) 1. Leadership. 2. Executive ability. 3. Creative ability in
business. 4. Business ethics. 5. Industrial management–Moral and ethical
aspects. I. Kostera, Monika, 1963– II. Koźmiński, Andrzej K. III. Title.

HD57.7.H3886 2005
658.4′092–dc22
2004007687

A catalogue record for this title is available from the British Library.

Set in Sabon 10/12$^{1}$/$_{2}$pt
by Graphicraft Limited, Hong Kong
Printed and bound in the United Kingdom
by MPG Books, Bodmin, Cornwall

The publisher's policy is to use permanent paper from mills that operate a sustainable
forestry policy, and which has been manufactured from pulp processed using acid-free
and elementary chlorine-free practices. Furthermore, the publisher ensures that the text
paper and cover board used have met acceptable environmental accreditation standards.

For further information on
Blackwell Publishing, visit our website:
www.blackwellpublishing.com

# Contents

Contents

# Preface

Our premise for this book is the observation that business leadership is evolving in the directions of artistry and spirituality, a trajectory that falls under the broad headings of organizational and management aesthetics. This is because businesses today, more than ever, need creativity to match the pace of change in their dynamic competitive environments, and ethics to attain and maintain the legitimacy necessary to attract resources and keep them flowing. As a result, the meaning of business leadership is changing from control, in the traditional sense of supervision and domination, to the use of powers derived from mythological consciousness including the powers of creative imagination and inspiration. We believe that this trajectory is apparent in the series of interviews with chief executive officers (CEOs) conducted by *Harvard Business Review* (*HBR*) between 1989 and 1998 that inspired this book and that it indicates the need to make creativity and ethics more explicit foundations of leadership training in the years to come.

We do not believe that successful twenty-first-century business leaders will completely abandon the techniques and ambitions of their predecessors, but they will need to redefine their purpose such that they do not focus all their energy on achieving pre-ordained goals like rationality, profitability, and excellence. Instead, we sense that the best business leaders will pursue inspiration to places where there is no safe haven or predetermined outcome. They will seek heroic adventures that demand even more creative courage, imagination, vision and ethical discipline than was practiced by their counterparts in the twentieth century. Artists question old assumptions and offer new ideas that awaken passions and motivate change by revealing the beauty and ugliness of our humanity. Priests exercise the discipline required to champion such a quest, to set an example of virtue, integrity, and devotion to purpose for others to follow. While the leader who emphasizes control is literally followed, the leader who is inspired will be emulated, which is why art and religion are such good developmental models for training a new generation of business leaders. Developing the potential to be worthy of the emulation accorded to admired artists and priests is the new meaning we see being given to the old idea of leadership and it is the meaning we explore in this book.

Although no one can isolate and deliver wisdom, inspiration or creativity as if they were technical skills or knowledge tools to be learned in an intellectual way, we feel that we all share the obligation to train future leaders in ways that enliven their human potential. Most would agree that it is within the remit of educational establishments to offer all contending perspectives on a subject and we would like to see this remit extended to the subject of business leadership. In particular we would like to see leadership studies embrace the aesthetic approach to business leadership we promote throughout this book.

Through the aesthetic approach we hope that concern for developing leaders with the virtues and values that build character will be renewed. We advocate giving attention not only to the character of admired leaders, but to the symbolic expressions they give to the qualities we so admire, such as what they say and do and the policies and practices they establish to lead their businesses. Furthermore, we believe that using the interpretive methods of literary and dramatic criticism we adopt in this book to influence and assess the policies, practices, and behavior of business leaders will give a much-needed boost to developing imagination for and ethics in business.

The aesthetic perspective on leadership that this book presents features clear and accessible explanations of aesthetic philosophy applied to key aesthetic concepts including creativity, imagination, courage, virtue, inspiration, faith, and ethics. It presents techniques for developing aesthetic sensibilities and the associated capacities of storytelling, dramatizing, and mythmaking that express these sensibilities and communicate them to others. Finally, it links aesthetic leadership practices to several important and perennial themes of business education and the development of human potential: organizational culture, change, vision, values, and identity.

Below you will find three versions of the story of how *The Three Faces of Leadership: Manager, Artist, Priest* came into being.

## Mary Jo Hatch's Tale

When Monika Kostera and Andrzej Koźmiński first contacted me and proposed the project that became this book, they had an idea about resisting Western managerialism. In what I have come to regard as a Polish proclivity to subversion, they initially wanted to slow or even stay the advance of Western management consultants whom Monika, in one of her published papers (I thought astutely), had cast as modern crusaders. They were each responding to their mutual observation of the rapid encroachment of Western values and practices into Polish management territory.

As they were both affiliated with the first MBA program to be offered in Poland, Monika and Andrzej were perhaps as conscious as anyone of the extent to which publications from the West were having a profound influence on Polish

management students (Andrzej was a founder of the Leon Koźmiński Academy of Entrepreneurship and Management (LKAEM) that offered Poland its first MBA program, and Monika, who had been his student, was a member of the Academy's founding faculty). Of the management publications being widely read at the time, *HBR* stood out as deserving special attention both because of its popularity in Poland, and because of its renown in the West, which was rapidly spreading to eastern Europe. Having already cast the "invasion" of Western management consultants in terms of a religious crusade, it was not surprising that Monika and Andrzej saw Harvard as the Vatican of Western management faith – their own students were indeed reading *HBR* with the same religious zeal that reborn Christians bring to the Bible.

Monika and Andrzej approached me wondering if I, as an American who had been living long enough in Europe (nearly a decade by this time), shared their wish to critically examine the Western management model offered by *HBR* in its series of interviews with CEOs. The interviews had become especially popular among their students and Monika and Andrzej suggested that these materials could provide us with data. A method close to my heart – text analysis – would guide our approach. I was intrigued. They invited me to spend three days at a hunting lodge in Wetlina (in southeast Poland just across the mountains from the Ukraine). I flew to Warsaw and Monika and I drove to the remote hunting lodge where we were to meet Andrzej.

When we initially agreed to work together, we decided the best way to begin was for each of us to read all the *HBR* interviews we would use before arriving in Wetlina. It was then that we decided to start with the November 1989 issue and read all the interviews published from then right up to the current time (September 1998). We chose to begin with November 1989 because that date followed closely upon the first free election in the post-communist world that took place in Poland in June 1989 and the subsequent fall of the Berlin Wall. These events initiated the full opening of central and eastern European countries to business news and publications from the West (not to mention to hordes of invading consultants). We studiously did our reading and thus we arrived in Wetlina unaware that we were in for a big surprise.

In contrast to our critical intention to deconstruct the texts and reveal their propagandistic wiles, we each independently reached the similar conclusion that we had met extraordinary individuals in the pages of these interviews – true leaders whose stories and examples taken *en masse* represented some of the best management thinking available. We had expected to find much to resist; instead we were seduced! Discovering that this had happened to each of us independently caused us first surprise, then ironic laughter, and then commitment to discovering how these texts had worked their magic on us. Thus was born the book you hold in your hand. In it we have attempted to share with you what inspired us. Through it we hope to unmask some of the magic that makes leadership work.

MJH, Jablonna, Poland
June 29, 2001

## Andrzej K. Koźmiński's Tale

Between 1990 and 1997 I was leading a "double life" of sorts, sharing my time between Poland and the University of California Los Angeles where I taught one trimester a year in the Anderson Graduate School of Management. In Poland I was busy promoting Western-style management education, teaching, and building "the business school of my dreams." This involved a variety of activities including consulting, advising Polish and foreign managers, researching companies undergoing painful processes and dramatic change in the whole region of central and eastern Europe. In Los Angeles I was able to reflect upon my hectic activities and to attempt to make sense out of them. I also had an obligation to my students, who wanted me to explain what was going on in Poland and in other "transition economies."

To meet this expectation I wrote a book *Catching Up? Organizational and Management Change in the Ex-Socialist Bloc* that was published in 1993 by SUNY Press. In addition, I wrote two articles presenting ethnographic research on the transformation of management in the post-communist countries of central and eastern Europe. My UCLA students, however, and managers whom I was meeting in the US and in other places where my travel took me, were quite inquisitive and continued asking more and more penetrating questions, all pertaining to one underlying issue: Why? Why did change take such an enormous variety of forms and paths? What made managers behave so differently producing such dramatically different results?

To answer these puzzling questions, Monika Kostera and I decided to look for the values embraced by Polish managers. To interpret the results of our empirical research we used a metaphor of theatrical styles (Kostera & Koźmiński 1995; 2001). We visualized managers as performing in four different types of theatrical shows (Japanese Kabuki theater, modern European and American theater, happenings and global shows). When using this metaphor we discovered that in performing their roles, some managers exhibited much more than simple value-driven behavior; they showed aesthetic feel with marked spiritual undertones. We asked ourselves if this was in some way time and place specific. We suspected that this was not the case, and to investigate this matter we needed to look for behavioral patterns of archetypal Western managers.

Looking for clues I started reading the interviews with the world's leading CEOs published by *Harvard Business Review*. During my last trimester at UCLA (in 1996) I started analyzing them using the framework of theatrical performances that I developed with Monika. When I sent her this analysis we both came to the conclusion that we needed a co-author with a strong Western (preferably American) background and skills in quantitative analysis and cultural empathy as well as imagination and the ability and willingness to work in a multi-cultural team. "Such people do not exist!" I said to Monika, but I had to change my mind soon after reading Mary Jo Hatch's book *Organization Theory*, and meeting her personally at the Standing Conference on Organizational Symbolism (SCOS) at LKAEM in

Warsaw in 1997. Mary Jo agreed to join us and our journey into the aesthetic and spiritual dimensions of management began, along with our adventure with the most outspoken managers of the Western world. For me, this book is a road map of this journey. We hope you enjoy it!

PS. I am writing these words one day after the attack on the World Trade Center in New York. I intuitively feel that spiritually and aesthetically sensitive management can prevent such acts of barbarism. Management is building reality from pieces of chaos. Reality has to make sense, not only practically and financially but also spiritually and aesthetically. Otherwise chaos wins.

AKK, Warsaw, Poland
September 12, 2001

## Monika Kostera's Tale

We all had met before and liked and respected each other as persons and authors but did not meet all together until 1997, when Andrzej and I were hosting an international conference. We were supposed to open the conference on a reflective note and thought of Mary Jo – for some reason it seemed like a great idea to invite her to be the third host, even though she did not work at our Academy. But we both immediately figured that she would be a great person to join in the conversation at the conference. And the conversation continued even after the conference ended – when we thought of working on a book together.

The idea was Andrzej's – to see what the *HBR* interviews with famous CEOs were about and whether they had a message for East European readers. As I saw it, we started to work with them with a positive intent to look for powerful metaphors and ideas that had the potential to move people in different parts of the world.

It was clear to me that management was not just about making money and that there was much more to it than met the eye of the average East European consumer of the mid-1990s. While the Polish business press, which I had repeatedly analyzed, was pretty straightforward and utilitarian as well as managerialist (in the traditional sense) in its rhetoric and declared orientation, the CEOs interviewed by *HBR* talked about beauty, passion, and vision. While Polish mass media dropped topic after topic from its cultural program, the CEOs talked in a cultured way and consciously tried to charm the reader. The ironic part was that, according to the Polish media, Poland and the rest of Eastern Europe should, after the fall of the Berlin Wall, try to imitate the West as best they could. Why not, I thought, if we use the right language – like the powerful language of the CEOs – the imitation process may actually become a creative route. Who knows where it leads?

As you can see from our individual contributions to this preface, the three of us had different ideas and perspectives, as well as different assumptions about this project. But we were all willing to talk and test our assumptions. I believe that the conversation we had was really a good one, both constructive and enjoyable. I wish

the same to the reader who is now welcome to join in – not as a passive receiver of this book but as our interlocutor.

<div align="right">

MK, Warsaw, Poland
January 3, 2002

</div>

## Acknowledgements

We are grateful to Philip Mirvis and Gib Akin for their many helpful comments and suggestions on drafts of our manuscript. Suzy Wetlaufer, former editor-in-chief of the *Harvard Business Review*, was generous with her time in giving us her views of the CEO interviews and of *HBR*'s role in shaping managerial culture. Our editor, Rosemary Nixon, was supportive and helpful throughout the editing process. We are also grateful to the Leon Koźmiński Academy of Entrepreneurship and Management Research Fund for financing our seven working meetings in Poland.

# 1

# The Aesthetics of Leadership

There is always some art introduced in anything produced by man ... [but when man] does things for the pure idea of functional reasoning, then the idea of aesthetics disappears.

*(Marcel Duchamp, quoted in Naumann 1999: 20)*

## Management as Art and Aesthetics

When scientific management was proposed by the American engineer Frederick Taylor nearly one hundred years ago, no one imagined that professional managers would one day take over business enterprises in the name of rationality (Shenhav 1999). In fact, when the famous Scottish economist Adam Smith, author of *An Inquiry into the Nature and Causes of the Wealth of Nations* (1937), advised against the use of management in industry, most of his contemporaries agreed with him. They believed that management would destroy invention by undermining freedom and honesty. This belief was one reason why scientific management was so strongly resisted at its inception during the early years of the twentieth century. Eventually, however, engineers demonstrated that professional management brought functional efficiency and with it came financial gain. Thus the profession of management as we recognize it today was built on faith that those with rationality would win the quest for profit. This quest became the central theme of the story of business in the twentieth century.

As life in the twentieth century unfolded, more and more business leaders aligned themselves with the rational principles and practices of the profession of management. Eventually, both managers and their societies came to take this body of rational principles and practices for granted. Another way to put this is to say that the profession of management became institutionalized. However, while the twentieth century saw the profession develop into an institution through many profitable applications of technical rationality and functional efficiency, it is likely that the twenty-first will witness substantial changes in business, and, along with it, management will have to change. The litany of sources of change includes: constant

technological advances (e.g., computing power, the Internet, broadband); global-ization of markets, and the democratization of politics with consequent rearrange-ment or, in some cases, the total disappearance of political, economic and cultural boundaries and barriers; not to mention some recent flagrant abuses of executive privilege.

The broad question this book addresses is, in what directions is the institution of management moving in response to these changes? To address this question we begin with the recognition that modern management has not merely been institu-tionalized within societies that depend upon business, its members are rapidly form-ing a global culture of their own. That is, through the dissemination of the MBA degree and other professionalizing activities, along with the democratization that has accompanied the spread of capitalism in the late twentieth century, the interests and activities of managers in many countries are merging into a discernable culture with its own values, norms and institutionalized practices. In a world where many international businesses control more resources than some countries possess, the global influence of this emerging managerial culture is practically a foregone con-clusion. Anticipating the direction in which such an influential group moves is of obvious importance.

In preparing to write this book, we looked to the most influential members of the emerging global culture of managers for indications of the direction of changes underway. Ironically, we found that although business acumen is glorified within this culture – the legacy of its twentieth-century trajectory – its celebration is increas-ingly taking on a distinctly artistic and moral tone. That is, our study of some of the most influential business leaders of the late twentieth century indicates that the artful side of management is reasserting itself. So it was that we set our sights on a fresh look at an old theme: the art of management. What makes it fresh is that we take up where Adam Smith left off, expanding the domain of art into that of aesthetics. Put another way, we seek not only to reassert the artful side of manage-ment, but to explore the aesthetics of business leadership as well.

Aesthetics is a term that covers interests ranging from the creative to the ethical. We employ the term here in this wide-ranging sense – when we refer to the aesthetics of business leadership we assert the values of artistic courage and an ethical conscience and place these alongside the value for technical rationality associated with scientific management. We also use the term aesthetics to highlight the humanistic aspect of leadership and to emphasize the importance for society of using virtue as a criterion for judging business leaders. Thus, we aim to complement the now institutionalized technical/rational face of the manager with the faces of the artist and the priest, asserting that business leaders must show all three faces in order for their culture to realize its potential as a dominant and positive influence on the world.[1]

---

[1]  Howard Gardner, author of *Leading Minds* (1995) and other books, first proposed the need to combine intellect with creativity and ethics to achieve greatness in leadership. His work was based on analysis of world leaders such as Gandhi, Martin Luther King Jr, Churchill and J.F. Kennedy, and artists such as Picasso. One of his major findings is that great leaders throughout history have relied upon

## The Three Faces of Leadership

The managerial face of business leadership is probably already familiar to you because the majority of books and articles on business speak to this subject. Technical management is what rational organizing is all about and it is the distinctive achievement of the institution of management in the twentieth century. Painted with a very broad brush, technical management is what business leaders try to achieve when they introduce order into a chaotic world, for example with financial reporting and control systems, inventory management, or with processes for enhancing and monitoring manufacturing or service output and quality.

Although ordering is necessary and useful, successful managers today recognize that it should not become an obsession; it should not deny opportunities to change organizational realities by unleashing some of the organization's creativity. While creativity may threaten current ways of organizing, it is also a source of invention, innovation, and lust for life. We need some of the chaos creative forces bring to the world to constantly challenge our technically ordered organizations so that they do not stagnate or fail to adapt to changing circumstances. Since creative forces are generally most strongly felt by artists, we characterize the second face of leadership as the face of the artist.

Doing new things calls forth that which was hitherto untamed. Through the undermining of old beliefs and the release of imagination, artists open us to chaos in both destructive and productive ways, and thereby to the opportunities for change that chaos brings. This may be one reason why, historically, artists often operated outside the boundaries of social normalcy and were generally left to their own devices. Today, however, successful artists are accorded the status of icons in Western society. Just as artists have become revered role models, acceptance of the chaotic element introduced by creativity has spread to the point where we sense that business is ready to acknowledge its need for chaos openly. The increasing interest shown by managers in complexity theory as a means to explain organizational change or to develop new business models attests to this readiness. Furthermore, many businesses require as much creativity from their leaders as does the art world from its artists. It may not be merely ironic that a counter-movement is taking place in the art world, which has become progressively more business-like (Becker 1982). These opposing movements within the realms of business and art suggest to us that the forces of creativity and rationality are aligning, confirming the importance of both the faces of the manager and the artist for business and art alike.

Unfortunately for business leaders, change often feeds fear. Artists and other innovators may be feared precisely because people are afraid that the chaos they unleash will negate all the benefits of order and the security it brings. The forces of

stories to inspire their followers. *The Three Faces of Leadership* extends Gardner's research from the domains of politics, science and art, to that of business and broadens the examination of stories to include drama and myth.

order need to be willing to embrace the forces of chaos, otherwise we get religious wars and the burning of heretics. Leadership plays an important role here. Inspired leaders can find the courage to embrace an organization's creative potential and the change it brings. This is because inspiration not only fuels the imagination required to change, it also reassures us so that we can face our fears.

Business leaders innovate when they play the role normally occupied by artists, but to fully realize their leadership potential they need to spark creativity in others as well as convince them to accept innovations they did not themselves produce. Functioning as role models and influencers, managers take on the character of priests, especially when they symbolize the deep values and beliefs that nourish their organizational cultures in order to make their members comfortable with change. This ability to inspire the courage to change while providing comfort and reassurance to face the fears change brings is the third face of leadership, the face of the priest. Showing the face of the priest reassures organizational members that needed changes will not destroy cherished beliefs but will instead keep them alive.

For the reasons given we argue that creativity and inspiration, alongside technical rationality, will define effective business leadership in the years to come. Table 1.1 defines and compares the three faces of leadership: manager, artist, priest.

In preparing this book we looked closely into the faces of the artist and the priest. We explored how a group of highly successful business leaders revealed these two aesthetic faces even as they celebrated their managerial (i.e., technical/rational) achievements. We found that when we looked into the artist's face, we saw creativity play out in organizational dramas and heard its voice in managerial storytelling. When we looked into the face of the priest we saw ancient myths inspiring business leaders with the virtues that shaped the roles they play on behalf of their organizations, including their roles as storytellers and dramatists.

You may be wondering in what ways thinking about aesthetics enhances our understanding of business leadership. Can businesses benefit from aesthetic

Table 1.1 The three faces of leadership: manager, artist, priest

|  | Manager | Artist | Priest |
| --- | --- | --- | --- |
| Common description | Disciplined | Curious | Empathic |
|  | Rational | Independent | Ethical |
| Core competences | Organizing | Creating | Inspring |
|  | Controlling | Provoking | Comforting |
| Helps others develop their | Skill | Imagination | Faith |
| Psychic domain | Intellect | Emotions | Soul |
| Type of vision | Strategic | Artistic (sensory) | Transcendent (metaphysical) |
| Source of power and influence | Expertise | Originality | Purity |
| Heroic ideal | Decision-maker | Innovator | Savior |

interpretations of what their leaders do? Since art and ethics are the natural realms of creativity and inspiration, we believe that describing how respected business leaders show the faces of the artist and the priest will help you develop your potential for creative and inspirational business leadership and will help us to explain how and why the institution of management is changing.

## Art and Religion at the Foundation of Cultures

On September 13, 1940 four young Frenchmen climbed into a dark hole in the ground near Lascaux, France. One of them, 17-year-old Marcel Ravidat, had discovered the place a few days earlier when his dog tumbled down a sink hole that led into a cave. Now, armed only with an oil lamp, the boys descended into its depths. By dim lamplight they saw a beautiful array of cave paintings that turned out to be some of the oldest known aesthetic remains of humankind, since dated to between 16,000 and 17,000 years of age. Some scholars, such as David Lewis-Williams from whose account in *The Mind in the Cave* we borrow liberally here, have suggested that, not only do the cave paintings of Lascaux indicate the artistry of Paleolithic man, but that this site was also used to perform the magical rites and ritual dances that developed over the course of human history into what we now know as religion.

Hard evidence such as that presented by Lascaux and other ancient cultural sites makes the existence of art and religion in the lives of the first humans practically incontrovertible. This evidence was important for anthropologists working at the time of these discoveries because it settled a longstanding argument about whether human aesthetic consciousness developed before or after more practical concerns. American cultural anthropologist Melville Herskovits (1956: 347) made the point vividly when he concluded over a decade after the discovery of Lascaux that: "Man contrived to surmount the requirements of daily life and achieve aesthetic gratification long before he was agriculturalist or herder, or knew how to make pots or weave cloth". The Polish philosopher Leszek Kolakowski (1984) similarly concluded that a spiritual dimension is embedded in every culture, and a culture's oldest assumptions are those harboring its sacred beliefs. For those who study management or practice it today, the recognition that management is forming its own culture suggests that artistic and spiritual forces are as important for contemporary business leaders as they were for the Upper Paleolithic humans who decorated the caves in France and practiced magical rituals within them.

An elite group of people typically carries out the most important functions of any society and many would argue that those who lead businesses increasingly dominate the elite of our times. Evidence can be found in the observation that today's business leaders are listened to like the religious leaders of earlier times and have much the same political influence that their religious counterparts had in earlier periods of history, such as when popes helped to choose kings and emperors. Consider, for example, the global popularity of books and articles written by GE's

former chief executive officer (CEO) Jack Welch and Bill Gates of Microsoft, or the political influence business leaders such as Ross Perot and Dick Cheney have exercised in the US.

At a time when many are mourning the loss of ethnic cultures across the globe, it is interesting to consider the possibility of new cultures emerging. In our view, managerial culture represents possibly the most influential new cultural formation in the world today. Recent rapid changes in the economic sectors of most parts of the world suggest that business provides a contemporary cultural frontier and that those most actively engaged in culture building along this frontier are its entre- preneurs and executives. We argue that, if this is the case, it is sensible to look to these business leaders to see who is manifesting the world's newest expressions of the artist and priest. If our conjecture is correct, business leaders today will carry the ancient aesthetic traditions of humanity forward into the cultural frontiers of the twenty-first century. Our intention, therefore, is to shine a spotlight on the creative and ethical practices of some of the world's most successful business leaders in whose images the modern institution of management is being reformed.

## Taking an Aesthetic Approach to Leading

The fact that many anthropologists and religious scholars now believe that, wherever culture is found, art and religion will attend its founding, means to us that man- agerial culture should also evidence artistic and spiritual origins. It is our ambition to explore the world of business in a way that appreciates the artistry and ethics of the global managerial culture that began to emerge in the roaring 1990s. We will conduct our exploration using interviews with CEOs that appeared in the pages of the *Harvard Business Review* (*HBR*) from 1989 to 1998. We believe that these interviews will provide evidence of the aesthetic aptitude of the CEOs featured. It is our intention to reveal the faces of the artist and the priest in business leadership through presentation and discussion of their example.

Managerial culture as captured by the *HBR* interviews with CEOs is worth study- ing for at least two reasons. First, the most advanced managerial techniques, eagerly copied and rapidly proliferating throughout the world, are deeply rooted in the managerial culture these interviews both represent and help to create. The inter- views conducted and published by *HBR* reveal the aesthetics of business leadership that are an integral part of those management techniques. Second, knowledge of managerial culture helps us to understand the changing nature of the institution of management as the pendulum swings from the extreme of technical rationality to its realignment with creativity and ethics.

We chose 1989 as a starting point because much that is associated with the twentieth century was upended in that year. For instance, this is roughly the date of the return of central and eastern Europe to the free world. It was also the year when Asian markets were liberalized, several countries in South America became

democracies, the International Monetary Fund (IMF) bailed out Argentina, and Nelson Mandela was released from prison. Thus 1989 marks the opening of major regions of the world for economic development, the spread of democracy, and the emergence of contemporary managerial culture as a global phenomenon. These events suggest 1989 as an interesting point to begin investigating the changing nature of the contemporary institution of management and mark a good spot to seek out the origins of this new cultural formation.

To produce this book we conducted text analysis of the 30 interviews published in *HBR* between 1989 and 1998 (see Table 1.2) and interviewed *HBR*'s then editor-in-chief, Suzy Wetlaufer. This set of interviews represents managerial culture as it was expressed by the CEOs that *HBR*'s editors selected from mostly American companies based on their success on some dimension or dimensions of organizational performance (e.g. financial success, technological or organizational innovation, globalization). In regard to the face of the priest, we feel that it is important to note that none of the CEOs who appeared in the *HBR* interviews we read has been implicated in the corporate scandals that took place during the first years of the twenty-first century. Just as a few Catholic priests during the same period gave the priesthood a black eye, we feel the business scandals only increase the need to re-establish the virtues of business leadership.

## Overview of the Book

The French artist, Marcel Duchamp, who became notorious by signing a urinal and putting it on display at an art exhibition, devoted a considerable part of his life to works that he called Readymades. Readymades, like the urinal, were manufactured objects purchased in hardware or department stores. By signing and displaying these everyday objects as works of art, Duchamp provocatively asked the question: What is art? Duchamp claimed his Readymades took aesthetics out of art. In our view, however, instead of taking aesthetics *out* of art, Readymades offer a way to find aesthetics *in* the everyday world of manufactured objects. Duchamp's Readymades showed that aesthetic consciousness – manifested in the creativity of our approach to life and its things – can transform the most mundane object, even a urinal, into art. Thus, although art helps us to develop our aesthetic consciousness, art is not *in* the object unless and until aesthetic consciousness is applied to it. Art, artist, and an appreciative audience emerge together in aesthetic consciousness.

The capacity to enjoy beauty and the possibility to experience wonder are present in all of us. While it may be difficult for us to agree on a single standard of beauty that explains all aesthetic pleasures, or one set of pleasures that defines a universal canon of the beautiful, we can nonetheless appreciate one another's aesthetic experience and thereby connect with it and with each other. This co-appreciation of beauty and wonder may lie behind the existence of art and religion at the foundation of all cultures. It might be that the development of human community and

**Table 1.2** Chronological list of *HBR* interviews with CEOs (1989–1998)

| Date | Company and CEO | Title of interview |
|---|---|---|
| Nov–Dec 1989 | Motorola, George Fisher | Customers Drive a Technology-Driven Company |
| Mar–Apr 1990 | Raychem, Paul Cook | The Business of Innovation |
| May–Jun 1990 | Thomson, Alain Gomez | From National Champion to Global Competitor |
| Jul–Aug 1990 | Compaq, Rod Canion | Consensus, Continuity, and Common Sense |
| Sep–Oct 1990 | Levi Strauss, Robert Hass | Values Make the Company |
| Nov–Dec 1990 | Citicorp, John Reed | Citicorp Faces the World |
| Jan–Feb 1991 | Bell Atlantic, Raymond Smith | Championing Change |
| Mar–Apr 1991 | ABB, Percy Barnevik | The Logic of Global Business |
| Jul–Aug 1991 | VW, Carl Hahn | A European Platform for Global Competition |
| Sep–Oct 1991 | USAA, Robert McDermott | Service Comes First |
| Nov–Dec 1991 | TRW, Frederick Crawford | A Voice of Experience |
| Jan–Feb 1992 | Softbank, Masayoshi Son | Japanese-style Entrepreneurship |
| Mar–Apr 1992 | Stride Rite, Arnold Hiatt | Building Corporate Character |
| May–Jun 1992 | Globe Metallurgical, Arden Sims | Trial-by-fire Transformation |
| Jul–Aug 1992 | Nike, Phil Knight | High-performance Marketing |
| Sep–Oct 1992 | Xerox, Paul Allaire | The CEO as Organizational Architect |
| Nov–Dec 1992 | Greater SE Community Hospital, Tom Chapman | Profits with a Purpose |
| Mar–Apr 1993 | Swatch, Nicolas Hayek | Message and Muscle |
| Sep–Oct 1993 | Vitro, Ernesto Martens | From Complacency to Competitiveness |
| Nov–Dec 1993 | Silicon Graphics, Ed McCracken | Mastering Chaos at the High-tech Frontier |
| Mar–Apr 1994 | Whirlpool, David Whitwam | The Right Way to Go Global |
| Nov–Dec 1994 | Merck, Roy Vagelos | Medicine, Management and Mergers |
| Mar–Apr 1995 | Allied Signal, Lawrence Bossidy | The CEO as Coach |
| Sep–Oct 1995 | Nature Conservancy, John Sawhill | Surviving Success |
| Nov–Dec 1995 | British Airways, Sir Colin Marshall | Competing on Customer Service |
| Jan–Feb 1997 | Monsanto, Robert B. Shapiro | Growth through Global Sustainability |
| Sep–Oct 1997 | British Petroleum, John Browne | Unleashing the Power of Learning |
| Jan–Feb 1998 | Ahlström, Krister Ahlström | Governing the Family-owned Enterprise |
| Mar–Apr 1998 | Dell Computer, Michael Dell | The Power of Virtual Integration |
| Jul–Aug 1998 | Eni, Franco Bernabè | Leadership When There Is No One to Ask |

society provides a positive reason for association (i.e., mutual wonder and delight) as a counterbalance to the usual negative motives used to explain collective life (e.g. physical necessity, fear, psychological or social dependence). We believe the aesthetic approach to business leadership develops positive reasons for organizing that will inspire the greatest performances that organizations and their leaders can achieve.

Leaders work with people, and the most successful of them inspire the creativity of their employees. To fully understand people in organizations, we contend that you need to add the perspective that aesthetic consciousness brings to rational models of human motivation and performance. This is because aesthetics enables you to address and inspire people in ways that lie beyond rationality – emotion, creativity, and ethics. In taking up this point of view, we offer an aesthetic perspective that we hope will enable you to see management as art, and the well-managed firm as beautiful. As the American philosopher David White (1996: 204) put it:

> if there is an art to management, and if in general the purpose of art is to create objects of beauty, then it would follow that whatever is managed, if managed well, must be in some sense beautiful. For how could the art of managing be practiced in the fullest sense if the product of that art remains neutral and colorless in value – in short, a product without an essential sense of beauty?

This way of looking at management is not new, and aesthetic philosophy is much older still. Nonetheless, using the category of beauty for interpreting organizational life is only a very recent interest for those who study management. According to Italian organization theorist Pasquale Gagliardi (1996: 566):

> When I call the aesthetic experience "basic", I intend the adjective also in the literal sense of the term, to indicate, that is, that the aesthetic experience is the basis of other experiences and forms of cognition which constitute the usual object of organizational studies and that it therefore implies that aesthetic experiences have a profound influence on the life and performance of the organization.

This book aims at addressing two aesthetic domains of business leadership: the creative and the ethical. We claim that both are crucial to the functioning of organizations, and that, to fulfill their creative and ethical responsibility, business leaders need to develop the faces of the artist and the priest. In this book, we offer ideas and examples to show how successful business leaders use these faces, and suggest ways for you to develop the artist and the priest in your own leadership style and practices.

In taking previously published interviews as our data material, we of course invoke well-known biases. These interviews were carefully constructed to bring to light desirable aspects of business leadership so they hide from view other, perhaps less seemly, characteristics and practices. We are not particularly concerned to give a complete rendition of everything business leaders do. Instead we play the role of an appreciative audience for the aesthetic performances of CEOs presented by

*HBR.* We believe that the interview material is worthy of unreconstructed appreciation precisely because art, drama, and myth can only be fully experienced through appreciative engagement. Thus we adopt the willing suspension of disbelief that literary critics claim is necessary to appreciate literature.

Because we ourselves were inspired by these performances and believe others have been or will be as well, we offer our interpretations as an invitation and a provocation to you to make your own interpretations and thereby to engage your aesthetic sensibilities with those of the successful business leaders portrayed in the *HBR* interviews. Thus our approach is consistent with our focus on the faces of the artist and the priest in that it departs significantly from the rationalistic methods of scientific management or positivistic science. We use instead an appreciative method built upon the academic practice of textual interpretation that traces to hermeneutics and reader response theory. However, we will provide enough raw material from the interviews that you will be able to make interpretations based in other perspectives as well, and we encourage you to do this.

**Figure 1.1** The three faces of leadership all rely upon the practices of aesthetic management

In this book we will reveal the aesthetic means that a group of business leaders employed in their narrative, dramatic, and mythological constructions of themselves and their organizations (see Figure 1.1). While, in their ordinary awareness, managers are perhaps more prone to dwell on technical than on aesthetic matters, we will show that creativity and ethics are practiced everyday by some of the world's most highly regarded business leaders. In the following chapters we will illustrate this via the stories and types of theatrical production CEOs employ as well as in their complicity with the mythologizing by which managerial culture expresses itself through them.

In Chapter 2 we will use storytelling to describe one aesthetic practice in which the CEOs in the *HBR* interviews revealed the faces of the artist and the priest. Chapter 3 looks at the ways in which the CEOs dramatized their organizations and their own leadership, not only through their responses to critical events, but also in their day-to-day activities, many of which revealed the faces of the artist and the priest. In Chapter 4 we describe how we believe the CEOs embodied mythic gods in their interviews and how the interviews themselves celebrated the god-like virtues the CEOs displayed as well as revealing their vices. There we will explain how the expression of virtues and vices reproduces the ancient myths of the gods the CEOs represent. In Chapter 5 we continue to examine the mythology theme by exploring how Harvard Business School and the *HBR* editors acted as mythmakers to bestow god-like status on the CEOs they selected for their interviews. Chapter 6 presents our final reflections on the aesthetics of business leadership and proposes ideas for aligning the face of the manager with the faces of the artist and the priest in your leadership style and practice.

# 2
# Telling Business Stories

Do not despise the story. A lost gold coin is found by means of a penny candle; the deepest truth is found by means of a simple story.

*(Anthony de Mello, SJ)*

Storytelling occurs in all human cultures. It takes precedence on many occasions from a child's bedtime, to sharing a campfire, birthday parties, reunions, retirement dinners, wakes, funerals, and all manner of gatherings, whether joyful or mournful. In the *Poetics*, the ancient Greek philosopher Aristotle argued that stories make it possible for us to share our world. When we imitate the dramas of our lives by weaving them into plots peopled with characters, we participate in the means by which human culture is built, sustained, and changed. When we repeat stories to others we help to form collective memory retained as cultural myths and sagas, or in our contemporary times, as history, novels, films, and other "poetic" forms.

As such a pervasive and significant aspect of our humanity, it is not surprising to find storytelling in business organizations and we were not surprised to find the chief executive officers (CEOs) interviewed by *Harvard Business Review* (*HBR*) telling their stories. What *did* surprise us was the volume of stories we found in the interviews and the prominence they were given by those who told them. The CEOs used their stories for many purposes, for instance to illustrate their points, convey their corporate or personal history and to celebrate acts of courage, their own or those of others. In approaching the storytelling done by the CEOs, we winnowed out the stories and read them as a set. When we did so, we saw more clearly how the interviews had attracted and seduced us – their sheer aesthetic force made characters come alive and events more memorable. The depth of meaning that stories convey exerts enormous persuasive power and exudes the capacity to create and inspire, suggesting that storytelling reveals the faces of the artist and the priest. We decided to look carefully at the stories contained in the *HBR* interviews to see if we could find some clues to how the CEOs worked their magic on us.

We begin this chapter with a discussion of what storytelling is. We then describe organizational storytelling and distinguish it from non-storytelling, contrasting the

modes of speaking that emanate from the rational manager's face with the voices of the artist and the priest. We then describe four basic types of stories and illustrate each of them with examples of organizational stories from the interviews with CEOs. We finish the chapter by drawing a few conclusions about the three faces of business leadership in regard to storytelling and suggest how you can develop the faces of the artist and the priest by telling your stories to others.

## Stories and Storytelling

Stories have been with us for a long time. They are found in ancient religious books such as the Bible, the Torah and the Qur'an, in the myths and epics of ancient Greek culture, and in Aristotle's philosophy. Aristotle discussed five topics in relation to narrative that are relevant to storytelling today: mythos (plot), mimesis (re-creation), catharsis (release), phronesis (wisdom), and ethos (ethics).[1]

In regard to *mythos* or plot, Aristotle's *Poetics* suggests that every life is a story in that it has a beginning (birth) and an ending (death) with lots of subplots in the middle (the events that comprise that life). As the Scottish moral philosopher Alasdair MacIntyre (1984: 117) stated in *After Virtue*: "It is not just that poems and sagas narrate what happens to men and women, but that in their narrative form poems and sagas capture a form that was already present in the lives which they relate." In this sense, stories have the same structure that life has, and this is what gives humans their natural affinity for stories. This affinity, in turn, encourages people to tell stories to one another and, having heard hundreds of stories while growing up, individual members of a culture easily come to see their life as a story having significance, at least for them. They then craft that story into an identity with which they live out their time together with others whose stories affect theirs and whose own stories are in turn affected. Combined, these stories produce and leave their trace on human history and culture. And since stories pervade identity, culture, and history, their central themes serve as foundations for our self-development and self-understanding.

*Mimesis*, or re-creation, points to the fact that life becomes storied when it is given a verbal accounting. This accounting is not simply a repetition of events, actions, and consequences, it is tailor-made to the circumstances of the telling. Stories are re-creations of the circumstances and events of life, not simply copies of them; they are inventions as much as they are imitations. But the links between life lived and life told are highly complex because these two domains are mutually influential. One lives, and tells and hears stories about that living, but the stories that one hears and tells affect how one subsequently lives. Thus mimesis means repetition with a license to shape the story as it in turn shapes the teller.

---

[1] Our presentation of Artistotle's five topics is based on Kearney (2002: 129–56).

*Catharsis* or release is the purging of pain, guilt, shame, or horror that a story can provide to its hearer by invoking their pity or fear. It offers a functional explanation for the pervasiveness of storytelling in all societies, an insight into the powerful and documented therapeutic effects of storytelling (storytelling has been used as a successful therapy with victims of torture as well as neurosis, and in family therapy). Since all humans suffer negative emotional states at some point in their lives, all humans respond to the catharsis offered by hearing an appropriate story of the suffering of others. For example, by being put in the role of spectator, we can vicariously confront the terrible events that befall humans. The distance the story places between us and those about whom the story is told allows us to appreciate the larger meaning of events and actions, thus allowing us to confront, come to terms with, and purge our fears. But stories also invoke our sympathetic and empathic emotions, and thus involve us in the lives of others. Through our empathic responses stories connect us to fellow sufferers of life's indignities and sorrows and thus reassure us that, when we suffer similar fates, we do not suffer alone. Because catharsis gives us the capacity to see life through the eyes of others, it can also open us to novel approaches to life and to new ideas. The capacity to face our fears and empathize with others grows through exposure to stories.

*Phronesis*, or wisdom, involves human understanding and practical reason. In pursuit of phronesis, we are not after the precise truth science seeks, but rather the realism of ordinary experience; a truth that emerges from reflection on our shared existence and its meaning. Aristotle argued that, to be appreciated, stories have to make even their most impossible claims seem realistic. They do this by invoking phronesis, or the linking of the particulars of everyday events and personal experiences with the universals of human existence.

*Ethos*, or ethics, refers to the use of stories to communicate values and to help listeners learn to distinguish right from wrong. MacIntyre claims that we construct the subject that is our self, that is, we construct our identity, by telling the story of our life. His model of narrative selfhood suggests that even in a postmodern world of fragmented being, and even after the denial of subjectivity, there will still be selves to tell and hear stories. These storytelling selves will continue to construct actors who make choices and take actions with consequences and who will ultimately pass judgment on all of these matters. In their capacity to communicate judgments, storytelling taps the ethical dimension of our being even as it serves to help us determine the criteria by which we judge.

In addition to the functions of catharsis and ethos described by Aristotle and MacIntyre, many other functions claimed for storytelling have been offered. Other functions that have been associated with storytelling include: entertainment (Georges 1969; 1980; 1981) and amusement (Campbell 1975); reassurance and the stimulation of imagination (Bettelheim 1976); justification and explanation (Levi Strauss 1978); providing information, advice and warning (Van Dijk 1975); building and retaining memory (Martin 1982); and making experience meaningful and renewing a sense of community (Boje & Dennehy 1993: 156). Gabriel (2000: 9) claimed that entertainment is the most important function in business settings in that it crosscuts

all the other functions. This is not to suggest that stories are mere embellishments grafted onto the serious activity of business, but rather to argue that entertainment is a more important part of business than we normally realize.[2]

One final point to keep in mind about storytelling is that it requires both teller and listener; thus, like drama, both an audience and an actor are necessary. And it is in the act of listening as much as in the telling, that the sharing of experience is produced and justified. As we put ourselves into a story through empathic listening, we share not only in the events the story recreates, but also in the emotions the story evokes. While sharing the events that are told is largely a vicarious experience, and thus keeps us once removed from participation in those events, the emotions that listening evokes are immediate and engage us directly. The emotional impact of a story is what draws us in – personal emotional engagement on the part of the listener is a hallmark of a good tale and its telling.

## Storytelling in Organizations

Contemporary organizations have their own stories. Organizational stories, according to Yiannis Gabriel (2000: 22), author of *Storytelling in Organizations: Facts, Fictions, and Fantasies,* are "narratives with simple but resonant plots and characters, involving narrative skill, entailing risk, and aiming to entertain, persuade, and win over". Swedish organizational researcher Barbara Czarniawska and German sociologist Bernward Joerges (1996) tell us further that story plots consist of beginnings and endings held together by action, and that stories are not only entertaining for their audiences, they are challenging for their tellers. This last point emphasizes the active nature of stories – they are told – hence our focus on story*telling*.

When an organizational story entertains us, we are drawn into aesthetic consciousness by the pleasure that storytelling brings. This aesthetic consciousness – which amounts to being sensitive to beauty and pleasure as well as to ethical responsibility – introduces the faces of the artist and the priest. As Italian organization theorist Antonio Strati (1992: 576) explained it:

> The charm of a story, the beautiful way in which things are described, the evocations and the allusions conjured up by the listener in order to understand the story, and its seductiveness, these notions leave fragments of organizational life impressed on the . . . memory. If the story is beautifully told, it will act as a structuring factor in the relation between [individual and organization] and transform these encounters into part of the organization's aesthetic dimension.

Most important of all, because organizational storytelling is an act involving others, it has the power to engage and thereby the possibility to motivate and

---

[2]  This point is the thesis of *The Experience Economy* (1999), a popular book by B. Joseph Pine and James H. Gilmore.

inspire. Hummel (1992: 36) described the factor of engagement in storytelling this way:

> as we hear the story, the events are not meaningful for us until we have read ourselves into the story. This is how a story, and the telling of it, functions in a fundamentally different way for us than does analytic science. Analytic science gives us events that are objective fragments of reality and leaves us detached from them; the story always gives us events that are intended to be coherent and meaningful to us, something that cannot happen unless we become involved with them. . . . Engagement in this context means participating with others – the story-teller as well as those about whom the story is told.

Not all business talk, of course, is storytelling. Business leaders speak in many ways, and only when they invoke the face of the artist or priest do they involve storytelling. Furthermore, not every business leader is a storyteller (Appendix A lists the CEOs from the *HBR* interviews and gives the story type of each story they told, showing considerable variability in their use of storytelling). In explaining the factor of engagement, Hummel distinguished storytelling from analytic modes of discourse and Gabriel distinguished storytellers from those who do not or cannot spin a yarn. Since becoming a storyteller rests on knowing how to tell a good story, it also depends on knowing what a story is and what a story is not.

All CEOs interviewed by *HBR* displayed considerable skill in rational explanation and factual description, which are both non-storytelling modes of speaking. The contents of the interviews were quite varied, of course, and interesting in their own right, for example as displays of the CEOs' considerably different theories of their businesses, and as illustrative descriptions of their management practices. For example, Lawrence Bossidy of Allied Signal, stated in his interview (Tichy & Charan 1995: 75):

> There's no rocket science to strategy, but you're supposed to know where you are, where your competition is, what your cost position is, and where you want to go. If you don't know those four things, you're not going to have a very effective effort. We needed a better database – key measures such as market share over time, for example – followed by issue identification and some options for solutions. So we put together a corporate training program to expose people to a more external way of approaching strategy. The result is a much more exciting conversation. And after every strategy review we have, I write a three- or four-page letter to the business head that solidifies our agreement about what the issues are and what we're going to do about them.

In this example, a theory of how Allied Signal uses strategy is intertwined with a description giving some of the factual details of implementing this strategy in relation to developing and using a better database. While the description leans toward storytelling when Bossidy introduces a sequence ("So we put together a corporate training program" which he claims was followed by "a more exciting conversation"), there is not enough detail given in the text to constitute a plot. What is more, the

use of "we" and "these people" scarcely contributes any characterization. Thus, this passage remains in a non-storytelling mode even though it drifts toward storytelling at the point mentioned above.

Another typical example of non-storytelling comes from British Airways' Sir Colin Marshall (Prokesch 1995: 103). Offering first his theory and then some description to illustrate it, Marshall stated:

> There are two sides to the business equation: costs and revenues. Any business that focuses on one at the expense of the other is going to pay very heavily. You can't walk away from the fact that if somebody can do the job better and cheaper, you have a problem and you have to do something about it. But you can do it without undermining the fabric of what you have built up. When business conditions got tough in recent years, we did not take meat cleavers to our product. We did not reduce costs indiscriminately. We did not reduce the quality of the wine. We did not stop investing in airport lounges and in training people. We continued making that investment despite the fact that it would have been very easy not to. Why is it that people prefer to fly business class with us? It's because our product is better.

As in the example from the Bossidy interview, Marshall begins in strictly non-storytelling mode with a statement of his theory of the business of British Airways ("You can't walk away from the fact that if somebody can do the job better and cheaper, you have a problem and you have to do something about it. But you can do it without undermining the fabric of what you have built up"). Then, like Bossidy, Marshall drifts toward storytelling when he says "When business conditions got tough in recent years" followed by several examples of things BA did not do and concluding with a sales pitch ("Why is it that people prefer to fly business class with us? It's because our product is better"). Although some elements of this latter sequence are story-like, they do not constitute a story because no specifics are given about the events alluded to, no characters are introduced, and no plot tying the elements together ever emerges.

This brings us to the matter of distinguishing storytelling from non-storytelling modes of speaking. According to Gabriel (2000: 26–7), stories can be distinguished from other forms of speech such as opinions, reports, and proto-stories. These terms are defined in Table 2.1.

The difficulty with applying Gabriel's scheme lies in the ambiguity of distinguishing stories from other forms in practice. This difficulty can be seen with reference to the Bossidy and Marshall examples given above. Or it can appear in the form of terse stories (Boje 1991), which are stories that are so well known in an organization that they can be invoked in memory simply by making a terse reference to them (e.g., "you know the Dallas story"). Using Gabriel's scheme, where shall we draw the line between opinions (e.g., presented in the first part of both examples), reports or proto-stories (e.g., offered in the second part of both examples), and stories? The distinction between storytelling and non-storytelling modes of speaking depends upon your interpretation of whether a certain bit of speech or passage of text contains a plot and characters as well as referring to a specific incident, and whether

**Table 2.1** A sampling of narrative types

| | |
|---|---|
| Opinions | A personal statement of belief or feeling |
| | Generalized assertions based on grounds short of proof |
| | Lack a particular incident around which to construct a story |
| Reports | Historical accounts in which accuracy is valued above effect and where evidence is weighed |
| | Attitude taken is factual, meaning is not read into the events reported |
| | No poetic license is accorded to the reporter who invites an instrumental rather than a symbolic interpretation of events reported |
| Proto-stories | Story fragments, sometimes highly charged emotionally and symbolically but plots are rudimentary |
| | Lack character development, do not have beginning, middle and ending, though they may have a subset of these elements |
| | May be overlooked by listeners who have not heard them previously because they take a great deal for granted; make reference to a story in lieu of actually telling it |
| Stories | An account of past or imaginary events in which effect is valued over accuracy, facts presented play a poetic rather than informational role |
| | Have plots with beginning, middle and ending that involve characters; in the most highly valued stories characters undergo some type of development |
| | In order to appreciate them, the listener enters a state known as the willing suspension of disbelief via which the storyteller is granted poetic license |

it gives symbolic expression to experience. As the distinction is ultimately a matter of interpretation, we might best represent Gabriel's modes of speaking on a continuum ranging from opinions to stories with gray areas between the categories, and admit that it will sometimes be difficult to reach consensus with others about whether a particular instance of speech is a story or not.

There are practical reasons to distinguish non-storytelling and storytelling modes of speaking. One is that without this distinction, the contribution of storytelling to business leadership might go unnoticed – after all, much of what is known about top executives comes in the form of opinions, reports, and sound-bites. However, once we realized that executives use stories to complement their other modes of expression, we began to suspect that some of the power attributed to the rational and analytic face of CEOs in fact is rooted in their storytelling skill. In this chapter we examine *how* storytelling contributes to effective business leadership by looking more closely at the stories and storytelling of the CEOs in their roles as managers, artists, and priests.

The idea to distinguish storytelling and non-storytelling modes of speaking and thinking lies close to a distinction the American psychologist Jerome Bruner (1986; 1990; 1996) made between narrative and logico-scientific ways of knowing (what, in the earlier quotation, Hummel called "analytic science"). The important

observation made by Bruner was that narrative thinking can be observed in children before they develop logico-scientific reasoning (we appreciate stories long before we learn to make coherent arguments or try our hand at rational analysis). Bruner argued that narrative thinking is more deeply rooted in our past and therefore engages us in a way that logico-scientific discourse never will. The invocation of narrative thinking through storytelling may well be a means of connecting us, not only to our childhood, but also to one another, through those deeper roots of human culture discussed by anthropologists in relation to the presence of art and religion at the beginning of human history (see Chapter 1). One practical implication of this possibility is that storytelling can make a meaningful connection between business leaders and those they seek to influence – a connection that can help them to address that often problematic translation of strategic vision into action.

Bruner's distinction between narrative and logico-scientific thinking relates to the difference between fact and fiction that is often raised in relation to storytelling. In providing entertainment, stories invite repetition and embellishment, but they do *not* demand or even welcome factual verification (Gabriel 2000; Kearney 2002). Stories depend upon the willing suspension of disbelief (listeners collude with the storyteller in making even fantastic claims seem plausible so long as they contribute to a good story) and upon poetic license (e.g., to alter and embellish details of the story for effect). As such, they are often accused of being non-factual. But this alone is insufficient to deny their claims to truthfulness. Understanding this may help to explain both the allure and the power of storytelling. In freeing speech from the constraints of pure reason and fact, the storyteller causes listeners to recognize similarly experienced moments in their lives, inciting a deep resonance and potential emotional bond between storytellers and their audiences, and among audience members as well. This is what literary critics refer to as verisimilitude. In other words the story "rings true" because it allows listeners to resonate with the personal truths invoked by storytellers (notice the similarity to Aristotle's notions of mimesis and phronesis).

Whether the preponderance of logico-scientific modes of speaking (i.e., rational explanation and factual description) in the interviews with CEOs is an artifact of being interviewed for an *HBR* article, or a manifestation of everyday managerial discourse, is difficult to say on the basis of the texts alone. However, based on our own experiences and those of others who study managers in organizational settings (e.g., Watson 1994), we do not find the preponderance of non-storytelling talk surprising. Nor, we suspect, will you. After all, ever since Frederick Taylor's scientific management was accepted, managers have been encouraged to adopt the language of logico-scientific reasoning. Today it seems quite natural for them to use this language. In fact it is our contention that most business writing in the twentieth century turned the face of the manager toward logico-scientific reasoning and thereby institutionalized its use.

That said, it becomes even more surprising that we found such frequent use of storytelling intertwined with non-storytelling modes of speaking in the pages of the *HBR* interviews. In the interviews we read, an explanation for a business decision

or action was often followed by a story to illustrate the point. However, just as often the CEO would begin with a story that would trigger an explanation or factual description. This intertwining of explanation and story is exemplified by Rod Canion of Compaq Computer who told interviewer Alan Webber (1990: 116):

> Low turnover is fundamental and distinguishes Compaq from lots of our competitors, particularly those in Silicon Valley. Most companies would point to compensation plans, stock options, and bonuses as the way to keep people. But really, they're just there to prevent people from being stolen. It's not pay or stock or anything else that keeps people. It's whether they're drained or charged emotionally. People stay when they enjoy what they do. People stay when they fit the culture, when they are working in a supportive, helpful environment, and when they get fulfillment from working as part of a winning team. It's dissatisfaction, more than money, that leads people to leave. I learned that lesson early in my career. Halfway through my tenure at Texas Instruments, I left to go to a small company here in Houston. I did it basically for money. I wasn't looking for a job. They came to me and showed me all this money, and I thought, "That's great." Six months later, I realized that there's a lot more to life than money. Money is important, but even more important is enjoying what you do and being really excited about it. So I went back to TI. Compaq wouldn't be here today if TI had continued to be a challenging place to work. I enjoyed most of my career there, and it was only in the last year that I really got frustrated. That was the critical factor in my deciding to leave.

In this example, explanation ended and a story began when Canion stated "Halfway through my tenure at Texas Instruments, I left to go to a small company here in Houston." The story ended with "So I went back to TI." Then a partial or proto-story was told about Canion's leaving TI to form Compaq. Because it followed the story of Canion's hiatus from TI, we assume this proto-story would take a similar shape if Canion were to tell it in full. But all Canion really told us is that frustration at TI caused him to decide to leave, which points back to his theory about employee turnover that began the passage. At this point in the interview Canion returned to the non-storytelling mode and continued to the topic of growth. This example clearly shows the intertwining of different modes of speaking in the interviews and shows the interpretive subtlety needed to make the distinctions between types suggested by Gabriel and underscored by Bruner and Hummel, not to mention the ability needed to weave stories and their power into everyday talk within your organization.

Even though the distinction between storytelling and non-storytelling modes of speaking may at times be difficult to pin down, we hope you will see that it is worth the effort. The value of storytelling is most likely to become clear to you when you tell stories yourself and notice their effects on others. Our basic proposition is that when you engage in storytelling, even where it is intertwined with rational explanation and factual description, it brings emotional and sometimes ethical dimensions to organizational life, as is clearly the case with this story told by Paul Allaire of Xerox (Howard 1992: 118):

My favorite example comes from the management team that designed our new architecture. Here is a group of 20 people who, more than anybody in the company, have internalized the new approach to running things. And yet, when it came to deciding how to organize the business divisions, this group recommended that we start with the business division staff – the head of personnel, head of finance, etc. – and that the staff help each division president choose his or her key operating people. In other words, they immediately fell back into the traditional top-down, functional approach.

I said, "Hold on. Don't we have it backwards? I thought we were trying to run this business by the line? Why would you select the staff people to help the presidents select the line? Why don't we do it just the reverse? Who are the key line managers required to run these businesses? We can help them figure that out. They don't need to hire individual staff people to do that. We can help them put their team leaders in place, then the presidents and their team leaders can decide together what kind of staff support they need."

At first, they were convinced I was wrong. But as we talked it through, you could see a shock of recognition go through the group. Everyone started to say, "Well, I think we just violated one of the principles with this recommendation." They began to realize that it would send exactly the wrong message to the organization. Finally, somebody said to the person who had made the original proposal, "I think you'd better back off on this. Not only is he the boss, but I think he is right on this one."

The faces of the artist and the priest appear in Allaire's story in the celebration of the team's creativity in designing a new structure and processes for Xerox (what Allaire called architecture) and the managers suddenly realized that their redesign also applied to them, which inspired them to transcend their old ways of thinking and being in Xerox. If you engage with it, the storytelling mode adopted by Allaire will draw you into this experience by allowing you to feel the change the managers made. This is a demonstration of the power of storytelling to take you there, to give you the vicarious experience that transfers cultural knowledge from storyteller to listener.

There was an enormous range of storytelling in our sample of interviews. The 30 CEOs interviewed by *HBR* editors told anywhere from 1 to 13 stories. Anchoring the multiple storytelling end of this continuum were three CEOs for whom storytelling overshadowed explanation as the primary mode of speaking in their interviews – the storytelling voices of these individuals were so strong we took to calling them storytelling CEOs.

One of the three storytelling CEOs was Frederick Crawford of TRW, a gifted yarn spinner who demonstrated a strong proclivity to moralize. Listen to this accomplished storyteller spin a tale (Dyer 1991: 116):

When I took over our Detroit plant, it was having a terrible time coming out of the recession after World War I. The year before, it had lost more money than it brought in revenue – some kind of record, I think. I was sent to Detroit with orders to close the plant or sell it.

When I got there, I spent a lot of time talking to the employees, and I was surprised to find that they had no idea that anything was wrong. The place was operating

without discipline, so everything was careless. People came late and loitered in the rest rooms. We produced as much scrap as we did finished product.

Well, my interests being human, I felt so sorry for these people that I decided to tell them what my orders were. The only place large enough for all of us to meet was the parking lot out front. I rented some undertaker's chairs and got some canvas to hang over the fence to keep the public from looking in, and then I got up on a soapbox and told the employees the condition of the plant and what I was supposed to do about it. I'll never forget the look of shock and disappointment on their faces when I said the company wanted to close the plant.

Then, on impulse, I said, "if I disobey orders and try to save this plant, how many of you will go all out to help me?" Every hand went up. Then I said, "Wait a minute. Do you know what you're voting for? If you vote yes, that means you'll be here on time and work a full day. No making scrap. No smoking breaks in the toilet room." They all voted yes again. Then I said, "Wait a minute. I want you to vote again. Will you come in here – everyone – and work as if you own the business and you are fighting for yourself?" Everyone voted yes again. It was like a religious revival.

In the days that followed, those people looked different. They walked different. They talked different. They were in early, and they were working when the bell rang. The response was amazing. Fantastic things – the kinds of things that the Japanese are doing now – began to happen.

The second storytelling CEO in our sample was Masayoshi Son of Softbank. Son's entire interview was one long saga of Son and his company, composed of numerous stories like this one (Webber 1992: 93–4):

When I first started the company, I only had two part-time workers and a small office. I got two apple boxes, and I stood up on them in the morning as if I was giving a speech. In a loud voice, I said to my two workers, "You guys have to listen to me, because I am the president of this company." I said, "In five years, I'm going to have $75 million in sales. In five years, I will be supplying 1,000 dealer outlets, and we'll be number one in PC software distribution." And I said it very loudly.

Those two guys opened their mouths. They stood up and opened wide their eyes and mouths, and they thought, this guy must be crazy. And they both quit.

That was in 1981. About a year and a half later, we were supplying 200 dealer outlets. Now we supply 15,000. In ten years, we've gone from two part-time employees doing software distribution and making about $12,000 to 570 employees doing software distribution, book and magazine publishing, telephone least cost routing, system integration, network computing, and CAD-CAM and making about $350 million.

The third storytelling CEO was Arnold Hiatt of Stride Rite. Hiatt told more stories and used a greater range of story types than any other CEO whose interview we read. Listen as Hiatt tells a story about his past (Stone 1992: 98):

I didn't set out to run my own company as much as I ran away from a big one. My first job was in the executive training program at Filene's. I felt threatened all the time. I knew there were fifteen other candidates for five positions three rungs up. The

situation was designed to make carnivores of us all, and my teeth just aren't that sharp. That kind of environment works for some people. It didn't work for me.

Fortunately an opportunity presented itself. I had heard about a small company in Lawrence, Massachusetts that had gone into Chapter 11. The Bank of Boston was willing to put up some money. My father was willing to put up some money. I bought Blue Star and became totally absorbed.

Comparing Canion, Allaire, Crawford, Son and Hiatt's stories to the quotes from Bossidy and Marshall presented earlier underscores the differences between storytelling and non-storytelling modes of speaking. Take particular notice of how the storytellers use characterization and how the stories have a beginning and an ending, whereas these features are missing from the examples of non-storytelling provided by Bossidy and Marshall. The comparison should also give you an experience of the differing entertainment values of storytelling and non-storytelling and of their different abilities to engage and inspire listeners.

## The CEOs' Tales

The stories told in the pages of the *HBR* interviews were arranged using a categorization scheme suggested by Gabriel (2000: 84–5). This scheme, outlined in Table 2.2, differentiates four primary story types: comic, tragic, epic, and romantic. These story types were occasionally found in combination, but the numbers of these more complex types of stories were quite small (15 combined story types vs. 98 primary types). The story types are not original to Gabriel but come from folklore and literary theory, disciplines that draw upon sources as ancient as Aristotle and about which a great deal has been written. We will not go into the history of this typology here as we expect that these types will be familiar to you already.

Most stories told in the context of our set of *HBR* interviews were epics, as were those of Canion, Allaire, Crawford, Son and Hiatt given as examples above (Appendix A gives the storyteller, story type, first line of each story and page numbers of the interviews on which each story begins). Eighty-eight out of a total of 113 stories (78 percent) were pure epic tales and another 15 (13 percent) were hybrid types involving epic (two were epic-romance; three were epic-comic; eight were epic-tragic; one was epic-comic-tragic; and one was epic-comic-romantic). This brings the total percentage of stories involving epic to 91 percent of all stories in the interviews we examined.

### *Epic tales*

Paul Cook of Raychem provided a clear example of the epic story type (Taylor 1990: 98–9). In fact, he told four very similar epic stories, all of which reiterate the company's basic innovation strategy. The first was told as a fairly generic corporate

**Table 2.2** Four primary story types

|  | Comic | Tragic | Epic | Romantic |
|---|---|---|---|---|
| Protagonist | Deserving victim, fool | Undeserving victim | Hero | Love object |
| Other characters | Trickster | Villain, helper | Rescue object, assistant, villain | Gift-giver, lover, injured or sick person |
| Plot focus | Misfortune or deserved chastisement | Undeserved misfortune, trauma | Achievement, noble victory, success | Love triumphant, love conquers misfortune |
| Predicament | Accident, mistake, coincidence, the unexpected or unpredictable | Crime, accident, insult, injury, loss, mistake, repetition, mis-recognition | Contest, challenge, trial, test, mission, quest, sacrifice | Gift, romantic fantasy, falling in love, reciprocation, recognition |
| Emotions | Mirth, aggression, scorn | Sorrow, pity, fear, anger, pathos | Pride, admiration, nostalgia | Love, care, kindness, generosity, gratitude |
| Function in business | Amusement | Catharsis | Inspiration | Compassion |

origin story, which is barely a story at all in that it lacks richness of detail and characterization:

> When we started the company, we didn't know what products we were going to make. We knew the first electron-beam machines were coming to market from General Electric, and we knew there were potential industrial applications for the technology. So we bought a machine. And pretty soon we started running out of money. We were under enormous pressure to find successful products – and we did. We came up with lots of good ideas because we had to. People need a fair amount of pressure to have creative ideas.

This example qualifies as a story in our view because it has a beginning ("When we started the company . . .") and an ending ("we did it") and because it recorded a specific incident, namely the buying of an electron-beam machine that helped Raychem develop successful products. The pressure from the marketplace was the challenge that indicates that this story is an epic tale of Raychem's struggle to succeed.

Following Cook's initial, quite general, success tale are three more specific stories each illustrating the implementation of Raychem's innovation strategy and the difficulties encountered, in epic fashion, on the way to achieving it. All three follow the

generic epic plot of the first story but do so in relation to different new product lines built from the core innovation strategy. In their own way these stories show how time and again Raychem repeats its own history as it produces one successful product innovation after another. The stories also reinforce the heroic character of Raychem's leadership with its success strategy (underpinned by its god-like vision for the company's future) as well as its stoic insistence on staying the strategic course (the quest). First came this story about Raychem's applications of radiation chemistry (Taylor 1990: 98–9):

> Too many people still think innovation is about one brilliant technologist coming up with one breakthrough idea. It's not. When we started Raychem, we began to learn what radiation chemistry could do. Within three or four years, we had generated virtually every idea behind the products we're selling today, and we're still working on that original inventory of ideas. Ten years ago, after we began work on conductive polymers, we identified a market for all the manifestations of the technology that totalled $747 million a year. We made our "747 list" and began working through it. At the time, it was a $5 or $10 million business. Today we're up to $150 million a year. So we still have a long way to go.

Next was the story of shape-memory alloys (Taylor 1990: 105):

> About 25 years ago, we learned that the Naval Ordnance Laboratories were experimenting with metals that shrunk with incredibly high force when heated. We were in heat-shrinkable plastics, so we thought this was something we should know about. We started some research. We developed a metal coupling to join hydraulic lines for the F-14 fighter, and the Navy bought it in the second year we had the technology. So we continued the research and made major investments. We kept pushing to get manufacturing costs down. We searched for markets in which these shape-memory alloys could have explosive growth.
>
> Last year, for the first time, we made money on that technology. We stayed with it for more than two decades. We are without question the world's pioneer. We have patents coming out of our ears. After 25 years, shape-memory alloys are on the verge of becoming a big and profitable business. And believe me, we are going to stick with that technology.

Finally Cook told virtually the same story about Raynet, except that this time the villainous Wall Street was the antagonist to Raychem's heroic efforts (Taylor 1990: 105–6):

> Wall Street does apply pressure; Raychem's market value dropped by 10% in one day last year when we reported disappointing quarterly results. But the analysts aren't totally unreasonable. Our fibre-optics subsidiary, which is one of the most exciting new ventures in the company, is a good example. We started exploring the fiber-optics area more than ten years ago. After we worked with the technology for a few years and made some technical discoveries, we began to see what was possible. We concluded it would take several hundred million dollars to bring the technology to market and

make it profitable. So far it's taken $150 million to get Raynet on its feet, and we haven't made the first sale yet.

Wall Street was shocked when we told the analysts about Raynet. We had been secretly working on the technology for years so the competition couldn't find out. Wall Street is still nervous. But the more it learns about our system and the potential markets, the more comfortable it gets. We've also tried to be smart about the financing. We brought in BellSouth as a partner to share some of the costs. And we break out Raynet's financials so the analysts can evaluate our existing businesses on a stand-alone basis.

Sure, it takes some courage to tell Wall Street, "Dammit, I'm going to spend a couple more percentage points of revenues on R & D and let my profits go down. But I'm going to show you how over a period of time that investment is going to pay off." That's not an easy story to sell. But it is sellable – especially if you have a track record of effective technology innovation.

Product lines rather than people were the central characters in Cook's tales, and management commitment in the face of opposition was the heroic factor. The plot was the same in all four stories: Raychem (the protagonist) was challenged – first by pressure, then by the long time it takes to get a product to market and finally by Wall Street – but the company and its heroic management prevailed when the market (the antagonist) accepted and rewarded Raychem's new products with patents, licensing agreements and revenues. In a way, the four stories fit neatly together into one long narrative history of Raychem (try reading straight through all four stories to get the full effect).

The ten non-epic stories we found fell into the three remaining pure categories and included two comic, two romantic and six tragic tales.

## Comic tales

A highly simple comic tale was told by Carl Hahn of Volkswagen (Avishai 1991: 106):

> Our van business was born, for example, when a Dutchman told us how nice it would be if our indestructible, indefatigable vehicle had a box on the top of it so that he could transport eggs around Holland.

What makes this short story a comedy is the effect it has on most people, it brings a smile. It is an unexpected explanation for a serious success story, the VW van.

The other instance of a purely comic tale was provided in a story told by one of our three storytelling CEOs, Frederick Crawford of TRW (Dyer 1991: 117):

> There was a machine in the plant that was water-cooled. The water was discharged through a hole in the floor, and it splashed everything, the floor was a hell of a mess. A week or two after my meeting with the employees, the operator of that machine

asked me to take a look at his invention. He had rigged an awning over the machine from canvas and wire that he had bent himself. The awning channeled the water so that it dropped down neatly into a pan. He had solved the problem. For the first time, that fellow had begun to think about the efficient operation of the business. I asked him why he didn't think of this before. He said, "I didn't know I was supposed to think."

## Tragic tales

Purely tragic stories were told by six of the CEOs interviewed by *HBR*: Crawford, George Fisher of Motorola, Arnold Hiatt of Stride Rite, Phil Knight of Nike (who told two tragic tales), Nicolas Hayek CEO of SMH, the company that created Swatch, and Ernesto Martens of Vitro. Crawford's tragic story (Dyer 1991: 117) is particularly interesting because it followed immediately after his comic story (see previous example) and was in many respects the same tale told in a different mood:

> About a month later, another worker came to see me with a tie-rod end (a steering part made by Steel products) and a blueprint. This fellow couldn't speak good English, and he had never had much schooling. But he had spotted something in the way two pieces of the part were joined that seemed awfully complicated. He then showed me a much simpler way to put the parts together. Nothing fancy, just pure common sense. That single idea saved us 40 cents per part. And we were making a lot of parts. I asked him why he didn't bring the idea up before. He said he did, but he was told to shut up and do his job.

The difference between Crawford's comic and tragic stories is that the worker in the comic tale is the deserving victim of misfortune. This story invites us to laugh at the protagonist when he declares to his CEO "I didn't know I was supposed to think." The worker in the second version of this story, however, invokes pity rather than mirth. Having attempted in vain to solve a problem at work via an ignored suggestion, this worker is presented as an undeserving victim of the same system that prompted the worker in the first story to assume he should not think.

Fisher's tragic tale tells of Motorola's difficulty introducing portable telephones due to the intervention of a regulatory agency (Avishai & Taylor 1989):

> Motorola jumped way out in front on the car phone – so far out in front that there were pictures in magazines two or three years before the systems were actually available. We didn't have thousands of people saying, "We want portable telephones that look a certain way and have particular kinds of features." We presented it to the world. Unfortunately, the regulatory bureaucracy slowed us down once we introduced the product. Other people were able to catch up while we were forced to sit on our hands.

In this story Motorola was the undeserving victim whose injury at the hands of the regulators resulted in a failure to succeed (and thus undermined the telling of this

tale as an epic story of success). It plays on our sympathies for the firm and thus belongs to the category of tragedy.

In the first tragic tale of Nike, Knight presented a strategic mistake as traumatic thus inviting pathos (Willigan 1992: 92):

> We went into casual shoes in the early 1980s when we saw that the running shoe business, which was about one-third of our revenues at the time, was slowing down. We knew that a lot of people were buying our shoes and wearing them to the grocery store and for walking to and from work. Since we happened to be good at shoes, we thought we could be successful with casual shoes. But we got our brains beat out. We came out with a functional shoe we thought the world needed, but it was funny looking and the buying public didn't want it.

Here Knight makes no apologies for Nike's mistake, but instead invites our pity for Nike's rejection by the buying public.

Knight (Willigan 1992: 92–3) presented a second, even more tragic, story involving the loss of good people as a result of poor fiscal performance. His last sentence seems to be an overt cry for sympathy, indicative of the tragic story type:

> By the mid-1980s, the financial signals were coming through loud and clear. Nike had been profitable throughout the 1970s. Then all of a sudden in fiscal year 1985, the company was in the red for two quarters. In fiscal 1987, sales dropped by $200 million and profits headed south again. We were forced to fire 280 people that year – our second layoff ever and a very painful one because it wasn't just an adjustment and trimming of fat. We lost some very good people that year.

Nicolas Hayek of SMH/Swatch told his interviewer, William Taylor (1993: 105), this tragic story about his company's Omega watch brand in its darkest hour:

> Omega is one of the Swiss watch industry's great brands. Its history goes back to 1848. You should visit the watchmaking museums and look at the pieces Omega made 50 or 100 years ago. They are wonderful. Few brands had or have Omega's potential power.
>
> The problems started in the early 1970s. There were bad business practices. The people there became arrogant. They treated their agents and dealers badly. If an agent from, say, New Jersey needed 200 units of a particular model, Omega would say: "You're crazy! Don't bother us with such nonsense. We'll give you 50."
>
> Second, and much worse, Omega became greedy. Rolex sells 600,000 watches per year. That's about as many as you can sell before a luxury brand begins to lose its prestige. That's about how many Omega was selling in the late 1970s. But Omega wanted to grow more rapidly. So they took the easy route. They figured, "If we can sell 600,000, why not a million? Or 2 million? Or 3 million?".
>
> Which meant, of course, they had to lower the price radically. A jeweler would say, "Omega is wonderful, but it is too expensive for my clients. How about giving me an Omega that is cheaper?" Now, if you are crazy, or I guess if you are greedy, you agree.

That was the kiss of death. Omega was everywhere: high price, medium price, precious metals, cheap gold plating. There were 2,000 different models! No one knew what Omega stood for. By the end of 1980, the company was again in a deep crisis, its deepest ever.

*HBR*: How did you develop the recovery plan?

It was very painful. Early on, before the SMH merger, we spent days behind closed doors with the company's managers and bankers. Some of the people suggested that we sell Omega to the Japanese, who had offered to buy it. It was still a powerful brand despite the problems, and it would fetch a lot of money. Of course, that would have been tragic for Switzerland.

Some managers from Omega were pleading that we take the brand down-market to face Citizen and Seiko in the middle segment. That was absurd! I fought them tooth and nail on that. At one point, the people at Omega would not even let us on their premises. It was bitter.

We made the investment in SMH in 1985, and we were free to act. I pushed out practically the entire management of Omega. I fired a lot of people, I got the reputation as a brutal guy, I am not a brutal guy. But the organization was so full of arrogance and stupidity that I didn't have much choice.

In telling the tragedy of Omega, Hayek carefully distanced himself from the victims of the trauma that overtook this brand and the organization behind it. The mistakes made in overextending the Omega brand led to Hayek's firing many of the managers of the organization, but instead of filling us with awe for Hayek's bravery, he invites us to feel pity for the poor arrogant managers he was forced to fire. This makes the Omega story tragic rather than epic.

The last tragic story in the set of interviews we read was told by Ernesto Martens of Vitro (Nichols 1993):

our real problems began in 1982. . . . Overnight the peso went kaboom. It went from 25 pesos to 70 pesos against the dollar. Instead of needing $18.7 billion in pesos to pay our bankers in the United States, we needed nearly three times that number, or roughly $52.5 billion. We had the pesos, but because of the currency controls, we couldn't get them out of the country. We couldn't pay our suppliers either. We had an executive studying at MIT, and we couldn't pay his tuition. It was traumatic because we hadn't failed in running our company, our company had failed.

This story is clearly a tragedy in that in it Martens represents his company as an undeserving victim of Mexico's financial difficulties.

## Romantic tales

Two purely romantic tales were told, one by Robert McDermott of USAA (Teal 1991) and the other by Arnold Hiatt of Stride Rite (Stone 1992). The care, kindness

and generosity McDermott expresses in this next story marks it as a romance (Teal 1991: 118):

> Whenever a war starts, most insurance companies are quick to invoke the war clause in their life insurance policies so they won't have to pay off on people killed in combat. Since we serve military officers, we have no such clause. So, for example, we're one of only a few companies that didn't invoke a war clause as soon as Desert Storm began. On the contrary, we sold new life insurance to people who'd just been called up.
>
> If an officer had a $100,000 policy with us and he got orders for Desert Storm, we not only kept the full $100,000 in force, we let him increase his insurance. We didn't suggest it, exactly, but we allowed it. We even sold new policies to people who suddenly panicked when they got their orders and realized they might need some protection for their families. We put a $50,000 limit on increases and new policies, but we were the only insurance company I know of that sold those people any new coverage at all.
>
> We also encouraged them to leave a power of attorney with someone at home. And we set up a hotline – the Desert Storm Assistance Center – so that should a member be killed, the survivors could call in and we'd take care of everything: life insurance, bank account, investment management, property insurance – everything with one phone call. When they mobilized, we mobilized. But that's how we see our mission. We insure fighter pilots and tank commanders. We sell life insurance to astronauts. We insured those guys on the moon.

In the other pure romance in the *HBR* interviews we read, Arnold Hiatt expressed his company's concern for the children who lived in the community where Stride Rite operated its factory, as he told how Stride Rite happened to start the first corporate day care center in the US:

> We started the center for the community, for the children living near the old Stride Rite factory on Harrison Avenue in Boston's Roxbury neighborhood. Until the late 1960's, when an aging work force and high labor costs led us to start moving production out of Boston, Stride Rite made all its children's shoes in that building. And in 1971, when we opened the center, our distribution center and corporate offices were still located there. But the neighborhood was falling apart around us. Businesses were pulling out, housing was in disrepair, crime and violence were more and more common. And every time I looked out my window, I saw a lot of small children with nothing to do and no place to go.
>
> It didn't take a great deal of imagination to make the connections. We were in the children's shoe business. We were in a decaying neighborhood surrounded by children in need. We had resources available in the form of empty manufacturing space. And we had a perfect model in the federal government's Head Start program. That's how the center got started.
>
> Remember this was 20 years ago. The employees were taken aback. Their position was cogently expressed by the head of the union. He stopped me in the corridor one day and said, "Hey, if you guys can spend so much money on that" – he didn't say nonsense, but that was the implication – "why don't you put it into a pay increase instead?" I said the two things weren't related and told him that if any of

the employees were interested in having their children come to the center, it was available for them too.

About six months later, one employee did bring her child in. It caused a great deal of concern because most of the employees were white and almost all of the children in the center were black. But over time, as people saw that the center worked, more employees started to enroll their kids. Eventually we decided to make it 50–50, half community children and half the children of employees. We kept expanding as the demand increased, and when we moved our offices out of Roxbury and over to Cambridge in 1981, we opened a second center here. This center also serves both the community and our employees.

Hiatt's story is romantic in that it expresses love for the children of the community in which the Stride Rite factory was located. In the story the community is portrayed as injured or sick ("a decaying neighborhood surrounded by children in need") and even when Hiatt encounters resistance from the union, he sticks to the company's position as protector of the children. In the end, love triumphs over Union greed. A secondary plot in the story unfolds as white employees begin to bring their children to the day care center and thus the center becomes racially integrated, a further indication of the story's romantic nature.

Two additional stories with romantic elements were told by Tom Chapman of Greater Southeast Community Hospital, although both of these were mixed with epic tales. It is probably not accidental that these stories of love, kindness, and generosity were told about a hospital where these emotions are part of everyday work life for many employees. Like Cook's four tales of Raychem, Chapman's two tales show how similar stories of the same type can be, especially when told by the same person. The first was the story of Gloria who started up the hospital's senior daycare center (Nichols 1992: 92–3):

For instance, there is a senior citizen apartment complex right across the street from the hospital. Years ago, we found that a lot of residents would come and sit for hours in our lobby. Maybe they were waiting for the bus, maybe they were lonely, or maybe they just thought the hospital was an exciting place to be. Eventually we gave them a room at the back of the emergency ward, and gradually our staff started some arts and crafts activities on a volunteer basis. After working with the elderly for a while, Gloria Anderson, who was then a social worker at the hospital, recognized a need for elderly day care. Using the basement of one of our buildings, she started our community's first senior day care center.

*HBR*: So what led you from day care to nursing homes?

It was a logical next step. When our elderly patients could no longer stay at home, we saw them shipped off to a nursing home on the other side of the river, where they were isolated from this community. Working with Gloria, we made the decision to build a nursing home here in Anacostia so they wouldn't have to leave the community.

Today, through our center for the aging, we operate three nursing homes in the District of Columbia and Maryland, and we have purchased a van called "The Dr. Feel

Good Van" to provide home visits for seniors who can't travel – and Gloria is in charge of the whole operation.

In the second epi-romantic tale, Chapman told about Lester Scheuermann creating a program for feeding the elderly patients in the hospital (Nichols 1992: 93):

> If you can't find more financially attractive patients, you have to find more attractive and cost-efficient ways to treat the patients you have. That is our basic approach. In fact, one of our employees, Lester Scheuermann, has just won a national award for doing that. He created a program called Service Spoons using a Freedom Grant, which we give out to employees who have a novel idea. Each year, we give out a few Freedom Grants of up to $5,000 to help employees create programs that solve an identified problem in our delivery system.
>
> From his work as a social worker, Lester knew that elderly hospitalized patients often have trouble feeding themselves. They can't swallow or they aspirate, taking food down into their lungs. This can be dangerous for a number of reasons: the patient can choke or get pneumonia.
>
> To avoid this problem, we had been tube-feeding many of our elderly and frail patients. Yet the tube feeding also had its drawbacks. The patients hated the tubes and often tried to dislodge them. Then they had to be restrained, which caused them further physical and mental problems. In addition, there is an increased risk of infection from tube feeding. Infections mean lengthier stays and, since the hospital is reimbursed by Medicare on a flat basis, we can't afford to have extended stays. They aren't good for us, and they aren't good for our patients either.
>
> Seeing this problem, Lester began a program where employees would feed the elderly on their lunch hours and before and after work. At first, a lot of people around here doubted whether employees would choose to spend their lunch hours doing extra work. But we've found that clerical employees, who are detached from the caring mission of the hospital, like being involved in this nursing activity. They find it fulfilling. From the hospital's perspective, the program saves both time and money. We don't have to pay a highly trained nurse to perform a routine feeding, and we don't have lengthened stays brought on by infections resulting from the feeding tubes. The patients also benefit physically and mentally from the added nutrition and from the extra social contact.

The stories told by Chapman are not pure romances, however, as the main characters are both amply rewarded for their heroic leadership when it results in financially sound additions to organizational operations. Thus, alongside the romance of giving care to patients, Chapman told epic tales of organizational improvement in service delivery and overall performance of the company that were brought about through the romantically motivated efforts of two employees.

## Combinations of story types

Great storytellers do not stick to one story form. They mix comedy with tragedy or romance. Consider the delight many people find in a romantic comedy, or the

frequency with which playwrights and screenwriters use comic relief in tragic plays and movies. In spite of the ability of the best storytellers to blend forms, pure epic tales overshadowed all other story types by a substantial margin in the *HBR* interviews we read. While comic and romantic stories were extremely rare, and tragic stories got only slightly more airing, there were instances of combinations of these pure types with the by far most popular epic form.

Perhaps the proclivity to use the epic form goes along with being a CEO – this form fits the image of the powerful leader as hero – whereas the other three detract from the glamour or power of the role. Tragic stories position the protagonist as unsuccessful, while comedy reduces the protagonist's status and romance focuses attention on the love object (traditionally a woman!). Each of these moves either detracts from the heroic image of the leader or distracts the listener from focusing on this image. It should be understood, however, that by being interviewed in the pages of *HBR*, the risk of losing one's heroic image is greatly reduced. This is because, presumably, if you get asked to do an interview, you have survived your challenges, have achieved high status, and are secure. Hence, the very existence of the *HBR* interview marks you as glorious, regardless of the sorts of stories you choose to tell.

It is possible that tragic, comic, and romantic stories were so rare in our sample of interviews because they were deemed inappropriate by the CEOs and/or by *HBR*'s editors. This might be because tragic tales point to failure rather than the success that *HBR*'s readers hope to emulate by learning from the CEOs that *HBR* interviews. Similarly comic tales could undermine the serious import of the topics discussed in the pages of *HBR* and romantic stories might be seen as emasculating or as a sign of weakness. Perhaps this is why most of these forms of stories only appear in combination with epic tales that reclaim their teller's winning ways, masculinity, strength, or virility. In this regard it is interesting to note that, in the only two epic-romantic tales we found, the heroes were not the CEOs who told the tale, but were other individuals, one of whom represented the only female hero (Gloria) in the entire set of interviews we read. The only purely romantic tale we found was told by a maternalistic CEO, Arnold Hiatt of Stride Rite, who spoke about his company's concern for local children (for more about why we regard Hiatt as maternal, see our discussion in Chapter 4).

Like the two epic-romantic tales told above, all combinations of story types involved the epic mode of storytelling. There were no combinations of story types that did not involve epic in some fashion (i.e., no tragic-comic, romantic-comic or romantic-tragic tales were found in our sample). Consider this combination of epic and comic story types told by Hayek of Swatch (Taylor 1993: 103):

We built a giant Swatch. It was 500 feet high, weighed 13 tons, and actually worked. We suspended that giant Swatch outside the tallest skyscraper in Frankfurt, the headquarters of Commerzbank. It was really something to see!

I remember asking the chairman of the bank for permission. He thought we were crazy. We were crazy, but we had already gotten authorization from the city engineers

and the local government. And we persuaded him that this giant Swatch would show his customers that his bank had heart and emotion. So there it hung. And all it said was: Swatch. Swiss. DM60.

In Hayek's story the unpredictability of the request to hang a giant watch from the side of a bank in Germany provided the comic predicament. Meanwhile the persuasive power of the Swatch executive illustrated heroism at work, with the ultimate display of the giant watch presenting the sign of victory – both elements of the epic.

Bernabè of Eni provided an example of the combination of epic and tragic stories (Hill & Wetlaufer 1998: 85):

> There were times of terrible stress. Perhaps the worst was when I was charged with taking a bribe. That really destroyed me. It was on television that night, and my children were watching, and they were astonished. I felt like I was at the beginning of a nervous breakdown. It felt so violent – such an act of aggression against me that you cannot imagine. One of the things I have been most careful about in life is my integrity, and here was this person on TV saying, "Bernabè took a $5 million bribe."
>
> I went out, I took a walk. I didn't know how to react at first. But I walked and I thought. When I got back home I said, "This kind of attack is why I am fighting, and I will keep fighting even harder now. And if they think I will go away they are wrong. Before I am finished, they will all be left behind, the people who think they can control Eni with politics and rumors and lies."
>
> I was very focused, you see, very determined. If I had vacillated about my objectives and my vision for Eni, I would have been finished before I got started. It was really war. It was a question of survival. If I had lost the battle to clean Eni of politics and make it a commercial business, both the company and the country would have suffered. And I truly wanted to save Eni for the young people of Italy, who dreamed as I did.
>
> Now there were definitely periods when I said "What am I doing? Why am I standing? Why am I putting this stress on my family? It's too tough, too heavy." But I don't really think I gave serious thought to stopping or quitting. They weren't options because too much was at stake.

In this tale Bernabè told a highly personal story about misfortune and misrecognition that expressed feelings of sorrow and pathos and invokes these feelings in the reader. Yet, even as he told the tale, Bernabè reminded us, as does his presence on the list of CEOs interviewed by *HBR*, that he prevailed in the end. His demonstrated (or claimed) fortitude during a long and lonely vigil, indicated the heroism that accompanies an epic character.

An instance of a story combining three of the four primary forms was provided in Son's (Webber 1992: 95–7) epi-tragi-comic tale of his first trade show:

> When Softbank was only two or three months old, I decided that I needed to show the end users and dealers what software was available in Japan. There was a consumer electronics show in Tokyo, and I made a reservation for the largest size booth, the

same size as Sony, Matsushita, and Toshiba. I purchased the space, and I called all the software vendors I could find, maybe just a dozen at that time. I told them that I had bought the space, I was going to prepare the flyers, I was going to have decorations, displays, a model PC, and I was going to pay for everything. I told them, you guys can be in my booth for free. They all said, what? How can you do that? Why are you doing that? How can you make money doing that?

They had the software, but they didn't have the money to show it to anybody else. I had a little money, but I didn't have products to sell. And there were so many PC dealers who had hardware but no software. So, I thought, some matchmaking is needed. At the consumer electronics show, I had a booth the size of eight small booths. I had a huge sign that said, "Now the revolution has come for software distribution for PCs." I had more people come to my booth than Sony did. My booth was always packed, jammed with people. And they all said how good it was.

My plan was that a bunch of people would sign up to establish outlets and another bunch of people would order software through Softbank. In fact, I got almost nothing. Nobody signed up for a dealership. Zero. And I sold very few software products. Actually, most of the software vendors who attended the booth would tell people, if you can't make up your mind today, here's my card. You can call me directly if you decide to buy my software. So I was cut out of the deal completely. I probably made back one-twentieth of the cost of the booth.

After that, many people were laughing at me. They said, that guy's really dumb. He's a nice guy but dumb. I said, OK, I'm dumb. But I'm going to keep at it, and someday, somebody will find out what I can do and what real software distribution means.

In this story Son represented himself as the undeserving victim who created a successful event that benefited everyone but himself. Then, in the last paragraph, he switched to comic mode by presenting himself as the fool seen through the eyes of those who benefited from his actions. Beneath it all, knowing that he has since been highly successful or he would not appear in an *HBR* interview, we can hear the epic – the long-suffering hero prevailed in the end.

One last example of a combination of three of the four story types comes from Stride Rite Chairman, Arnold Hiatt who told this epic-comic-romantic story (Stone 1992: 103):

At one time we used to have an annual lunch for all the Stride Rite scholars. Not any more. I was no match for them. I'd thank them for all they were doing, using pompous words about making a difference. They'd look at me, and it was clear they were thinking, "I've got to be nice to this guy because he pays the bills. But he doesn't know what he's talking about." They knew they made a difference, and they felt they got more from the experience than any of the people they had helped. That had never occurred to me.

This story is particularly interesting in that it relates how Chairman Hiatt learned something through something he thought he was doing for others. Thus this story has a reflexive element to it that anticipates the next and last category of story type we will examine.

## Reflexivity and Complexity in Organizational Storytelling

While they are a subtype of epic tales, we found one additional category of story types interesting, given our focus on storytelling. These were stories that were themselves about storytelling, or reflexive tales. We find these stories particularly interesting because they give evidence that at least some of the CEOs were well aware of their storytelling ability and the importance of storytelling. The first was told by Robert Haas. Here is Haas's description of himself telling a story to Levi Strauss employees (Howard 1990: 139):

> When I talk to employees about the development of the Aspirations Statement, I describe the stark terror I felt when I took over this company, just having turned 43 years old. We were a company in crisis. Our sales were dropping, our international business was heading for a loss, our domestic business had an eroding profit base, our diversification wasn't working, and we had too much production capacity. I had no bold plan of action. I knew that values were important but didn't have the two granite tablets that I could bring down from Mount Sinai to deliver to the organization. I talk about how alone I felt as a senior manager and how tough it is to be held up as a paragon to the organization. It helps people realize that senior management is human, that we can't be expected to know everything, and that we're inviting them in as partners in the organization.

Another two stories about storytelling were told by the storytelling CEO Frederick Crawford (Dyer 1991: 122). Crawford illustrated this story about storytelling with another story about a woman who remembered a story she once heard him tell. It is not surprising to find Crawford reflecting about his storytelling given that this ability was touted by the interviewer (in the introduction) as a major reason *HBR* wanted to conduct this interview. Nonetheless, Crawford's two examples of reflexive stories show us his skill at storytelling and provide a benchmark that could prove useful to others.

> A few years ago on a street in Cleveland, I ran into a woman who had worked for us during the war. After we exchanged greetings, she recalled a story I had told at one of the mass meetings years before. She had forgotten the circumstances, but she remembered the story. It was about cooperation: I was talking about the need to plan things and work together. In those days, everybody used analogies from football, but I thought those stories were old and overworked even then.
> So I told a story about little Willie, who wears short pants but wants long pants like the big boys, and Christmas is coming. He tells Santa Claus that he wants long pants. Mother gets him long pants, but they are about six inches too long, and she doesn't have time to fix them. She and Willie's sister and grandmother wrap them up and put them in a box under the Christmas tree. Mother puts the lights out and goes to bed and then starts thinking, "Poor little Willie, he'll be so disappointed that he can't wear his long pants Christmas Day." So about midnight, she gets up and goes downstairs, turns on the lights, cuts the six inches off the pants, hems them, and goes back to bed.

At about one o'clock, grandmother does the same thing. At about two o'clock, sister does it again. The next morning, little Willie, tries on his new pants, and they're even shorter than his old ones.

The story is now dated, of course, but at the time it got a good laugh. It made the point that effort is fine, but you need cooperation to harness that effort. I had spoken for probably 20 minutes, but 40 years later, this woman remembered that story. That tells you something.

Crawford's second example of reflexive storytelling was a complex, three-part story about his approach to management wherein he again demonstrated his strong moralizing tendencies but also made clear how he used stories strategically to persuade his audiences to accept his views (Dyer 1991: 121):

There were three things we stressed in employee education. If you get these three lessons into employees' heads, then you've got the best employees in the world.

The first lesson involves an understanding of the sources of wealth. I used a simple formula, which I called "The Triangle of Plenty," to show how wealth is created by serving the interests of three constituencies; customers, investors, and employees. I'd illustrate the formula by telling the story of Henry Ford.

When Henry Ford started making real money from the Model T, he didn't raise wages right away. First he lowered prices, giving the savings to the customers and creating a mass market for the automobile. As he made more and more money with the prices going lower and lower, he reinvested in machinery and plants, which guaranteed tens of thousands of jobs that couldn't be guaranteed any other way. Finally, he said to his employees, "We've got the machine rolling and I'm going to pay everybody $5 per day minimum" – this at a time when $2.50 was considered good pay. He shocked the industrial world. If Elijah had seen what Henry Ford did, he'd have written three pages about it in the Bible.

After I made my point about increased production being the source of increased wealth, we got to the second lesson. The workers would say, "Yes, I know we're producing but do I get my fair share?" At this point, I'd tell the story of an old prospector who raises a grubstake in a saloon. I'd ask, "How should a gold strike be divided?" Everybody yelled, "fifty-fifty." I never had an audience say anything but fifty-fifty.

Then I'd pull out some slides based on our annual report. I'd show our total revenue, then how much we paid in bills for necessary expenses, including taxes, materials, depreciation, rentals, and other items, but not the payroll. The pot of money left over we called "money created," funds available for employees, for reinvestment, or for dividends. Then I'd show how we spent this total. Every year, more than 90 percent went to the payroll. The stockholders got less than 5 percent, with the balance plowed back, which really helped make work better for the workers. So I'd say to the employees, "you folks got more than 90 percent of the money. Is there anything wrong in that?" I'd get a big cheer. Then I'd ask "How about the stockholders? Are they making too much money?" "Noooooo!" Everyone would yell, "Hooray for the stockholders!" Now I defy you to go to any plant in the United States today and ask them to cheer for the stockholders. But that came easily at Thompson Products, where we gained, and worked hard to keep, employees' confidence.

The third lesson was to lay to rest the myth widely believed by intelligent people in this country that machinery puts people out of work. During the 1940s, Eleanor Roosevelt made a speech saying as much. Well, I'd quote Mrs. Roosevelt and then I'd say, "There's something damn wrong with that. In China, there's no machinery and wages are ten cents an hour." Then I'd tell them the story of welded pipe.

At one time, pipe for pipelines was made by curling up a sheet of steel into a tube and welding it by hand. Welding was a highly skilled job, and the welders were a big, tough union with several thousand members. Well, along came a fellow who invented a machine that would rollup a sheet of steel and weld the seam automatically, zip, just like that. The union tried to destroy the new machinery. There were strikes and violence. But what happened? Pipe made the new way was so cheap that the oil companies stopped shipping by rail. Oil pipelines were laid all over the country, and within ten years, 20,000 people were making steel pipe.

The moral of the story is that new machinery and equipment for automation is a paradox. The more you buy, the more you hire. I had everybody in our plants talking about paradoxes.

Crawford's stories (given throughout this chapter) demonstrate one reason why he was such an effective storyteller – Crawford used an enormous range of story types. Although he, like all other CEOs, showed a strong bias toward the epic, he also used comic and tragic forms. His mastery of storytelling types is confirmed by his ability to be reflexive about his storytelling and his consciously rhetorical use of stories to lead his company. A final indication of Crawford's extraordinary range was given in a story in which he appears as villain, at least in the eyes of his arch-enemies the unionists (remember that Crawford was CEO in an earlier era than the others in our sample having served immediately after World War II):

> Another time, during the war, Frank Graham, head of the War Labor Board, summoned me to Washington. He was a delightful person, but a screwball on unionism. He gave me a little speech about unions being the salvation of the American people and what you could call "strong encouragement" to let the CIO in. I also got a lot of bad press. After the war, I was described as labor's worst enemy in a book by a union organizer.

In our view this story is an anti-epic as it depicted Crawford as a villain ("labor's worst enemy"), nonetheless it allowed Crawford to maintain his heroic appeal. Because we know that Crawford was a staunch anti-unionist, appearing as a villain to the unionists was an act of courage, which makes this an epic with an ironic twist at its core, hence the label anti-epic. The use of irony provides further evidence of Crawford's mastery of the art of storytelling.

Arnold Hiatt of Stride Rite displayed an even greater storytelling range than did Crawford, though he did not appear to have to the same degree Crawford's ability to enchant his listeners. Hiatt's stories are shorter and more to the point, with less tension and surprise inherent in their plots. Another difference is that Crawford's stories contain much greater depth of characterization. These differences are also

apparent in the stories told by our third storytelling CEO, Mayoshi Son of Softbank, who shares Crawford's gift of enchantment but expresses it in quite a different way.

While Son did not display the range either Crawford or Hiatt achieved in their tales, he was nonetheless equally if not more complex in his storytelling. You can see his complexity in the number of interrelated stories he told and in his telling of an epic-comic-tragic story that was the most complex story in our sample (see pages 34–5). To give another indication of not only his complexity as a storyteller, but also of his sensitivity as a manager, we offer one last Masayoshi Son story (Webber 1992: 99):

When I started the company, I used straight bank loans. And that was really difficult. I went to the Dai-ichi Kangyo Bank when the company was only three or four months old. At the time, I had revenues of about $10,000 and I asked for a loan of $750,000. I told them, I have no collateral, I have no business experience, and I am not going to ask my family or my friends to co-sign my loan. I will sign myself, and I'll take all the responsibility. But unless you give me the prime rate, I'm not going to take a loan from you.

The people at the Dai-ichi Kangyo Bank said, are you crazy? What are you talking about? What are you doing here?

I said, I came to get a loan, of course.

The people at the Dai-ichi Kangyo Bank just started laughing. We can't give you a loan, they said. Do you have anything that can convince us?

I said, no, I don't have anything. But if you really think about business in the future, what we're doing might interest you.

Then they asked me, is there anyone you can use as a reference?

I told them to talk with Dr. Sasaki at Sharp because he was the person I had business experience with from selling Sharp my invention at Berkeley – my pocket language translator.

The bank branch manager was a really good guy. He didn't want to give up on me just because I couldn't give good reasons why his headquarters should give me a $750,000 loan. So he called Dr. Sasaki. Dr. Sasaki said, Mr. Son has good business potential, so please give him this loan. The branch manager also asked Joshin Denki, and they recommended me for the loan too.

Then it was up to the branch manager to fill in the formal scorecard of the bank using his judgment whether or not to make the loan. When he used the ordinary scoring, the total was –15 against making the loan. But the last column was "potential growth." He gave us 15 points for potential growth. So the total came out zero. He sent the scorecard to headquarters and they said, since the total is zero, you make the judgment. The branch manager said, I'm going to give him the loan.

Today at Softbank, we have a special day where we honor the few individuals who made contributions to help start Softbank. One of the people we honor is that bank branch manager.

This final Son story is a good example on which to close this chapter as it takes us back to many of the points raised along the way and thus serves as a summary. First, it is an unambiguous example of the story form. It has a beginning and an

ending ("When I started the company . . . Today at Softbank"). There is a particular incident that is related (Son getting Softbank its first bank loan). There is characterization (Son as the protagonist, Dai-ichi Kangyo Bank as antagonist, plus three helpers: Dr Sasaki of Sharp, Joshin Denki and the bank branch manager who approved the loan). And there is a plot (Son faces difficulties presented by the bank and its lending practices which, with the help of Dr Sasaki, Joshin Denki and especially the branch bank manager, are ultimately overcome and the ending is a happy one – Softbank succeeds). There is even a sub-story about the branch manager whose own heroism is glorified by Softbank on a special day honoring its heroes – a story about a Softbank drama that foreshadows our discussion of theater in the next chapter. For now, let us draw some general conclusions about storytelling.

## Developing Your Storytelling Skills

The presence of so much storytelling suggests that the CEOs featured in our sample of interviews use the faces of the artist and the priest. The frequency of storytelling in the interviews indicates that aesthetic consciousness is deeply embedded within the forms and contents of expression these business leaders employed in their interviews. Of particular note is that the epic tale was by far the most representative example of CEO storytelling in the *HBR* interviews we read.

One might suspect egotism, but many stories did not feature the CEOs themselves, or, when they did, did not glorify the teller. Many times the hero was not even a person, but was a product, a team, or the whole organization. We came away with the strong impression that their stories show us that CEOs function as heroes even though they often model humility. In Chapter 4 we give further consideration to the heroic aspects of the CEOs by defining their virtues in relation to those of the gods in Greek mythology. However, we want to summarize here what we think we have learned about storytelling from the *HBR* interviews.

First, managerial culture, like any other, needs its heroes and constructs them according to its key values. The values of the epic form are heroism and achievement in spite of the odds. Success stories, or stories of achievement (corporate, product/brand, personal) are epics and we only rarely found other types of stories in the pages of the *HBR* interviews we read. The Greek poet, Homer, believed that both epic and tragedy depended upon the hero being noble. Perhaps the CEOs' stories speak to their nobility, a point to which we will return in Chapter 4 where we discuss virtue. We can only speculate about the preponderance of epic stories. Were the 1990s the decade of the business epic or the epic manager-hero? Was *HBR* encouraging, via editorial license, stories told in this mode? Were they editing out stories that were not in the tradition of epic tales? Was there something about the interview situation that called for epic stories? Or is it that managerial culture, of which *HBR* is merely a part, prefers stories that celebrate its heroes? We will return to the question of celebrity and the role *HBR* plays in Chapter 5.

Second, communication is enhanced by storytelling. Storytelling allows business leaders to create more engaging and memorable messages than are constructed by those who are inept with the storytelling mode. This is because illustration gets points across in more concrete and colorful ways than making simple declarations, as was demonstrated by the examples presented in this chapter. The communicative power of storytelling engages listeners and encourages some of them to repeat what they have heard to others, further extending the influence of the storyteller and the tale.

Third, entrepreneurs' stories made extensive use of the first person and did so more conspicuously than any other category of CEO in the interviews (e.g., non-founders, retired CEOs). They were furthermore far more prone than other CEOs to strongly identify their organization with themselves. Why are entrepreneurs so often storytellers and why do their stories sound so similar? Perhaps they have greater ego needs than do other business leaders, or maybe they just have to sell themselves more often, but what appears plausible on the basis of the interview material is that they live in the first person, eagerly constructing themselves as heroes rather than waiting for someone else to do it. Like other CEOs in our sample, however, their storytelling was done mainly in the epic mode.

## Telling stories

Storytelling is one of the most important elements for building organizational culture. Its specificity makes culture concrete while reinvigorating values and maintaining the pedestals on which cultural heroes stand. Without it, organizational identity and uniqueness would be hard to sustain. Storytelling is undoubtedly a key skill for business leaders and imaginative storytelling can make a leader stand out and enhance the reach of his or her influence. This raises the question: how can storytelling skills be developed? The answer has three parts: by listening to or reading stories, retelling them to others, and learning to tell your own stories effectively.

To develop your storytelling ability you need to expose yourself to the best stories you can find. Read great stories and listen to gifted storytellers until you notice that the ways in which stories are told well have invaded the way in which you tell stories to others. Don't stop there, for you need to develop a personal style of storytelling, but this technique will help you begin to do just that. You will find that over the course of retelling your favorite stories and developing new ones, you will find your storytelling voice.

To get started on the path to becoming a storyteller, think about a good story you know well enough to retell from memory. Re-read this chapter and use Table 2.1 to find out what sort of story yours is and to make sure it has all the elements necessary to be recognizable to others. Then choose three stories of the same type, either from this chapter or other business writings, and read them several times until you feel their rhythms and experience the emotions they are capable of evoking. Now tell your story to others. As you tell it, look into the faces of your listeners

for cues to their emotional responses. Learn to ride the emotions of your story along with the audience. Be sure to notice what this does to your story. When you achieve a true storytelling groove, you should find yourself saying things you did not expect to say, or saying them in a way that you had not planned. Look for this improvisational element in your storytelling. When you find it you will know that you are telling stories well enough to begin to regard yourself as a storyteller.

A word of warning, don't expect to learn this skill overnight. It may take considerable practice to find your voice, particularly if you are not a natural storyteller. The first hurdle will be overcoming any shyness you may have that stops you from telling stories. The next is to overcome self-consciousness while you are telling a story. Self-consciousness impedes your empathy and will interfere with your ability to ride the emotions of your story alongside your listeners. But once you relax with the experience of a few successes, you will find your rhythm and your voice. Then it will be time to start experimenting with more personal material. We do not recommend starting with purely personal stories (though personalizing your story by explaining how you came to know it, or why you value it, is always a nice touch) because it is very easy to appear to be arrogant or narcissistic when you tell personal stories before you have overcome your self-consciousness as a storyteller.

When you have traveled some distance down the road to finding your storytelling voice, it is time to learn to incorporate your personal experiences into the stories you tell. By now you will have told enough stories to have intuitively grasped what your audience responds to when they hear a story, and this should have prepared you to draw aspects of your own life into readiness to help you to address the interests of those who like to listen to your tales. Remember, a little goes a long way, a good personal narrative is responsive to the interests and needs of the listeners, it is not a narcissistic rendition of what matters only to you. On the other hand, you are well advised to dig deep. Sharing only the bits of yourself that make you look good is another route to being considered arrogant by your audience.

There is an additional step you may want to take with your storytelling once you have begun to establish some influence within your organization. You should take advantage of every opportunity to spread stories through retellings, or by encouraging other organizational storytellers to tell them. Doing this will grow culture and deeply embed within it the values the storytellers express in their stories. Notice that using stories as a vehicle for communicating values permits listeners to derive meaning in their own preferred terms and gives them latitude to accept or reject the communicated values. As we know from years of studying culture and from goal setting theory, involvement in the setting of goals or the expression of values means the difference between accepted and imposed goals and values. Encouraging storytelling within your organizational culture will build community in and provide symbolic meaning to your organization, but you will never fully control this aspect of organizational life. Don't try. The danger in trying to control other people's meanings is that you become for them a symbol of manipulation and deceit.

Finally, bear in mind that the worst enemy of the storyteller is the constant rehearsal of facts and figures. When communication is free of anecdote, emotion,

fantasy, and history, life becomes dull indeed. As we have indicated by example earlier in the chapter, the technical face of the manager often revels in facts and figures. When this face is complemented by storytelling, the faces of the artist and priest will be revealed. Developing your storytelling ability and that of others will enhance the communicative capacity of your organization and enrich your life and the lives you touch with your stories.

# 3

# Dramatizing Leadership

Faith is always based in primeval revelation and revelation is a concrete event. In revelation, God, or ancestral spirits, or culture heroes create and mould the universe, manifest their will and power to man. All this is a temporal process, or concrete sequence of activities, a set of dramatic performances.

*(Malinowski, quoted in Strenski 1992: 135)*

Suspense, conflict, and tension are dramatic elements of life that are ever present in business just as they are in theater. The second approach we made to the *HBR* interviews with CEOs was as theatrical performances dramatizing business and its leadership. As with storytelling in Chapter 2, we will use drama in this chapter to reveal the artistry displayed by the CEOs interviewed in the pages of *HBR*. Furthermore, because theater emerged as an art form from the storytelling rituals associated with ancient cultures and their religions, the dramatic approach will provide a link between the two aesthetic domains of creativity and ethics that we are exploring in this book.

Those who study the history of theater trace its origins to primitive rituals practiced by early humans. The usual explanations they give for ritual include: the reenactment of successful hunts or battles, or of behaviors superstitiously associated with these events, and the worship of forces believed to control the movement of animals and the weather or to provide skill to hunters or warriors. Reenacting dramatic events and worshiping forces believed to control the universe gave early humans a sense of self-determination, that they could cajole the gods to come to their aid in times of need. Thus drama in life was ritualistically reenacted in ways that aligned humans with divine power and hence formed the foundation for developing religion.

Anthropologists think it is likely that all members of a tribe participated in the earliest sacred rituals, but that later the practice of rituals became the domain of a single individual who had potency where the desired outcome of worship was concerned, and whose role eventually evolved into that of the priest. They also believe that sacred rituals were associated not only with particular people, but with specific places, such as the caves of Lascaux that were found decorated with scenes from the

hunt, presumably to heighten the power of the rituals performed there. What is more, evidence exists to support the idea that time of year was important in the practice of these ancient rituals, changes in seasons seem to have been the favored time for performing them.

Time is important in another way. According to anthropologically oriented religious scholars such as Mircea Eliade, we can follow the trail of ritual all the way back through human history to the Great Time when people banded together to form the first human community. These scholars see the role of religion as preserving the sacred elements of the cultures they formed through ritual reenactment. These preservation efforts link each generation to its ancestors and ultimately to the original humans. It is in this sense that today's ritual reenactments of sacred practices carry their participants back to the Great Time when humans first appeared on earth. The practice of sacred ritual transports human consciousness from the ordinary mode of everyday existence to that of spiritual reality which Cassirer identified with mythological consciousness, as we will discuss in Chapter 4. Ritual reenactment does *not* imply, however, that cultures are static. To the contrary, if so many different cultures all trace to the same Great Time, then cultures must change. Yet, if the oldest knowledge, once proven worthy, is preserved in ritual and symbol, how do cultures change? The study of theater helps us to understand this seeming paradox.

The famous Polish theater creator and mystic Jerzy Grotowski (1965–9, cited in Osinski 1998: 175) noted that reenacting rituals makes us channels for past knowledge:

> is it possible to touch something that is connected not only to beginnings, but, if I dare say so – the beginning? I don't know anything about that. When I work close to spirit I have the impression that memory becomes reality. When spirit is being enacted it is as if very powerful potentials were enacted. Reminiscence is perhaps one of these potentials.

Grotowski believed that theater embodies and incarnates the sacred. Osinski (1998) added that theater (as with other forms of ritual reenactment such as religious worship) does this by allowing us to directly experience the sacred in the present moment even as it connects us through archaic memory to the distant past.

However, ritual reenactment also permits each generation to cast its own set of characters to play the roles and to define new situations in which to rediscover the truth of what has been preserved. An example of this occurs when an old play is reinterpreted in a contemporary setting, as in Shakespeare's retelling of an old Nordic tale in *Hamlet,* or as in *West Side Story*, which reset Shakespeare's Romeo and Juliet in 1950s New York. Thus ritual, whether in the context of religious worship or the theater, creates the possibility of simultaneously preserving and changing knowledge. Whether these memories are communicated by a single narrator, as in storytelling (see Chapter 2), or by a cast of players, as in theater (this chapter), sacred knowledge is preserved, renewed and revised via ritual reenactment.

## Theater through the Ages[1]

Theater developed out of primitive ritual into dramatic stories about gods and their relationships with humans and then about the humans themselves (e.g., noblemen, warriors, hunters). Both tragedy and comedy appear to have developed in ancient tribes, for instance, it is known that the Peruvian Indians had both. Tragedy was concerned with normative or prescriptive knowledge (what one should do) and focused on the ruling classes, while comedy concerned the everyday life (how people really are) of the lower classes. In Egypt, records of theatrical coronation rituals date to around 3000 BC. Greece, from which the rest of Western theater developed, had theater sometime before the sixth century BC. In India the earliest Sanskrit drama has been dated to 320 AD. While Japanese No (known today as either Noh or Kabuki) developed around the seventh century, and China had a school for scenic art and music in the ninth century, Westerners did not know much about Asian theater before the nineteenth century.

The fall of the Roman Empire in 476 and the concurrent rise of Christianity brought the end of most forms of theater for many generations of Westerners. In spite of church decrees against theater in all its forms, however, mimes and minstrels continued to practice their craft and some pagan rites and festivals endured. Ironically, when theater again appeared in Western Europe in the tenth century, it was as part of Christian worship services. Miracle plays (about the lives of saints), mystery plays (about the life of Christ) and passion plays (about Christ's crucifixion), performed by the clergy, were used to instruct followers by providing them with visual examples of biblical stories.

Medieval theater developed out of the secularization of liturgical drama when the priests realized that the dramas they enacted had become more popular than the rest of the worship service. Secularization was a slow process. First the plays were moved to the churchyard and some lay actors were involved, but eventually only lay actors performed the plays and ultimately they were removed from the church grounds entirely. By the fourteenth and fifteenth centuries the church was once again completely disassociated from theatrical productions, although religious subjects were still mandated by the church to be the subjects of dramatic presentations, such as those of morality plays depicting moral concerns, for instance, man's attempt to save his soul. Christopher Marlowe's *The Tragical History of Doctor Faustus*, about a man who sells his soul to the devil, is a well-known sixteenth-century example of the morality play.

The Middle Ages saw tremendous developments in the staging and geographical dispersion of theater, but these pale in comparison to the developments that accompanied the Renaissance. Along with the Enlightenment came more complex dramas that could be shared through the invention of the printing press. The appearance of the middle classes during this period provided a whole new audience for theater,

---

[1]   The material on the history of theatre is based on Marsh Cassady's *Theatre: An Introduction* (1997).

which heretofore had been the domain of the wealthy who made theatrical production possible with their patronage, although their patronage more often took the form of protection than financial support. While some playwrights of the Renaissance looked to the classics of Greece and Rome (especially to the recently recovered Roman plays of Seneca) for inspiration and sought to perfect classical forms (the Italian Renaissance with its development of opera led the way), others were more forward looking, building on the looser, often improvisational style of medieval drama and staging with its reliance on sensational effects and preference for romantic adventures.

It was in Elizabethan England (1508–1603) that the next interesting development took place. Queen Elizabeth I, concerned to avoid further inflaming the conflict between Catholics and Protestants, reversed the dictum that theatrical productions should focus on religious content, and in the spirit of nationalism ruled that dramatists now had to choose patriotic themes rather than religious ones for their plays. It was her intention to unite England by emphasizing a shared cultural heritage, an important part of which was the theater. Thus, Elizabeth drove religion out of the theater just as many years before the church had pushed theater out of its domain.

By the mid-seventeenth century most of Western theater came under the influence of the technical aspects of theatrical production so successfully developed in Italy for the opera. Nationalism was growing all over Europe, as well as in England and its fledgling America, and the elaborate costumes and complex staging of the Italian opera were copied in the national theaters of France, England, Spain, Germany, Poland, Hungary and across Scandinavia. In England, however, the Puritans gained control of the government and maintained it for thirteen years, during which theater was banned. Theater returned with the restoration of Charles II to the English throne in 1660, following which comedies about the shortcomings of the upper classes became extremely popular.

With the establishment of the Parliament in England and the advance of trade and industry, the conduct of the upper and middle classes started to converge and the artificiality of court life became a popular subject for plays, as did the sentimental and mundane existence of the idealized middle classes. Russia, Holland, and the Scandinavian countries all established theater outside the royal court during this period, a change that occurred in other Western countries thereafter. By the nineteenth century, with the spread of industrialization and the growth of the railroads that allowed theater companies to travel to all parts of the Western world, modern theater was both secularized and open to just about everyone in the West. The diversity and geographical reach of modern theater types probably owes its existence to this development.

## The Theater Metaphor in Organization Studies

The use of the theatrical metaphor has its own history in sociology and organization studies. For example, Erving Goffman (1959; 1974) used dramaturgical analysis to

investigate the ways in which social actors present themselves and help one another to construct and maintain social roles that allow for organization and coordination. He borrowed the fundamental ideas of actor and audience from theater, applying them to an understanding of everyday social life as a mutually contrived performance. Ian Mangham (1987; 1998) created a theatrical metaphor by describing leadership using terms borrowed from the Italian dramatic genre of *commedia dell'arte* in which stock characters perform known sequences for audiences trained to anticipate them. Heather Hopfl (1995) described the work of employees in a modern service company as play acting and also used the metaphor of the theater to question the propriety of regulating organizational performances through the application of hierarchical authority (Hopfl 1996). Monika Kostera and Andrzej Koźmiński (1995) interpreted the moral values of Polish managers in times of transition using four types of theater: traditional Japanese Kabuki; contemporary European and American drama; the happening; and Michael Jackson's global show, a typology we will build upon below.

In their book *Organizations as Theatre*, Mangham and Overington (1987) argued that the big stars of management simultaneously play the roles of actors, playwrights and show directors. Using the example of the autobiography of Michael Edwardes, the former Chairman of British Leyland, these researchers demonstrated that a theatrical analysis of the multiple roles performed by star business leaders can reveal their personal philosophies of management. According to Mangham and Overington, it is the Michael Edwardeses of the management world, the Watsons, the Proctors, the Gambles, the Hewletts, Sloans, Geneens and Fords, who not only interpret the scripts, but also supervise the details of their performance. In the strictest sense, of course, few of these star actor-managers actually wrote any scripts; the script arises from their actions, it is a summation rather than a blueprint. Edwardes and others like him evolved their philosophies of management over long periods of time and, for the most part, were masters of drama, highly creative practitioners of the art of management.

According to American literary theorist Kenneth Burke (1969), the theatrical metaphor is well-suited to jointly analyzing social actions and people's explanations of social actions which he claimed lie behind the patterns of culture. In Burke's hands the theatrical metaphor became a method of dramaturgical analysis consisting of five questions: what was done? (act); when or where was it done? (scene); who did it? (agent); how was it done? (agency); and why? (purpose). We begin our theatrical look into the CEO interviews with consideration of how Burke's pentad would apply to the interviews in a general way. Table 3.1 summarizes our application of Burke's five dramaturgical concepts (scene, actor, act, agency, and purpose) along with three other common elements involved in producing a play (audience, casting, and directing).

Table 3.1 suggests that business leaders should act as producers and directors of artistic dramas that build on the talents of actors by teaching them to collaborate to achieve aesthetic as well as practical ends. Rather than merely typing scripts for

**Table 3.1** Elements of the theater metaphor applied to the *HBR* interviews

| | |
|---|---|
| Script | Interview schema: answering (or deflecting) questions, disclosing (or concealing) information |
| | Co-written by the CEO and the interviewer |
| Act/Action | Exchange of talk between interviewer and interviewee |
| | Storytelling and dramatic enactment (gesture, pose, monologue, dialogue) |
| | Describing, reporting, giving explanations |
| Setting/Scene | The point in the CEO's career when the organization is doing well or when the CEO has reached a personal pinnacle |
| | Background information given at the beginning of an interview, provided by the company, *HBR*'s research, and/or the interviewee |
| | Context of interview: current business issues and/or management practices |
| Agent/Actor | Interviewee/manager |
| | Other organizational member or stakeholder |
| | May also be company |
| Agency | Non-storytelling – reporting, informing, theorizing |
| | Storytelling |
| Purpose | Garner attention, build or capitalize on image/reputation |
| | Inspire, inform, socialize |
| | Illustrate management concepts or ideas |
| Audience | Editor (present) |
| | Employees (anticipated) |
| | Business and financial analysts (hoped for) |
| | Other managers (peers, aspirants, admirers, rivals, challengers) |
| Casting | *HBR*'s selection of the CEO to interview |
| | Consciousness of diversity issues (gender and nationality of interviewees, company characteristics such as industry, size, etc.) |
| Directing | Editor (questions asked, framing of interviews, titles and tag lines, post hoc editing) |
| | CEO (leading the interviewer, negotiating which questions to address, correcting and revising interview text) |
| | Selection of themes |

other people to follow, business leaders should adopt the strategies of directors who inspire moods, invoke feelings and motivations and watch over character development. The dramas they produce should have purpose as well as action, and the actors they cast in the play should be permitted to develop the agency demanded by their roles. In order to let the organization be innovative, business leaders, like the producers and directors of plays and their casts, have to credibly dare themselves to face chaos, to accept uncertainty, and channel these forces to create new forms of organizational performance together.

## Theater in the *HBR* Interviews: From Morality Play to Global Show

Theater has global reach and a history almost as long as human culture. It accompanied very different cultures and distinctive social and moral orders, therefore different types of theater were created representing a highly differentiated spectrum of theater types. In order to grasp some of the variety of dramatic approaches to management entertained by the collection of CEOs interviewed by *HBR* we have adapted Kostera and Koźmiński's (1995) typology to include:

- morality play
- modern drama
- the happening
- the global show.

In a morality play, characters are fixed and the action is focused on an ethically charged situation with one morally superior resolution. Audience members are familiar with the story, know who is good and who is bad, and know how they are expected to react to characters who behave in stereotypical ways. This type of theater invites the audience to sit in moral judgment and dictates what that judgment should be. There is nothing ambivalent about the characters, each of whom symbolizes a certain virtue, vice or value such as courage, honor, waywardness, trickery, treason or love. The actors faithfully follow the script and always fulfill the expectations of their audience. The entire production supports the ethics of the society of which it is a dramatic representation. This type of theater is present in different epochs and cultures and includes, among others: Italian *comedia dell'arte*, the traditional Japanese Kabuki theater and the American western. The popular film *Star Wars* is a technologically sophisticated example of a contemporary morality play.

Modern drama in the West developed following the Renaissance in Europe and from there was carried to America. It is a theater of reflection, dilemma, and ambivalence. The situation in a modern drama is never fully defined in the script, thus this type of theater is deliberately ambiguous. Instead of the morality play's clear-cut judgments, the modern drama demands the audience member's own interpretation as well as the director's and actors' creativity. A good play of this type should be puzzling and leave space for varied interpretations. A new production of a modern play often renews discussion of particular moral matters but does so in an open way. The more open a play is to multiple interpretations, the more likely it is to become a classic of this genre. Shakespeare's plays are exemplary of modern drama in that they are open to perhaps infinite re-interpretation: each character, each role comes close to offering limitless possibilities for reconceptualization and moral re-evaluation. Both the characters and the actors have choice and seek to legitimate their choices in relation to their particular system of values and moral

sensibilities. The sequence of events, however, is logical and causal relationships between events are understandable on the grounds of a modern notion of common sense. The ambiguity involved in these plays is rooted in the complexities of human motives, norms, and values.

Happenings are plays structured in unconventional ways. For example, the actors' roles are often compartmentalized, that is, they are separated one from another in a way that allows novel interactions to occur between them when they are performed together. Because of this structure the action in a happening is often indeterminate and frequently without logic, which does not mean that it is completely improvised. Acts are premeditated and rehearsed by actors but only separately – interaction between them provides the element of surprise that is characteristic of this type of theater. The audience is integral to the happening and is expected to behave in a spontaneous and playful fashion that adds to the novelty of the performance. Nobody is in full control of the situation. What a happening produces is unpredictable and dynamic; for aficionados this product is the essence of creativity. The consequences can be evaluated after the fact, but those who participate often say that the process is more important than the product, with perhaps the element of expression being the most important of all.

The global show is a special kind of theater. It is special because it contains the other three types of theater. For example, the global show put on by Michael Jackson embraces all roles and values: he is black and white, a man and a woman, homo- and heterosexual, virtuous and wicked. He is Liz Taylor, Cleopatra, and Julius Cesar all rolled into one. Most characteristic of this type of theater is its elaborate, high-tech staging that requires extensive behind-the-scenes professional support. Everybody's expectations are met in a global show; it is designed to have universal appeal. This is not merely a matter of interpretation: while seeing one characteristic, one inevitably sees its opposite. The foundation for this type of theater is not interpretation, but rather a way of switching emphases that need not be ruled by a consistent rationality, nor rule out contradiction. It is universalized, globalized, a complete virtual reality comprising both the hyperreal and the modernist "really real." It is the theater of the self-conscious, of living in the postmodern age, the simulacrum of everything-at-once. And yet, the show is minutely planned. No real spontaneity is possible, or desirable. The global show is a discourse of total possibility where all the boundaries between cultures, nationalities, social groups, the "real" and the "not real" have been demolished. In this theatrical mode the star performer is a global product and the audience surrenders its imagination and identity to the performer who comes to life on the stage.

Our typology of theatrical styles is not meant to be used to typecast companies or their CEOs. While each interview was more suggestive of one theater type than the others, all CEOs demonstrated the capacity to use more than one form (see Table 3.2). Although no one in the set of interviews used all four types, it is worth noting that during the period 1989–98 *HBR* published two interviews with COOs (chief operating officers) – Judy Lewent of Merck and Gary Wilson of Disney – and

**Table 3.2** Theater types illustrated by the *HBR* interviews

| Theater type (theme) | Illustrated by interview with: | Secondary theater type(s) interview illustrates: |
| --- | --- | --- |
| Morality play (ethics) | Levi Strauss – Robert Haas | Modern |
| | Volkswagen – Carl Hahn | Modern + Global |
| | USAA – Robert McDermott | Modern |
| | Stride Rite – Arnold Hiatt | Happening |
| | Greater SE – Tom Chapman | Modern |
| | SMH – Nicolas Hayek | Happening |
| | Nature Conservancy – John Sawhill | Modern |
| | Eni – Franco Bernabè | Modern |
| Modern drama (ambiguity) | Compaq – Rod Canion | Happening |
| | Bell Atlantic – Raymond Smith | Happening + Morality play |
| | TRW – Frederick Crawford | Morality play |
| | Softbank – Masayoshi Son | Happening |
| | Nike – Phil Knight | Happening |
| | Xerox – Paul Allaire | Happening |
| | Merck – Roy Vagelos | Happening |
| | British Airways – Colin Marshall | Global show + Morality play |
| | British Petroleum – John Browne | Happening + Global Show |
| | Motorola – George M.C. Fisher | Happening |
| | Ahlström – Krister Ahlström | Happening + Morality play |
| Happening (improvisation) | Raychem – Paul Cook | Modern |
| | Globe Metallurgical – Arden Sims | Modern + Morality |
| | Silicon Graphics – Ed McCracken | Morality play |
| | Allied Signal – Lawrence Bossidy | Morality play |
| | Monsanto – Robert Shapiro | Global show |
| | Dell – Michael Dell | Modern |
| Global show (universality) | Thomson – Alain Gomez | Modern + Happening |
| | Citicorp – John Reed | Modern |
| | ABB – Percy Barnevik | Modern |
| | Vitro – Ernesto Martens | Modern |
| | Whirlpool – David Whitwam | Modern |

in both cases the interviewees used only one theater type. This leads us to wonder if CEOs have greater capacity or opportunity to develop and display a wider range of dramatic expression than do other managers, a question to which we will return later in this chapter.

Below we illustrate our typology of four theaters in business with examples based on some of the interviews we read. Certainly not all of the interviews are equally dramatic. Some have much less theater in them than others. We will linger over those with the most illustrative potential.

## Business as morality play

Morality plays are built around values and ideals. They are highly didactic; CEOs who perform in them often sound like preachers or evangelists. For instance, in his *HBR* interview, Stride Rite's Arnold Hiatt moralized about his company's obligation to society (Stone 1992: 103):

> You can't run a healthy company in an unhealthy society for long. The millions of Americans who live below the poverty line deprive us of a market equal to the combined populations of Holland, Belgium, Denmark, Norway, and Sweden. By failing to liberate the children who are imprisoned by poverty and inadequate education, we further compromise our future as well as theirs.

A similar moralistic tone can be heard in SMH's CEO Nicolas Hayek's expressed belief in the need to defend Swiss industry against foreign competition (Taylor 1993: 100):

> We are all global companies competing in global markets. But that does not mean that we owe no allegiance to our own societies and cultures.
> We must build where we live. When a country loses the know-how and expertise to manufacture things, it loses its capacity to create wealth – its financial independence. When it loses its financial independence, it starts to lose political sovereignty.
> We have to change that reflex: that instinctive reaction that if a company has a mass market consumer product, the only place to build it is Asia or Mexico. CEOs must say to their people: "We will build this product in our country at a lower cost and with higher quality than anywhere else in the world". Then they have to figure out how to do it.

Sometimes, as in Hiatt's and Hayek's cases, the values that are central to a morality play are related to societal or national interests, sometimes to the community or some group within it. Tom Chapman, CEO of the Greater Southeast Community Hospital in Washington DC, illustrated community-level interests (Nichols 1992: 88):

> At Greater Southeast we don't just treat the illnesses our patients bring to us, we try to treat the diseases that are racking our community – poverty, illiteracy, drugs and violence.
> Beyond that we've tried to make serving children our top priority. When we can we try to structure our services around their needs.

In the morality play CEOs often speak about their moral motivation. For example, Franco Bernabè, who took over Eni, the state-owned Italian oil giant, in the midst of the worst corruption crisis in its history, spoke directly to the issue of resisting corruption (Hill & Wetlaufer 1998: 85):

My basic motivation was moral. Eighty five percent of the people were paying for the wrongdoings of 15% of the people who were responsible for the corruption and misuse of politics. They were suffering because that 15% was stealing their professional pride. Their image of good honest, hard-working people was being stolen from them. I had to right that inequity.

In some interviews, such as those mentioned above, the values a performance was built around were highly idealistic, even messianic in their broad societal reach. In others the values were more pragmatic and inward-oriented. For example, Robert F. McDermott, CEO of the USAA insurance company serving predominantly US military officers, said (Teal 1991: 118):

The mission and corporate culture of this company are, in one word, service. As a company objective, service comes ahead of either profits or growth.

Robert Haas, CEO of the Levi Strauss company, explicitly saw values and morals as instrumental to the success of his company (Howard 1990: 134):

What we've learned is that the soft stuff and the hard stuff are becoming increasingly intertwined. A company's values – what it stands for, what its people believe in – are crucial to its competitive success. Indeed, values drive the business.
    Values provide a common language for aligning a company's leadership and its people.

In a similar way traditional family values (embodied in social programs) were perceived by Arnold Hiatt, CEO of Stride Rite, to lie behind his company's success in the highly competitive US footwear industry (Stone 1992: 96):

Our strength lies in building on classics, on knowing who we are. That is how we've succeeded as a company. And that same quality lies behind the social programs and policies we've introduced over the years. They are conservative in the best sense of the word because they restore something that was in danger of being lost – extended families, a healthy work environment. Moreover they reflect the same values and business principles that have driven Stride Rite's evolution and growth as a company.

As Robert Haas (Howard 1990: 142) pointed out, however, the value of honesty is important even when it places you in an uncomfortable position:

You can't promise employment security and be honest. The best you can do is not play games with people. You can't make any guarantees.

In the morality play CEOs represent and personify the values they are promoting. They are the stars on the *HBR* stage. Like cedar dolls in the Japanese Kabuki theater they represent the values they stand for in the show. Dark characters, who do not espouse the values promoted by our heroes, are not explicitly discussed in

the interviews, but their presence can be felt in the background of the morality plays that were enacted within the *HBR* interviews with CEOs. They are present in the setting of the scene, for example:

- unlike Tom Chapman they practice business-like technocratic medicine for the rich;
- unlike Robert Haas they concentrate on "hard" aspects of business and do not leave space for the expression of values at work;
- unlike Nicolas Hayek they transfer production to low wage regions of the world;
- unlike Franco Bernabè they get involved in corrupt exchanges.

The values emphasized by the CEOs whose interviews illustrate the morality play all communicate the key values of the CEO and/or his organization in terms of an ethical mandate. Interviews illustrating this form may include complex subplots or surprises that invoke other forms, but the dominant flavor of these interviews is the strong moral position taken. Relative to the other theater types, the morality play is simpler and highly focused on one core message couched in terms of an ethical position.

## Modern drama in business

Intrigue is the essence of modern drama that presents a complex set of unstructured problems to be solved by the characters. Ambiguity, uncertainty, suspense, and the absence of absolute or easy judgments are consequences of the intrigue. Dominating problems, proposed solutions and conflicts between them are the primary elements in the intrigue presented by the modern drama.

According to Krister Ahlström, CEO of the Finnish company owned by his family, Ahlström might be a stage set for a somber family drama by Ibsen that mixes such components as family pride, power games and generational conflicts in an increasingly unforgiving environment. Compared with the golden age of the founding fathers, chaos was rampant in recent times. Ahlström's rational, sometimes Machiavellian strategies form the action in this complex family drama, as illustrated by this example taken from his interview (Magretta 1998b: 117):

> The key is that people play multiple roles in a family business. At Ahlström, the cast of characters includes managers, board members and family members. Some people play all three roles at once. Others are owners only. Sorting out the different perspectives inherent in these roles and relationships can really help you make sense of any issue or decision.

For Xerox's Paul Allaire the intrigue was an old staff-driven functional organization that was in conflict with the demand for creativity and flexibility that Xerox faced (Howard 1992: 110):

It breeds dependence and passivity. In a functional organization there is a natural tendency for conflicts to get kicked upstairs. People are too accustomed to sitting on their hands and waiting for decisions to come down from above.

Allaire stated his goal in terms of a contradiction between the characteristics of large and small companies, both of which he saw as necessary for Xerox's success (Howard 1992: 111):

> In fact we intend to create a company that combines the best of both worlds – the speed, flexibility, accountability and creativity that come from being a small highly focused organization and the economies of scale, the access to resources and the strategic vision that a large corporation can provide.

The intricate plot and complexities of the modern drama are illustrated by Allaire's description of what must happen for Xerox to transform itself (Howard 1992: 112):

> By redefining the three key components that make up any organizational architecture. The first we call "hardware." These are the things managers usually think of as organizational structure, the formal processes by which we get things done: the business planning system, control mechanisms, measurement systems, reporting relationships, reward systems and the like.
>
> The second is "people" – the new skills managers need, including the kind of personality and character they must have to operate effectively in the new environment. Clearly if you are running a functional organization, you go with functional experts and you manage with a lot of staff who hold the functions together. But in decentralized, more entrepreneurial organizations, like we have now you, need a completely different kind of manager.
>
> Finally, the third component of our new architecture is what we call "software." This is the most difficult to describe but probably the most important: the informal networks and practices linking people together, the value system, the culture. Any company that leaves these out of its organizational change effort is making a big mistake.

The plot then unfolds as Allaire describes how suspense and uncertainty come with difficulties and failures linked to the implementation of the new architecture (Howard 1992: 118).

> But we were not doing it just to be perverse. The change process we have begun is extremely difficult. We have to be very diligent so that old habits, practices and behaviors don't sneak back in.

Several instances of resistance to change and ways to overcome it were put on the stage that made up Allaire's modern drama. Here is one example of his flair for the dramatic (Howard 1992: 118):

My favorite example comes from the management team that designed our new architecture. Here is a group of 20 people who, more than anyone else in the company have internalized the new approach to running things. And yet, when it came to deciding to organize the business divisions, that group recommended that we start with the business division staff – the head of personnel, head of finance etc – and that the staff help each division president to choose his or her operating people. In other words they immediately fell back into a traditional top-down functional approach.

At that critical moment our hero intervened:

I said "hold on. Don't we have it backwards? I thought we were trying to run this business by the line? Why would you select the staff people to help the presidents select the line? Why don't we do it just the reverse? Who are the key line managers required to run these businesses? We can help them figure that out. They don't need to hire individual staff people to do that. We can help them put their team leaders in place, then the presidents and their team leaders can decide together what kind of staff support they need".

This intervention of the CEO had dramatic impact (Howard 1992: 118):

At first they were convinced I was wrong. But as we talked it through, you could see a shock of recognition go through the group. Everyone started to say, "Well, I think we just violated the principles with this recommendation". They began to realize that it would send exactly the wrong message to the organization. Finally somebody said to the person who had made the original proposal: "I think you'd better back off on this. Not only is he the boss. But I think he is right on this one."

The plot twists and lively dialogue of this example amply illustrate the convolutions of the modern drama as they appear in the *HBR* interviews that we read. All the interviews we have categorized as illustrating this type can be relatively easily transformed into modern dramatic scripts similar to the one presented above. While Allaire's example takes the popular form of a success story (or epic, as explained in Chapter 2), in some cases a failure (tragedy) added dramatic flavor to the script. Nike's CEO Phil Knight provided a good example of the tragic plot twist within the modern type of theater (Willigan 1992: 94):

In the early days, when we were just a running shoe company and almost all our employees were runners, we understood the consumer very well. There is no shoe school, so where do you recruit people for a company that develops and markets running shoes? The running track. It made sense, and it worked. We and the consumer were one and the same.

   When we started making shoes for basketball, tennis, and football, we did essentially the same thing. We got to know the players at the top of the game and we did everything we could to understand what they needed, both from a technological and a design perspective. Our engineers and designers spent a lot of time talking to the athletes about what they needed both functionally and aesthetically.

It was effective – to a point. We were missing something. Despite great products and great ad campaigns, sales just stayed flat. We were missing an immense group.

Entering the casual shoes market was a response to that situation, but:

> From the start everybody understood that Nike was a running shoe company, and the brand stood for excellence in track and field. It was a very clear message, and Nike was very successful. But casual shoes sent a different message. People got confused, and Nike began to lose its magic. Retailers were unenthusiastic, athletes were looking at the alternatives, and sales slowed. So not only was the casual shoe effort a failure, but it was diluting our trademark and hurting us in running (Willigan 1992: 96).

The failure taught Nike a very important lesson:

> Understanding the consumer is just a part of good marketing. You also have to understand the brand. That's really the lesson we learned from casual shoes. The whole experience forced us to define what the Nike brand really meant, and it taught us the importance of focus. Without focus the whole brand is at risk (Willigan 1992: 96).

Highly focused brands usually limit sales growth, but Nike was able to grow rapidly putting the company back into the preferred epic mode (as explained in Chapter 2).

## Business as happening

In a happening the most important elements are situational parameters delimiting the physical, social and emotional space of the show. In other words the situation triggers the show by motivating the actors and the interaction between them, the show and the audience. The most compelling example of a happening in the *HBR* interviews we read was described by Nicolas Hayek of SMH who recalled an advertising stunt the company pulled for its Swatch watches (Taylor 1993: 103):

> How did we launch Swatch in Germany? Did we saturate the airwaves with paid advertisements? No. Anyone can do that. We built a giant Swatch. It was 500 feet high, weighed 13 tons, and actually worked. We suspended that giant Swatch outside the tallest skyscraper in Frankfurt, the headquarters of Commerzbank. It was really something to see!

The Swatch happening went from being a local event to a global show when SMH repeated the giant Swatch stunt in Japan (Taylor 1993: 103):

> We also hung a giant Swatch in Tokyo, in the Ginza. This message can work in Japan as well. By value, Swiss companies account for more than 50% of all the watches sold in Japan. SMH accounts for 75% of that 50%. Do you think we broadcast

these figures? Or that we act arrogantly in Japan? Of course not. The Japanese are sympathetic to us. We're nice people from a small country. We have nice mountains and clear water. They like us and our products, and we like them.

Turnarounds can be described as happenings in which crisis and danger trigger a show that ends in organizational renewal. Allied Signal's Lawrence A. Bossidy described Chrysler's turnaround as a happening, contrasting it to the lack of change at IBM (Tichy & Charan 1995: 70):

I believe in the "burning platform" theory of change. When the roustabouts are standing on the offshore oil rig and the foreman yells, "Jump into the water", not only won't they jump but they also won't feel too kindly toward the foreman. There may be sharks in the water. They will jump only when they themselves see the flames shooting up from the platform. Chrysler's platform was visibly burning; the company changed. IBM's platform was not visibly burning; it didn't.

Arden C. Sims, a manager who turned around Globe Metallurgical, a medium-sized US steel company, saw the fight for survival in terms of the risk of a happening (Rayner 1992: 129):

I consider myself a fairly conservative manager. But over the last eight years, I've had to take some pretty big risks just to survive, and I've had to fight some pretty fierce battles. There are a lot of companies out there, big and small, that face the same kind of challenges that we faced in the 1980s – low productivity, high costs, the wrong product line. They have to deal with their problems soon or they won't be around much longer.

In addition to turnarounds, looking for new unknown opportunities is another way to start a happening. This is particularly important in technologically advanced industries such as biotechnology, as illustrated by Monsanto's Robert B. Shapiro who emphasized the happening's unpredictable nature (Magretta 1997: 81):

We are entering a time of perhaps unprecedented discontinuity. Businesses grounded in the old model will become obsolete and die. At Monsanto we are trying to invent some new businesses around the concept of environmental sustainability. We may not yet know exactly what those businesses will look like, but we're willing to put some bets because the world cannot avoid needing sustainability in the long run.

Another reason to embark on the bumpy road of an innovation happening may be creative curiosity. As Raychem's Paul Cook illustrates, the happening is emotionally charged and highly involving (Taylor 1990: 99):

Innovation is an emotional experience. You can train people technically, but you can't teach them curiosity . . . You can't have a good technologist who doesn't wake up in the middle of the night searching for answers.

In some cases entrepreneurial spirit and a strong will to succeed motivate a happening. Masayoshi Son is an entrepreneur who started one of the world's most successful computer software companies – Softbank. In this passage from his interview, Son told about the conversation he had with his first big client illustrating the playful nature of drama as happening (Webber 1992: 97):

> He asked me many questions: How much capital do you have? How old are you? What kind of business experience do you have?
>
> I told him, I have very little money, very little business experience. I have no product, nothing. What I do have is the greatest enthusiasm, the greatest desire to succeed . . . If you want to be the number one PC dealer in Japan you have to find the number one guy in software distribution. That's me. I have no evidence, but I strongly believe in myself.

Important audiences for managers are employees, scientists and researchers, customers, investors, business partners and government. In a happening, these audience members are actively involved in the performance. For instance, Arden C. Sims of Globe Metallurgical told about involving workers' in his change effort (Rayner 1992: 129):

> I've found that one of the most important components of a successful transformation is to gain the respect of the work force. I don't mean the workers have to like you, although that helps, but they have to understand that you will stand your ground when it comes to forcing through big changes. To initiate change, you have to be tenacious, and you need to show that you are not afraid of getting a little dirt under your fingernails.

Similarly Raychem's Paul Cook acknowledged the importance of employee involvement in change (Taylor 1990: 99):

> One of my most important jobs is finding the right people to add to the Raychem environment – people who genuinely want to serve the customer, who want to build new products that are superior to anything that's come before, who are willing to stick their necks out to do new things. That means learning how their minds work, what they think about, what excites them, how they approach problems. The most important factor is individual recognition – more important than salaries, bonuses and promotions.

Softbank's Masayoshi Son told of how he got important business people on his board of directors by getting them to engage with his fantasies for Softbank's future (Webber 1992: 102):

> Look at our board of directors. We have a person who used to be second in command at Sharp. He was the head of all engineering at Sharp and a representative director there. We have the man who was second in command at Unisys Japan; he's now running SystemBank. We have the man who used to be a director of the Tokyo Stock

Exchange. He was in charge of making rules that control how companies go public and deciding which companies could go public. The way I attract these men to Softbank is to explain what my dream is.

## Producing a global show

The most important characteristic of the global show is its universal character, its ability to adjust to the needs, potential, values, norms, and cognitive structures of highly differentiated audiences around the world. The key question is how this universal character is accomplished. What are its enabling conditions? Answers to these questions may involve such elements as:

- mission and strategy
- organizational structure
- employees' orientations, attitudes, capabilities and skills
- technology
- marketing (e.g., use of brand names, symbols etc.).

As John Reed explained, the mission of Citicorp is global (Tichy & Charan 1990: 138):

> Let's do the whole world . . . Globality is our most important advantage, even over the Swiss, who have been the world's best private bankers. We have competitors in every country, but we don't have a single, unified, worldwide competitor.

Citicorp's global strategy is designed to have universal appeal and Reed intriguingly used the metaphor of a Chinese game that has become known the world over to explain his idea (Tichy & Charan 1990: 136):

> Global competition in banking is strategic as opposed to tactical. Competition among the top 30 players around the world is about occupying space. It's about positioning yourself wisely over time, not wiping out the other guys on specific products. I approach competition like the Chinese board game Go. You see where other players have put their chips, figure out why, and decide where to put your chips.

Citicorp's marketing was based on recognition of the similarities of consumers' needs around the world, which overcame their differences, thus illustrating the universalism of the global show in its ability to appeal to diverse audiences (Tichy & Charan 1990: 138):

> We also made an important discovery that drove everything we did later. It became apparent that there were more similarities than differences among customers around the world . . . The thing that separates us in the consumer business is our shared vision. Most bankers want to make loans, run branches and sell credit cards, but they don't identify with customers. We do. We don't say, "Consumers need credit cards". We

say, "Consumers need ways to buy things easily". That may mean credit cards, checks, or easy access to lots of cash.

Citicorp used multinational, multilingual staff on all levels, including top management. According to John Reed (Tichy & Charan 1990: 137):

> Our global human capital may be as important a resource, if not more important, than our financial capital. Look at the Policy Committee, the top 30 or so officers in the bank. Almost 75% have worked outside the United States; more than 25% have worked in three or more countries. Half speak a language other than English, more than a quarter speak two or more languages other than English. Seven were born outside the United States. Compare that with single culture competitors who are in a solid position financially.

The global show depends upon mobility – it must be transported around the world to reach its various audiences. In order to develop and improve operations worldwide a culture and operational system of sharing and transferring successful solutions had been developed at Citicorp (Tichy & Charan 1990: 139):

> We call this process "success transfer". The term was coined by a Citibanker; Rana Talvar, who came out of our Indian branch system to head up our consumer business in Singapore. He developed a new collection of mutual funds, and they became a great success in Singapore. He had the notion of transferring that success throughout the Asia Pacific region and it worked.

Volkswagen's Carl Hahn tried to build a global strategy out of the European platform his company developed (Avishai 1991: 104):

> I see Europe not as a fortress but as a platform for global competition. It is by concentrating on the European market that Volkswagen will establish the corporate structures and generate the enormous resources needed for world markets . . . We seek to turn Volkswagen AG into a "federated" European company: a true multinational emerging from the European theater, gaining the capacities to compete across the board worldwide. Poking fun at Lenin I have told my people, "All power to the marques". I want to pursue a vision of divisional autonomy: Volkswagen, Audi, Seat and Skoda.

French electronics giant Thomson went global through consolidation. As CEO Alain Gomez pointed out (McCormick & Stone 1990: 132):

> European companies have a choice: consolidate through acquisitions or ventures – or die by attrition.

According to Gomez, Thomson's strategy was based on mastering "critical" or "strategic" technologies while outsourcing less important ones (McCormick & Stone 1990: 128–9):

We grew our capacity as well as growing by acquisition. We took a very long view in measuring our return on investments. And when we had to, we licensed technologies and created joint ventures. But we always had the objective of attaining an in-house capacity in strategic technologies.

Thus the global show can have a predominantly internal audience that will help it perform more successfully on the world stage.

Rapidly globalizing American appliance manufacturer Whirpool pursued a highly integrated global strategy. According to its CEO, David Whitwam (Maruca 1994: 136):

> The only way to gain lasting competitive advantage is to leverage your capabilities around the world so that the company as a whole is greater than the sum of its parts. Being an international company – selling globally, having global brands or operations in different countries – isn't enough.
>
> Our vision at Whirpool is to integrate our geographical businesses wherever possible, so that our most advanced expertise in any given area – whether it's refrigeration technology, financial reporting systems, or distribution strategy – isn't confined to one location or one division. We want to be able to take the best capabilities we have and to leverage them in all of our operations worldwide.

According to Whitwam, organizational culture must be well orchestrated with that kind of strategy (Maruca 1994: 136–7):

> You must create an organization whose people are adept at exchanging ideas, processes, and systems across borders, people who are absolutely free of the "not-invented-here" syndrome, people who are constantly working together to identify the best global opportunities and the biggest global problems facing the organization. If you are going to ask people to work together in pursuing global ends across organizational and geographic boundaries, you have to give them a vision of what they're striving to achieve, as well as a unifying philosophy to guide their efforts.

The global show has a built-in mechanism of meticulous planning that is the result of its dependence on technical support to produce a show on the global scale. Thus the global show seems inherently linked to the modern drama that always appeared as a supportive drama in the interviews we read. As Whirpool's CEO, Whitwam, explained it (Maruca 1994: 143):

> Our strategy is based in the premise that world-class cost and quality are merely the ante – the price of being in the game at all. We have to provide a compelling reason other than price for consumers to buy Whirpool-built products. We can do that only by understanding the consumer better than anyone else does and then translating our understanding into clearly superior product designs, features and after-sales support. Our goal is for consumers to prefer the Whirpool brand because it offers greater overall value than competing products.

At ABB organizational structure played an important role in global strategy. The global matrix was ABB's invention and offers another form of technical support for the global show (Taylor 1991: 95):

> ABB is an organization with three internal contradictions. We want to be global and local, big and small, radically decentralized with centralized reporting and control. If we resolve those contradictions, we create real organizational advantage.
> That's where the matrix comes in. The matrix is the framework through which we organize our activities. It allows us to optimize our businesses globally and maximize performance in every country in which we operate.

Surprisingly, national values may be present in the global show but, unlike in the morality play national values are preserved as a means to compete globally. Mexican manager, Ernesto Martens of Vitro, put it this way (Nichols 1993: 164):

> We don't want to lose our identity as a Mexican company with a unique culture and relationship with our employees but we don't want to be battered in the world marketplace either.

Volkswagen's Carl Hahn had similar views but revealed that in VW's case globalization was not the primary ambition, it resulted from economic necessity (Avishai 1991: 106):

> But Volkswagen has never been an automobile company in the ordinary sense. We have been a monument and river of the postwar German recovery. Next to making profits our mandate was to motorize our country and large parts of Europe, to provide employment to tens of thousands of people. This responsibility meant that early on we were forced to concentrate on developing markets abroad.

## Dramatic Range

The four types of theater we identified represent four distinct themes in contemporary business: ethics (morality play), ambiguity (modern drama), improvisation (happening) and universality (global show). Based on our readings of the *HBR* interviews, we suspect that CEOs have a dramatic range that includes multiple dramatic forms because each of the interviews gave evidence of the use of at least two of the theater types (see Table 3.2, columns 1 and 3).

In the interviews we read, the morality play was most often accompanied by the modern drama type, where rational decisions helped to overcome ambiguity and chaos to enact core values. Missionaries armed themselves with rational modern tools, as McDermott of USAA illustrated with his complex plan to improve his company's performance (Teal 1991: 119):

By the time I took over, I had already made four basic decisions. First, we were going to automate our policy writing system.

Second, we were going to reduce the number of employees and do it by means of attrition – we weren't going to fire anyone. Turnover was very, very high at that time, so it wasn't a difficult promise to keep.

Third, we were going to have an education and training program to upgrade employee quality and enrich the jobs. "Enriched" was a word I'd seen on a loaf of bread, where it meant they'd added something to improve nutrition. I wanted to add interest and challenge to our jobs.

Fourth, we were going to decentralize. The decisions about how to serve our 650,000 members had to be made on the front line.

Management processes, however, can rarely be fully represented by pre-written detailed scenarios combined with actors' and directors' interpretations. Some place has to be left for spontaneity and improvisation within more or less rigidly set parameters. The CEOs in the interviews we read seemed to understand this, and we believe that is why they so often accompanied the modern drama with happenings. Happenings allow and even encourage unpredictable and unstructured processes of learning and development within a predetermined scenario, as British Petroleum's John Browne illustrated (Prokesch 1997: 150):

> The conventional wisdom is that excelling in incremental learning is a science – a matter of installing the right processes – while excelling in breakthrough thinking is more of an art. I disagree about the latter. I think you can install processes that generate breakthrough thinking. We have.
>
> Another conventional view is that it is harder to tap implicit knowledge, which is the experiential knowledge locked inside someone's head, than explicit knowledge, which can be captured in a database. But that hasn't been our experience. We have had great success in fostering the personal interactions you need to mine explicit knowledge.

George Fisher of Motorola started his play by introducing the purely rational principle of regular customer visits (Avishai & Taylor 1989: 108):

> First, we've established a massive program of increasing customer visits at all levels of the organization. We want everyone in Motorola, from top to bottom, to get out and see customers – to talk with them directly and to understand their business better.

The complexity and intricacy of events that followed are typical of the modern drama, but within this broad script can be found a series of happenings. Customers started talking, Motorola's people were listening and when these normally compartmentalized roles were jointly enacted, unanticipated solutions emerged (Avishai & Taylor 1989: 109–10):

> Take the radio data communication system we developed with IBM. We have an ongoing dialogue with IBM; I'm not even sure who came to whom on this project. One of the business problems IBM had talked with us about for a long time involved

customer service. How could they keep track of maintenance records on computers and the availability of spare parts across the country? How could they reduce the need for their service people to borrow customers' telephone lines while they are on their premises? How could their service people make calls from near a computer where there's no computer available? How could they better dispatch their field engineers?

IBM didn't identify radio communication solutions per se. They defined their problems. Talking through that situation led us to do something we had never done before. Together we saw how we could put up a nation-wide, interconnected radio system with a portable communicating computer in a very small package. It didn't exist, but we knew it was possible. So we worked together. IBM provided much of the software and the interface to their host computers. We put up the radio data network.

A happening is usually followed, accompanied or reinforced by some kind of a plan in the manner of the modern drama. Raychem is a good example of just such a combination of these two theatrical modes. The whole value system at Raychem is based on innovation (Taylor 1990: 98):

> We get innovation at Raychem because our corporate strategy is premised on it. Without innovation we die.

Developing new technology is a happening, but leveraging it on the market calls for a plan, which can best be represented by the modern drama (Taylor 1990: 106):

> The essence of innovation is discovering what your organization is uniquely good at – what special capabilities you possess and taking advantage of those capabilities to build products and deliver services that are better than anyone else's. Every company has unique strengths. Success comes from leveraging those strengths in the market.

At Dell Computers countless meetings with customers and special councils for the information executives of client companies helped to get customers involved in the Dell happening. According to CEO Michael Dell, the environment of new technology produces the happening to which his company responds in the rational way of the modern American and European drama that plays a supportive role in Dell's customer-engaged happenings (Magretta 1998a: 80):

> The councils are another way we're able to play more of an advisory role, trying to help our customers understand what the flow of new technology really means, how it will translate into specific products. We are trying to help the customer anticipate what's happening and be ready. And that helps us as well, with our own demand forecasting. So we're helping each other in important ways.

Although these two examples pair the happening with the modern drama, happenings are just as often paired with morality plays and global shows in the interviews that we read. Allied Signal's Bossidy recalled in a happening-like way forging a set of company values that creatively combined the happening with a morality play (Tichy & Charan 1995: 71):

But we had to unite ourselves with vision and values. And that effort begins with the team at the top. In November 1991, we had an off-site meeting with the top 12 managers of the company. We spent two days arguing – and I mean arguing – about values. That was helpful because at the end of the meeting, we not only had values, we also had a specific definition of each of those values. The seven values we settled on are simple: customers, integrity, people, teamwork, speed, innovation and performance. They're not unique. But they are important because they give all our people a view of what behavior is expected of them. And if you are a leader in this company, you risk being labeled a hypocrite if you don't behave according to those values. And you are going to get some heat – and I think that's terrific.

A similar happening-like philosophy of "letting things happen" was intertwined with the core values of innovation and customer service at Silicon Graphics in this example provided by CEO Ed McCracken (Prokesch 1993: 136):

Our philosophy is that the key to achieving competitive advantage isn't reacting to chaos: it's producing that chaos. And the key to being a chaos producer is being an innovation leader ... But I think the key to obtaining competitive advantage in the 1990s is making your customers feel you designed a product specially for them, that your product has special features or capabilities for which they would pay a premium. It's difficult to add values if you are removed from your customers.

The dramatic range of some CEOs combined happenings with global shows. Monsanto's Robert B. Shapiro is such a leader and he shows us how a happening became global (Magretta 1997: 84):

That off-site meeting in 1994 led to an emerging insight that we couldn't ignore the changing global environmental conditions. The focus around sustainable development became obvious. I should have been able to come up with that in 15 minutes. But it took a group of very good people quite a while to think it through, to determine what was real and what was just puff, to understand the data, and to convince themselves that this wasn't a fluffy issue – and that we ought to be engaged in it.

## Putting on a Show

In the set of interviews we read, corporate morality plays were quite often accompanied by dramas of the modern type, while modern drama-based interviews were more commonly paired with happenings. As these theater types developed in a historical sequence – morality plays predated modern drama, which in turn predated the happening followed by the global show – it would appear that use of the morality play and the modern drama anticipate their successive forms. However, when we turn to the improvisational happening, anything goes! As might be expected on the basis of the form, this type was equally likely to be paired with a morality play, a modern drama, or a global show. Interestingly the global show, in contrast

to the happening, was paired only with the modern drama, which is by far the most common form seen across all the interviews we read and may simply be a legitimating nod by the newest form to the currently dominant form.

It appears on the basis of the interviews that performances by business leaders and/or their organizations are staged in front of large audiences of different kinds of stakeholders (e.g., employees, customers, the public, *HBR* editors and readers) and are built around the messages business leaders want to convey to these audiences. Their need to inspire audience members is why the aesthetic faces of leadership are so important. As we hope to have shown by example, a beautiful, dramatic, seductive message has a much more powerful impact than does a dry and dull analysis. Students of management often neglect the issue of dramatic effect in favor of emphasizing the rational face of the manager. Our point is that purely technical management (based on scientific and analytical foundations) has a limited future because of the shift from an emphasis on control to inspiration. As demonstrated in this chapter and Chapter 2, successful business leaders often know instinctively how to practice the arts of storytelling and dramatic performance.

As the examples from the interviews also show, successful business leaders mix value judgments, emotions, prejudices, and vanity with rational analysis and the application of state-of-the-art scientific principles. Complex webs of relationships among these elements (clearly visible through the lens of the theatrical metaphor) are mostly absent in the scientific analysis that represents business leadership as a purely rational economic endeavor. The use of the theatrical metaphor reveals the artistic, emotional and ethical aspects of business leadership that stand alongside the rational. The rational and the aesthetic can be seen working in tandem in the modern theatrical script where intrigue is created by violating rational premises that are later restored by solving the intrigue. As Table 3.2 indicates, the modern drama dominates managerial forms of theater as it is depicted in the *HBR* interviews in that it is represented in some way in all but five of the interviews we read. We believe this indicates the extent to which the group of interviewed CEOs continued to present the face of the manager during the 1990s even as they practiced the skills of the artist and the priest.

The material presented in this chapter suggests that theatrical instincts and dramatic skill are a second vehicle, alongside storytelling (see Chapter 2), for building organizational culture through business leadership. Our readings of the *HBR* interviews with CEOs indicate the practical sense of conducting management development through theatrical activities such as playwriting, directing, acting, set design and staging. More passive ways of developing theatrical skill include analysis and critique of theatrical performances, which is also useful but not as powerful as direct involvement. Practiced along with storytelling, discussed in Chapter 2, these theatrical activities will develop the unique skills of capturing peoples' attention, building tension and creating drama, combining emotion with reflection, intuition with analysis, and moral judgment with cold calculation. We feel that our readings of the *HBR* interviews have shown that emotion, intuition and moral judgment are as essential to business leadership as they are to theater.

Dramatizing business consciously builds up the spectacle of the organization and its product and service experiences for customers, business partners, employees, shareholders and the general public and we have seen in recent years how public excitement can influence Wall Street just as it does Main Street or Broadway. Of course we have also learned that over-excitement on Wall Street can lead to disaster just as can the exclusive reliance on any one face of leadership expressed in isolation of the other two. Even though we are focusing here mainly on the faces of the artist and the priest in business leadership, do not forget that this is only because these faces have been underplayed in recent times. However, just as it is unwise to rely completely on the rational face of the manager, it is equally unwise to rely solely upon either the face of the artist or the priest – it is a broad-ranging aesthetic base we are after as well as a healthy balance between the technical and aesthetic faces of leadership. And so we move in the next chapter from storytelling and theater to our third aesthetic element – myth. But first, let us present some ideas for developing skill at dramatizing your business.

## Staging a show and engaging the critics

Plays are stories that are dramatized. To dramatize a story you must lift it onto a stage where you will act it out for an audience. Generally plays are performed by multiple players, so you will need to secure help from others to act the parts of the characters in your story. This means you will need to concern yourself with staging and casting as well as with attracting an audience for whom to perform. You may also want to create sets and scenery, assemble props, and/or make costumes. It is up to you how intricate or how simple you want the performance to be. Go back to the categories listed in Table 3.1 to help you think through your many options.

To begin the process of learning to dramatize you may find it useful to reverse engineer some of the dramatic events you find in the everyday life of your organization. For instance, take a close look at a business meeting, a product launch, retirement dinner, award ceremony, press conference, ad campaign, trade show, executive retreat, training program or team building effort. What dramatic elements can you find in these examples to represent the categories of Table 3.1? Describe how those who enact the dramas of your everyday work life use these elements. Which of these uses of dramatic elements are the most effective and why? What does not work?

Now get ready to put on your own show. Whether you do this in your imagination or on a real stage is up to you. Either way, take one of the stories you wrote for Chapter 2 or another you write for this purpose. You might start by thinking about relating a story about what happened yesterday or what you hope or fear will happen tomorrow. What sort of drama will you create: a romance, tragedy, comedy or epic? Whatever its form, imagine how you might translate your story into a play. Write a script. Design a set and assemble your dream cast by thinking of famous actors who could best bring your characters to life on a stage. Be sure to think about who should play you! How will you direct your actors to behave so that they

can communicate to the audience what happens in your story? What motives should they imagine they possess to explain their actions? How will you explain to them the idea behind your story? To whom will they present your play? What has inspired the audience to attend? How do you hope they will receive your play? What will they think about it? How will they feel as they are leaving? What will they say about it to their friends?

After you perform your play, either on stage or in your imagination, ask yourself: who are your critics? What reviews did your play receive? What did the critics like about your play? What did they dislike? Why? How will you respond to the criticism you received for your play? What would you do differently considering the criticism you were given? It is good to remember that artists and priests do not always respond to all of their critics or the criticisms given and you do not have to do so either. But consider that some of the things for which you get criticized may be of a great importance to you and defensiveness may cause you to overlook these. All artists and mystics get misunderstood and unfairly criticized at times. Anthony de Mello expressed it nicely when he said: "No one can be said to have attained the pinnacle of Truth until a thousand sincere people have denounced him for blasphemy." But also remember that it takes courage to face the critics and heart to find out the ways in which they are right. Provoke the critics, make them tell you more unpleasant things, and think about what they say. It is an uncomfortable and potentially dangerous game that will make you a better leader.

# 4
# Leading Mythologically

Mythology, no doubt, breaks out more fiercely during the early periods of the
history of human thought, but it never disappears altogether. Depend upon it, there
is mythology now as there was in the time of Homer, only we do not perceive it,
because we ourselves live in the very shadow of it . . .

*(Ernst Cassirer 1946: 5)*

Myths come from the sacred realm of experience and therefore are associated by
many people with spiritual belief and religion, though more often with the beliefs of
others than with their own. Because myths serve the sacred rather than the profane,
it may seem strange to associate them with business. However, because humans
have spirit, the spiritual element is available within business just as it is within more
overtly religious cultures and organizations. For example, the sacred stories of a
business culture are their particular renditions of the universal themes of creation,
divinity, and heroism. Thus, stories about the founding of a business, the glory of its
leaders, or extraordinary efforts by its employees, particularize the sacred within
settings normally misconstrued as strictly profane. While business leadership may
seem profane when reflected in the manager's face, it becomes spiritualized in the
face of the priest.

According to mythologists, in all cultures myths provide a foundation for narrative
understanding and offer templates for storytelling while ritual dramatizing literally
enacts myths. Thus, we argue, myths are expressed through the storytelling and
dramatizing practices of the business leaders we presented in Chapters 2 and 3.

Mythologists try to explain why myths occur in all cultures and why some of
them contain similar sets of characters and characteristics regardless of the culture
in which they occur. Different groups of mythologists explain mythology differently.
A culture's mythology is believed by some simply to be the repository of stories that
have served useful purposes long enough to be retained in cultural memory and
transmitted from generation to generation (e.g., Kirk 1970). According to these
historically and empirically grounded mythologists, oft-repeated stories become part
of a culture's heritage and are frequently incorporated into its rituals, such as when

a Catholic priest tells stories from the Bible as part of saying a Mass, or when a corporate executive tells founder stories at a company picnic or award ceremony. Over time, the cultural significance of retold stories broadens until their original function is forgotten and they become valued simply for the sake of belonging to tradition. Mythologists who use this historical-empirical line of reasoning define myths as stories whose genesis and authorship have been forgotten and whose claims are either fantastical or uncertifiable.

Other mythologists offer a metaphysical perspective on the genesis of myth. They believe myths are not just universal in their occurrence within human culture, but that they all have similar elements because they take divine inspiration as their common source. Myths are the means by which divine forces express their universal messages to the world in the forms of story and drama. In his 1946 book *Language and Myth*, the German-American philosopher Ernst Cassirer took this perspective a step further by claiming that engaging with myth leads storytellers, dramatists, and their audiences into mythological consciousness. In his view, mythological consciousness lies at the very core of humanity and offers us an alternative way of being in the world, one which, we argue, is reflected in the face of the priest.

Cassirer was concerned with the evolution of knowledge in civilization. In this regard he proclaimed mythological consciousness as a precursor to the rational mode of thinking so characteristic of modern civilization and, we would add, of the managerial culture to which modern civilization gave birth. He challenged the then dominant view of myth – as the product of ignorance, superstition, or dogma – with his view that myth is essential to our capacity to symbolize (e.g., form languages and use them to communicate meaning). Following Cassirer's idea, we propose to view myth, symbols, and mythological consciousness as fundamental to storytelling, dramatizing and other uses of language within managerial culture and business (depicted by the vertical axis of Figure 4.1).

Because he viewed mythological consciousness as pre-rational, Cassirer believed that myths cannot be explained using logico-scientific reasoning, they can only be experienced by entering mythological consciousness (depicted by the gray parts of Figure 4.1). Accepting Cassirer's view that myth can only be experienced, we reread the *HBR* interviews as mythic texts. In these readings we used mythological consciousness to experience the interviews, not as CEOs telling their tales (as we did in Chapter 2) or dramatizing their organizations or business practices (as in Chapter 3), but as ancient myths expressing themselves through the CEOs. In this chapter we present our readings of the CEOs as characters in myths that they created in collaboration with their *HBR* interviewers.

We used the oldest mythology in Western culture – Greek myths – to frame our readings of the *HBR* interviews for this chapter. This framing device transformed the CEOs into Greek gods and heroes whose characters were revealed by comparing each interview to the Greek myth or myths that we felt they expressed. This approach of representing the CEOs as gods may look like a simple trait theory of leadership in that it identifies characteristics associated with successful CEOs, but there are major differences. First, the Greek gods offer a pantheon of possible models rather than the single model of leadership set out in most trait theories.

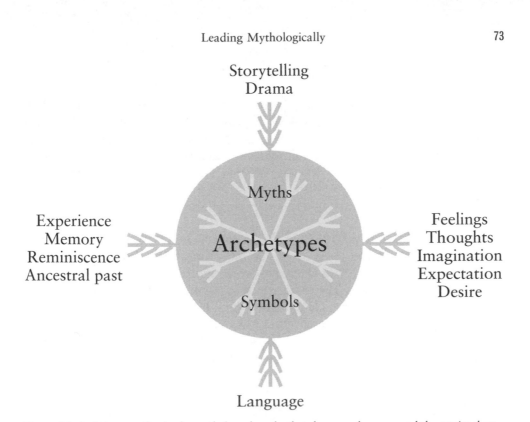

Figure 4.1 Archetypes underpin the symbols and myths that shape our language and the stories that we tell. They live in memories and reminiscences of our ancestral past embedded deep within the human mind. Mythological consciousness (shown in gray) gives us access to the myths and symbols that inspire imagination and produce the heroes, victims, clowns, and lovers that populate the epic, tragic, comic, and romantic stories that we express in our art, drama, and film as well as in our business lives

Second, the mythological approach aims more deeply than trait theory by emphasizing age-old virtues and vices. We claim that the virtues and vices of the gods represented in Greek mythology manifest in the different values CEOs symbolize in contemporary managerial culture. We take this to mean that leadership has a moral foundation as well as a mythological function and that exploring mythology in relation to the *HBR* interviews with CEOs will reveal the complex morality of managerial culture today as well as the individual mythos of its celebrated business leaders.

Of course we cannot completely escape the rationality of our times, and so in Chapter 6 we will complement analysis inspired by mythological consciousness with an explanation of the *HBR* myths that focuses on demystifying those who act as mythmakers. There we will address the question: who creates the gods who populate the *HBR* pantheon of business leaders? But first, in this chapter, we discuss myth and the closely related notion of archetype. Following this discussion we will present our interpretations of the *HBR* pantheon of business leadership filtered through the lens of Greek mythology. We will conclude with some ideas about how you can stimulate your own mythological consciousness.

## Myths and Archetypes

Mythologists find evidence for the existence of archetypes in the universal symbolism of dreams and schizophrenic delusions (Moreno 1970) as well as in the myths of all cultures (Campbell 1976). The co-presence of archetypes in dream and myth encouraged Carl Jung, the primary proponent of archetypal analysis in psychology, to argue that myths are the dreams of collective unconscious. Jungian psychology tells us that archetypes express themselves through myths by providing us with the symbolic material and imagination necessary to tell stories and to create our lives in their images (see Figure 4.1).

According to Kołakowski (1967), myths do not contain words, they are accounted through, or translated into words. Myths become stories when they fire the imagination of the storyteller who puts them into words in order to create characters and describe their relationships. The characters that populate myths express archetypes such as of the mother, father, child, hero, villain, master and servant. That is, the gods embody these and other archetypical characters that appear in Greek myth. But the gods of Greek mythology are much more than archetypal symbols, rather they live through us and therefore through them we may find the divine spark within ourselves.

Paralleling the two approaches to mythology described above, organizational scholar Martin Bowles (1993) distinguished two theories of the archetype, one historical-empirical, the other metaphysical. The historical view assumes archetypes evolved along with humans and looks for empirical evidence of their development in the historical record. The metaphysical view asserts the presence of myth at the dawn of human life and suggests that archetypes provided early humans with the capacity to form ideas and develop language, and thereby differentiated them from other animals. In other words, like mythologist Joseph Campbell, author of the popular book *The Power of Myth* (1988), metaphysically inclined mythologists believe that archetypes are responsible for making humans human.

Jung was, according to Bowles, ambivalent regarding the two views. While most often referring to archetypes as historically evolved, Jung also described them in metaphysical terms such as: "Archetypes are the riverbeds along which the currents of psychic life have always flowed" (Jung 1969: 227, cited in Bowles 1993: 398). According to Jung, archetypes express themselves through our images (e.g., archetypes as riverbeds) and thereby inspire our ideas. Archetypes are so deeply rooted in our humanity they can only be found in our subconscious. However, they resurface in the symbols and myths that appear and reappear as cultural artifacts throughout human history (e.g., stories, paintings, poems, plays). According to Jung (1971/81: 362), archetypes are:

> ex-ante meanings formed out of the collective unconscious; a gestalting form of fantasy, given a priori. At the surface of the archetype are concrete images of hidden motives.

In other words, archetypes exist as latent images of all that moves us to action and inspires our being. They are harbored by the unconscious but shared by all humans. Thus it is that, through myth and symbol sharing, people can cease being individuals and become a group capable of experiencing *communitas*, the foundation of culture and society.

According to Jung (1974) an archetype provides a model or prototype for recognizing and acknowledging an aspect of our deep existence. We know archetypes objectively when they manifest in behavior (action or speech) or in objects, and in the interpretations we give to those objects and behaviors. In their pure form, archetypes are inexpressible because they lie beyond culture and beneath meaning. They are made expressible only through culture and its meaning making (symbolization) processes. Archetypes are universal and unchangeable although they are used and reused by humans to produce culture and inspire its ever-changing array of ideas and practices. As Bowles (1993: 399) put it:

> The fact that the contents of the archetypes are ultimately interwoven with the conscious mind, and, as such, with the everyday world, provides the clothing through which the archetype speaks. The content with which archetypes are represented will vary according to the history and culture of a society, and will be filled out by individual experience.

Bowles traced the notion of archetype to Plato's myth of the cave. According to this parable, humans are imprisoned within a cave, chained facing the rear wall. The light of truth streams in behind them, casting shadows that they take to be reality because it is all they have ever seen. Thus, according to Plato's myth, humans see only the shadow of truth unless and until they escape from the cave.

Interestingly, Plato discussed the means to escape the cave in terms of "the rational knowledge of the soul" (see Bowles 1993: 390), which he defined with the term "logos". Logos shares its root with the root of our word logic. Today it is common to interpret Plato's myth as saying that rationality can deliver us from the chains of superstitious belief. However, Platonic rationality is different from our scientific objectivity in that it invokes imagination, which is linked to divine inspiration. In this interpretation, the imagination that carries humans out of the cave to confront reality directly is filled with archetypes. Bowles (1993: 399) arrived at this interpretation by associating Plato's rationality with St Augustine's "principal ideas" that are "laid down in the mind of an individual through the hand of a divinity". Thus archetypes are, in Bowles' words (1993: 399): "forms of apprehension which give rise to ways of thinking, feeling, imagining and experiencing." The link to experience is the thread that connects archetypal ideas and images to the empirical world of thought and feeling as well as to divine inspiration and to our ancestral past (see the horizontal axis of Figure 4.1). In this view imagination and mythological consciousness are conjoined.

The link between humans and their ancestral past is an important one for mythologists. Because of the universality of their archetypal symbolism, myths

transcend time – time may pass, but the human condition remains the same. Myths have an almost infinite potential for interpretation and retelling because their symbols are so rich that, as Jung noted in *Man and his Symbols* (1964: 67, 69): "[symbols and myths] can vary a great deal in detail without losing their basic patterns." Through storytelling and dramatizing based on archetypal symbols, a culture can maintain currency without sacrificing its heritage. As time passes, old myths are told anew in ways that speak to contemporary sensibilities as well as to tradition. The human condition remains unchanged while contemporary tales based in myth relate the universals of human existence to current cultural realities and practices. Consider, for example, the tragedy of romantic love told in the Middle Ages as *Tristan and Isuelt*, retold in Elizabethan England as *Romeo and Juliet*, and told yet again in modern America as *West Side Story*.

Because myths can be adopted by any culture and translated to fit the current social context, they contain both archetypal and particularistic elements. Within organizational cultures archetypal elements include the god, the hero, the mother, the judge, the servant and the soldier, which can be translated, for example, into the roles of CEO, executive, secretary, customer, administrator and salesperson to be associated with particular individuals who will bring these universal characters to life. Given our focus on business leaders, the question we faced was how do we identify the mythic gods that the CEOs embodied in their interviews? We concluded that the reason archetypes and myths are so hard to discern in contemporary business practice is that they hide behind the face of the manager. We realized that our rationalized view of business needed to be set aside to discover the faces of the artist and the priest in business leadership. Adopting mythological consciousness permitted us to set aside the rational view and gave us the following reading of the CEO interviews as presenting a pantheon of business leaders.

## The *HBR* Pantheon of Business Leaders

In his book entitled *Work, Death, and Life Itself*, Burkard Sievers (1994) criticized mainstream and popular approaches to business leadership, organizational participation, and employee motivation for not recognizing that, as a human universal, work must be placed in the context of other human universals, most importantly, life and death. Sievers adopted Greek mythology as a means to provide this context. He claimed that Greek myths approach life and immortality from a dichotomous yet ambiguous perspective that is useful for understanding work in contemporary organizations. For example, in Greek mythology the boundary between immortality and mortality is imprecise and blurred. Hades is inhabited by the souls of dead people, but also by gods and goddesses. The gods are immortal, but sometimes annihilate each other. And even humans can be immortalized, as when the hero Heracles was promoted from man to god. According to Sievers, participation in contemporary work organizations is a metaphor for our struggle with immortality.

The psycho-social processes of organizing operate "to establish and sustain a limited access to immortality" that allows humans to blur the boundary between life and death in much the same way that Greek myth blurs this boundary (Sievers 1994: 130). By applying the metaphor of Greek mythology to business, the business organization is mythologized as immortal, while its leaders are deified and its workers are reified. Thus, Sievers argued, psychologically speaking all organizational members work to achieve immortality.

In this section of the chapter we adopt an approach similar to that of Bowles (1993) who used the gods and goddesses from the Greek pantheon to represent divinities in contemporary organizations. Thus, Bowles was interested in the same group of people that we are, namely business leaders. However, he focused on delineating the role of myths in the structure of consciousness and on the effects of myth on human experience and on images of power and leadership, whereas we are interested in how a group of business leaders invoked and embodied myths and expressed archetypes when they gave their interviews. We chose Greek mythology as the framework for our analysis because it is our personal way of imagining myth and because we agree with Bowles that Greek myth has an archetypal influence that is shared across many cultures and ages, particularly in the West.

Myth is not only present in the stories the CEOs told, but it can also be a useful lens for addressing each interview in its entirety as a portrayal of an individual CEO as an embodiment of a Greek god or hero. In his book *After Virtue: A Study in Moral Theory*, Alasdair MacIntyre explained how myth underlies our identity and manifests in the roles we play in the drama of life (1984: 261):

> We enter human society . . . with one or more imputed characters – roles into which we have been drafted – and we have to learn what they are in order to be able to understand how others respond to us and how our responses to them are apt to be construed. It is through hearing stories about wicked stepmothers, lost children, good but misguided kings, wolves that suckle twin boys, youngest sons who receive no inheritance but must make their own way in the world and eldest sons who waste their inheritance on riotous living and go into exile to live with the swine, that children learn or mislearn both what a child and what a parent is, what the cast of characters may be in the drama into which they have been born and what the ways of the world are. . . . Hence there is no way to give us an understanding of any society, including our own, except through the stock of stories which constitute its initial dramatic resources.

We contend that the *HBR* interviews with CEOs present us with myths of business leadership that link the featured CEOs to the gods of ancient Greek mythology. The mythic connection gives us a language of virtue (and vice) with which to talk about business and its leaders and thus provides a moral foundation upon which to build our relationship to them. As we showed in Chapter 2, this language is predominantly concerned with characterizing heroism and defining leadership via the epic tale. It gives, as MacIntyre suggested, a moral ground to managerial culture by documenting and enlivening its virtues (1984: 149):

> Virtues are dispositions to act in particular ways, but also to feel in particular ways. To act virtuously is not, as Kant was later to think, to act against inclination; it is to act from inclination formed by the cultivation of virtues.

Thus myth plays a large role in encouraging virtue, which MacIntyre claimed has been defined in three different ways (1984: 185):

> We have thus at least three very different conceptions of a virtue to confront: a virtue is a quality which enables an individual to discharge his or her social role (Homer); a virtue is a quality which enables an individual to move towards the achievement of the specifically human *telos*, whether natural or supernatural (Aristotle, the New Testament and Aquinas); a virtue is a quality which has utility in achieving earthly and heavenly success (Franklin).

The *HBR* interviews with CEOs are linked with the organizational archetype of the leader, and, through this culturally influenced character, to the basic archetypes represented in Greek myth as the gods. It is via this route that Greek mythology gives us language and imagination to talk about leadership, just as it gives business leaders language and imagination to talk about their organizations and themselves. The gods are archetypal images and thus are invisible to most people in their archetypal forms; however, when used to tell the stories of business leaders, the archetypes express themselves in the characters and situations portrayed. The traces of these archetypes have lived with humanity from its beginning, and so they can be used to explain the values in which the current role of the business leader is rooted. In other words, people carry with them archetypes, just like they carry with them the fairy tales they listened to as small children, and upon them they build their basic understanding of the social and professional world that is their organization. Western business cultures are in this respect still inspired by Greek mythology and, even if unknowingly, business leaders present themselves as mythical characters based on the stories of Hermes, Athena, Zeus, and the other Greek gods and heroes.

We have not focused our interpretations of individual CEOs on single virtues but on sets of virtues. The virtues we have selected as typical of a given CEO are those that recur as leitmotifs in the whole of their interviews. This can mean that a particular CEO is a composite of two or more gods in that he has virtues normally associated with different gods. Below we present the CEOs from the interviews we read using the virtues of the Greek gods that we feel they represent. According to our readings, it is not the business leaders themselves that are living and personified myths, it is the way they construct themselves in the interviews that is mythological.

The characters constructed in the *HBR* interviews were remarkably consistent throughout each interview, every CEO constructed himself as only one or at most two of the gods found in Greek mythology (see Table 4.1). We also compared our *HBR* interviews with a few *Fortune* articles from the same period. These comparisons showed that CEOs presented as one god in *Harvard Business Review* (e.g. Zeus), were depicted as another in *Fortune* (e.g. Athena). This indicates that in

**Table 4.1** CEOs as Greek gods and their virtues

| The Gods | Their virtues[a] | The CEOs who portrayed them |
|---|---|---|
| Hermes | Communication, exchange, wit, innovation and risk-taking | Percy Barnevik (ABB) <br> Paul Cook (Raychem) *Hermes + Ares* <br> Phil Knight (Nike) <br> Paul Allaire (Xerox) *Hermes + Apollo* <br> Ernesto Martens (Vitro) *Hermes + Persephone* <br> Arden C. Sims (Globe Metallurgical) <br> Ed McCracken (Silicon Graphic) <br> Frederick C. Crawford (TRW) <br> Michael Dell (Dell Computers) <br> John Browne (BP) *Hermes + Athena* <br> John Sawhill (Nature Conservancy) *Hermes + Demeter* |
| Athena | Rationality, strategic thinking, control of emotions | David Whitwam (Whirlpool) *Zeus + Athena* <br> Krister Ahlström (Ahlström) <br> Robert B. Shapiro (Monsanto) <br> Roy Vagelos (Merck) <br> George Fisher (Motorola) <br> John Browne (BP) *Hermes (or Hephaestus?) + Athena* |
| Demeter | Care, locality, growth, renewal (maternalism) | Alain Gomez (Thomson) <br> Rod Canion (Compaq) <br> Nicolas Hayek (Swatch) <br> Arnold Hiatt (Stride Rite) <br> John Sawhill (Nature Conservancy) *Hermes + Demeter* |
| Zeus | Global vision and supreme power (paternalism) | Robert Haas (Levi Strauss) <br> John Reed (Citicorp) <br> David Whitwam (Whirlpool) *Zeus + Athena* |
| Ares | Aggression, competition, desire to win | Carl Hahn (VW) <br> Paul Cook (Raychem) *Hermes + Ares* <br> Lawrence A. Bossidy (Allied Signal) |
| Hephaestus | Craft, exactness, concern for the product | Robert F. McDermott (USAA) <br> Tom Chapman (Greater Southeast Community Hospital) <br> Colin Marshall (BA) *Hephaestus + Apollo* |
| Apollo | Art, creativity, prophecy | Colin Marshall (BA) *Hephaestus + Apollo* <br> Paul Allaire (Xerox) *Hermes + Apollo* |
| Persephone | Contradiction, duality | Ernesto Martens (Vitro) *Hermes + Persephone* |
| Hades | Generosity and severity | Raymond Smith (Bell Atlantic) |
| Heracles (demi-god) | Bravery, perseverance, entrepreneurship | Masayoshi Son (Softbank) <br> Franco Bernabè (Eni) |

[a] The characters of the gods are our personal readings of mythology. Although we consulted with a historian who confirmed our interpretations were reasonable, others may want to interpret them differently.

other contexts, such as privately, or in their everyday construction of their pro-
fessional roles, the CEOs may be entirely different people than the god-like figures
they presented in their *HBR* interviews. However, we were interested in the myths
retold in the *HBR* interviews, and not in tracing the roles that the CEOs may
have played in other contexts. Neither did we focus explicitly on gender issues,
since there were no female CEOs in the interviews we read. However, gender *is*
implicated in the mythology perpetuated by *HBR* in that 12 of the 30 CEOs in the
interviews were constructed, in whole or in part, as Athena, Demeter or Persephone,
all female gods.

## The In-crowd: Hermes, Athena and Demeter

As shown in Table 4.1 Hermes, the messenger, was the most popular god in the
*HBR* interviews that we read. The other gods active in the interviews were Athena,
Demeter, Zeus, Ares and Hephaestus. Apollo, Persephone, Hades and the demi-god
Heracles appeared only once or twice each. Though relatively rare, their presence
was still felt within the pantheon of business leaders *HBR* presented to its readers in
the interviews published from 1989–98.

In this section of the chapter we will present the three most popular gods of
*HBR*'s pantheon of business leaders – Hermes, Athena and Demeter – and their
CEO representatives. We will focus not only on the virtues, but the major vices of
each of these god types. In the next section we will explore the characters of Zeus,
Ares and Hephaestus as these were brought to life in the *HBR* interviews. Here we
will consider both the ways in which these gods play into and refute common
stereotypes of managers. We will then discuss the gods who were rare and those
who were notable by their absence in the set of interviews we read.

### *Hermes, innovator and communicator*

Hermes was Zeus's cleverest son, born to the immortal nymph Maia. On the day
of his birth he invented the lyre, which he later gave to his brother Apollo as
compensation for stealing 50 of his cows. Known for his nimble fingers, cunning,
and ingenuity, Hermes became the god of travelers, merchants, and thieves. His
cunning, humor, and gift for innovation are illustrated in the story that, while being
tried by Zeus for the theft of his brother's cattle, Hermes stole Apollo's bow and
quiver. However, he returned all his brother's possessions at the behest of their
father and gave Apollo the lyre, which Apollo greatly desired. In return Apollo gave
Hermes the office of messenger between earth and the Underworld and a golden
staff that bestows wealth. Zeus then granted Hermes the power to communicate
with both immortals and mortals. Hermes' identity as the messenger god was thus
bestowed upon him by his brother Apollo and his father Zeus, both of whom
forgave him his thievery.

Hermes' virtues[1] are clearly rendered by the myth that tells of his birth. He is an innovator, inventing the lyre on the morning he was born. He has guile but also great wit. He takes risks but, when he gets into trouble, uses his charm and natural humor to convince Zeus to protect him from the consequences of his actions. He bears the staff of wealth and plays the role of messenger or communicator between heaven, earth, and the Underworld (i.e. throughout the universe). Hermes was also a protector of heroes who could send good luck unexpectedly, as he did for the traveler Odysseus when Circe trapped him on her island.

The role of communicator and the virtue of being understood at all levels of the hierarchy are the aspects of Hermes most often illustrated by the interviews in which Hermes-like CEOs appear. Their willingness to take risks and their wealth producing abilities are other virtues their tales divulge. The association with thievery, underplayed by those invoking Hermes' character in the *HBR* interviews, should not be overlooked. Quite often CEOs find themselves in the position of judging a very gray area between honest business practice and thievery. Hermes-like CEOs need to be particularly vigilant in regard to ethical matters because their natural capacity to beguile means that they will be able to get away with things that others might not, thereby putting their businesses at risk, along with their own reputations, as Hermes did on several occasions.

The *HBR* interview with Michael Dell (Magretta 1998a) begins with the rhetorical question: "How do you create a $12 billion company in just 13 years?" Reminiscent of the precocious Hermes, Dell Computer Corporation's founder seems blessed from his birth into business with abilities to innovate that others do not have. We learn from his interview that, just as Hermes invented the seductive lyre, Michael Dell invented a direct business model that attracts and mesmerizes customers. Through this model, Dell Computer Corporation has a Hermes-like capacity to communicate with everyone in the supply chain, no matter what position they hold. In Hermes' fashion, Michael Dell referred to the virtue of information sharing throughout his interview. You can almost see him strapping on Hermes' famous flying sandals as he explains how Dell works the miracle of fast shipment of custom-configured PCs (Magretta 1998a: 76):

> We tell Airborne Express or UPS to come to Austin and pick up 10,000 computers a day and go over to the Sony factory in Mexico and pick up the corresponding number of monitors. Then while we're all sleeping, they match up the computers and the monitors, and deliver them to the customer. Of course, this requires sophisticated data exchange.

According to the company's CEO, the secret to Dell's success is that "We substitute information for inventory" (Magretta 1998a: 77). In this regard Dell has

---

[1] Another version of his character was accounted in later myths, where he was presented as Hermes Trismegistos – the god of knowledge, science, and writing. Here we will concentrate on his image as the god of merchants, travelers, and thieves.

created innovative ways to let customers communicate with company information systems, such as via its customized intranet sites (Premier Pages) which are available to Dell's largest global customers. The company also set up regional forums for communicating with their customers, called Platinum councils (Magretta 1998a: 80):

> Our Platinum councils, are regional meetings – in Asia-Pacific, Japan, the United States, and Europe – of our largest customers. . . . In these meetings, our senior technologists share their views on where the technology is heading and lay out road maps of product plans over the next two years. There are also breakout sessions and working groups in which our engineering teams focus on specific product areas and talk about how to solve problems that may not necessarily have anything to do with the commercial relationship with Dell. For example, Is leasing better than buying? Or How do you manage the transition to Windows NT? Or How do you manage a field force of notebook computers?
>
> People in businesses as dissimilar as Unilever and ICI can learn from each other because, amazingly, they have very similar problems when it comes to PCs. And we send not only our top technologists and engineers but also the real engineers, the people who usually don't get out to talk to customers because they're too busy developing products. All of our senior executives from around the company participate, spending time with the customer, listening to how we're doing. The ratio is about one Dell person to one customer. At our last session, we had about 100 customers.

CEO Dell continued his discussion of communication pointing out what the company has learned as a result of being willing to listen:

> At every Platinum council, we review what they told us last time and what we did about it. We keep an ongoing record of the issues. Let me give you a concrete example: A few years ago, the engineers responsible for our desktops were operating on the theory that customers really wanted performance from these products – the faster the better. But what I really want is a stable product that doesn't change. Because if I'm trying to run a bank or an airline, I don't care if it's 2% faster or 3% slower. What really matters is stability." So our engineers thought one thing, the customers thought another thing. It took the direct feedback from the Platinum Councils to spotlight this failure to communicate. We responded by building product with intergenerational consistency over many years. The same feedback has helped shape the creation of our brands. For both our desktop and notebook businesses, we created different brands designed to deliver greater stability to corporate customers, as opposed to the fast technology changes that consumers demand.
>
> As I think back to some of those council meetings, things that would seem fairly small at the time have often turned out three or four years later to become the basis for billions of dollars of revenue – notebooks with longer-life batteries, for example, or loading customers' software for them in our plants.

Clearly Dell combines Hermes's two most important virtues – innovation with communication. Furthermore, the last statement above speaks to Dell's capacity for wealth generation, another of Hermes' gifts.

One final quote from the interview shows Dell acting as a go-between for customers and suppliers (Magretta 1998a: 82):

> A big piece of our brand is being the most efficient and effective way for customers to buy Intel or Microsoft technologies. But beyond that, we're evolving into a technology selector, or navigator. We often talk to customers about "relevant technology." Intel and Microsoft tend to launch into a massive variety of things, some of which are speculative and aimed at exploring new technologies. We think it's our job to help our customers sort out the technology relevant to today's needs from the bleeding edge.

Here, Dell's capacity to help customers understand what suppliers have to offer them is reminiscent of Hermes' gift to communicate between heaven and earth.

Percy Barnevik of ABB is another example of a modern Hermes. Like Michael Dell, he constantly refers to communication, but Barnevik also brings into play Hermes' connection to travelers (Taylor 1991: 91):

> We are a federation of national companies with a global coordination center. We are not homeless. We have many homes.

Barnevik is comfortable with all the layers of people that populate his organization and with the decentralized structure ABB maintains (Taylor 1991: 99):

> ABB is a huge enterprise. But the work of most of our people is organized in small units with P&L responsibility and meaningful autonomy. . . . all of our operations . . . function as closely as possible to stand-alone operations.

Barnevik claims that ABB is both decentralized and centralized, big and small, and he sees these paradoxes as natural and desirable. The decentralized dimension is about action and responsibility. The centralized dimension is about communicating with each other. Thus for Barnevik, communication is central, nothing should stand in its way: a manager should not just inform but over inform, which is "about breaking taboos" (Taylor 1991: 104).

An international traveler himself, Barnevik believes in global management and he associates this with a Hermes-like concern for innovation. Global managers are, according to Barnevik, innovators with "exceptionally open minds" (Taylor 1991: 94). Global managers should respect other cultures but that does not mean accepting everything the people of the cultures say. "They sort through the debris of cultural excuses and find opportunities to innovate" (Taylor 1991: 94). One thing a manager definitely should learn, according to Barnevik, is languages, because they enable communication. In his view global managers are "made, not born" by rotating them around the globe, "forcing" them to make international alliances as they travel (Taylor 1991: 95). After such a heroic quest, a person becomes an excellent manager.

In his interview, Phil Knight of Nike also presented himself as Hermes (Willigan 1992). As with Michael Dell and Percy Barnevik, this modern-day Hermes believes

in the creative powers of communication. In the beginning, according to Knight, the company and its customers were alike, as Nike was (Willigan 1992: 94):

> just a running shoe company and almost all our employees were runners, we understood the consumer very well . . . We and the consumer were one and the same.

But now, Knight claims, understanding should involve communication with customers, identification with them is not enough (Willigan 1992: 94):

> Whether you're talking about the core consumer or the person on the street, the principle is the same: you have to come up with what the consumer wants, and you need a vehicle to understand it. To understand the rest of the pyramid, we do a lot of work at the grass-roots level. We go to amateur sports events and spend time at gyms and tennis courts talking to people.

Apart from direct communication with athletes at sporting events, the company does all sorts of traditional market research, "but lots of it – spending time in stores and watching what happens across the counter, getting reports from dealers, doing focus groups, tracking responses to our ads" (Willigan 1992: 94). It is thus that Nike has managed to build a focused brand through communication: "A brand is something that has a clear-cut identity among consumers, which a company creates by sending out a clear, consistent message over a period of years" (Willigan 1992: 96).

True to Hermes, Knight relishes taking risks: "Our basic philosophy is the same throughout the business: take a chance and learn from it" (Willigan 1992: 99). One example of risk-taking Knight described was the 1987 Revolution advertising campaign (Willigan 1992: 99):

> We launched the [Nike Air] product with the Revolution campaign, using the Beatles song. We wanted to communicate not just a radical departure in shoes but a revolution in the way Americans felt about fitness, exercise, and wellness. The ads were a tremendous hit, and Nike Air became the standard for the industry immediately thereafter.

Nike's CEO also demonstrated humor as a way to communicate, perhaps also to empathize and inspire, thus Knight's interview exudes Hermes' boyish charm.

Ed McCracken from Silicon Graphics (Prokesch 1993) is portrayed in his interview as another Hermes-inspired CEO. As was true for Dell, Barnevik and Knight, McCracken perceives communication as desirable and a value in itself. However, in the case of Silicon Graphics, even the product is portrayed as a medium for communication (Prokesch 1993: 136):

> I think the key to obtaining competitive advantage in the 1990s is making your customers feel like you designed a product specifically for them, that your product has special features or capabilities for which they would pay a premium.

Like Knight, McCracken stressed the importance of having fun: "Silicon Graphics is all about making technology fun and usable, and that means that working here should be fun" (Prokesch 1993: 142). He blamed US and Japanese companies for having taken the fun out of work. "Irreverence is also important in a highly creative environment" (Prokesch 1993: 142), because too much reverence decreases productivity. "Fun and irreverence also make change less scary" (Prokesch 1993: 142). Hermes-McCracken's playfulness in the face of change is illustrated in this example from his interview (Prokesch 1993: 142–4):

> For example, we recently replaced two old divisions with five new ones. We brought a New Orleans band and held a wake on our Mountain View campus. We filled two coffins with paraphernalia from each division and then buried them. This ceremony reinforced our philosophy that we must view life as it is and how it might be rather than how it was.

According to McCracken, his company wants to be big, but not boring, and he wishes it to remain "vital." Vitality is an additional characteristic easily associated with Hermes.

Of all the CEOs who appeared as Hermes, Phil Knight comes closest to revealing Hermes' darker side as well as his capacity to work his way out of difficult situations. Nike first encountered serious competitive problems as the result of not knowing their customers and, more recently, in not recognizing problems in their Asian factories. In both instances, a combination of charm and good communication has helped bring Nike back from the brink of disaster, but the repetition of the lesson to listen suggests that there is a problem with this Hermes. Perhaps it is revealing that Knight is the only CEO in the interviews we read who told multiple tragic stories (see Chapter 2).

Knight's case offers a reminder that there are no guarantees of virtue. God-like virtues will not save you from expressing your god-like vices and bearing their consequences. The Greek gods all had their failings as well as their gifts, and we must take care not to ignore the warnings that come with a focus on the gods and their CEO counterparts.

## Athena, the rational strategist

Athena was the daughter of Zeus and Metis. After learning of her pregnancy, Zeus tricked Metis into turning herself into a fly that he then swallowed to avoid her child taking his place as ruler of the gods, as he had done to his father, Cronus. Later Haphaestus split Zeus's skull with an axe thus freeing Athena who sprang from his head fully grown and armored. Although Athena was his equal in wisdom and strength, she had none of Zeus's ambitions to rule the world and never challenged his position. In fact, even though she was the goddess of war, her cool rationality and lack of emotion inspired most Greeks to worship her as the goddess of civility

and wisdom. Her symbol is the owl, which represents wisdom in Western cultures even today.

An active goddess, Athena aided heroes and adventurers such as Perseus, Heracles and Odysseus. Although she remained a virgin, when Hephaestus dropped his seed on the ground while pursuing her and it turned into the serpent king Erichthonius, Athena raised the child in her temple on the Acropolis. In due time Erichthonius was made king of the Athenians and, in gratitude to Athena, promoted her as the city's goddess. Thus Athena came to be associated with citadels and, because Athens was an ancient commercial center, she was also known as the patroness of arts and crafts. One of her titles is Ergane, which means working-woman. In this regard one story indicates that she taught people important skills, and eventually presented them with the gift of fire, which she took from Hephaestus' smithy.

Although to modern, rational tastes, Athena often seems nearly perfect, it is well to remember she has a weakness. Her lack of emotion leaves her remote from the people who revere her. Her Olympian vantage point gives her a strategic view, but also an aura of disconnectedness from the events of everyday life. Thus she is able to oversee war without being touched by its consequences. There is a coldness to Athena that CEOs who take on her character should guard against, if they are able.

Athena's virtues and vices are clearly communicated in the stories told about her. The circumstances of her birth from her father's head symbolize her intelligence and her strategic orientation to life but also represent her tendency toward emotionless decision-making. The story about her gift of fire shows her benevolent side and also represents her connection to craftwork (the smithy's fire) which is associated with many traditional occupations and the businesses that grew out of them (e.g. tanner, blacksmith, cobbler). Since businesses are sometimes regarded as the citadels of contemporary times, her patronage of Athens suggests that Athena-inspired CEOs might be conceived as rational, if remote, guardians of the business-citadels under their god-like protection. Although she was the goddess of war, she was obsessed with the strategic element of warfare rather than with fighting per se, which she left to her brother Ares. Today's Athenas are the epitome of the strategic manager – calm, cool, emotional rocks in the face of uncertainty or crisis. CEOs who appeared as Athena were quite common in the interviews we read, though they were not as prevalent as Hermes. You will recognize the Athena-inspired CEOs by their devotion to the virtue of rationality, their intellect outshines all other aspects of their being.

One such rational guardian is Ray Vagelos, who was a university professor before he joined Merck as head of its research labs, only later becoming CEO of the firm. In the introduction to his interview, *HBR* editor Nancy Nichols emphasized the intellectual heritage Vagelos brought to the company. She presented an image of Vagelos reigning over the citadel of Merck in which Vagelos seems to be as closely linked to Merck as Athena was to Athens (1994: 105):

Occasionally, a company and its CEO become so inextricably linked that the image of the CEO becomes inseparable from the image of the company. Sometimes it is the CEO's accomplishments that come to represent the organization, and other times it

is his or her personality. In the case of Merck's P. Roy Vagelos, his unusual blend
of scientific knowledge and leadership abilities turned Merck into a pharmaceutical
powerhouse.

This depiction of Vagelos as an Athena-like scientific leader appears again and
again throughout his interview. For example, Vagelos explained how Merck achieved
its success through state of the art science and its rational application to human
problems. Here, Vagelos reminds us of Athena bringing fire down from Mount
Olympus to aid human progress (1994: 106):

> Our goal is to maximize the effectiveness of our drugs. First, we must develop the
> safest and most effective drugs possible in the labs. Then, once the drug is on the market
> and has been prescribed to the patient, we must be sure that the patient is taking the
> right drug, that he or she has the appropriate information to take the drug properly,
> and that the drug will not interfere with other medications the patient is taking.

Like Athena, Vagelos is concerned about the welfare of humans and wants to be
able to help them but this is not an emotional urge, it is an application of reason
(1994: 108): "our research is contributing to the war against cancer, not by making
a frenetic let's-save-the-world effort, but by focusing on a specific problem".

Vagelos's calm rationality shines through as he explains why Merck acquired
Medco and the strategic role the acquisition played (1994: 106):

> We saw a tremendous opportunity to create a new model for the pharmaceutical
> industry that would simultaneously improve the quality of health care, help contain
> costs, and increase Merck's market share. Expanding our information base is critical to
> achieving these goals; Medco has data on 38 million patients, which allow us to learn
> a lot more about how our drugs are prescribed and used and, ultimately, how effective
> they are in fighting disease. Whether it is cutting-edge scientific information or the
> reams of data on how doctors prescribe Merck products, information lies at the heart
> of what the company does. Our ability to leverage information will set us apart.

Vagelos shows his penchant for rational decision-making when he says (Nichols
1994: 107):

> At Merck, we must be able to condense reams of information and let our best judg-
> ment, not our worst fears, prevail.

His Athena-like detachment from the emotional side of healing is clear when he
goes on to explain that (1994: 107):

> I believe that the company that best controls the information flow from doctor
> to patient to pharmacist to plan sponsor has the best chance of succeeding in this
> industry.

The final extensive quote, like so many others throughout the interview, shows that Vagelos is devoted to applying scientific knowledge. Vagelos clearly is the Athena-like rational strategist whose emotions are under control even when dealing with the emotionally charged issue of finding a cure for cancer (Nichols 1994: 107):

> During the so-called war on cancer, which had been declared by President Nixon, it was very popular to say that the United States was on the brink of finding a cure for cancer, although I and many others doubted that there was any scientific basis for this claim. People would come to the labs and ask us to find a cure for cancer, but that was too diffuse a goal for us to undertake. The science hadn't evolved far enough, and the target itself was too broad – there are more than 100,000 genes in each human cell, and, to this day, nobody knows how many of them are cancer causing or cancer suppressing.
> . . . We began by setting out some basic criteria: we would look for areas where there were no therapies or drugs available, where the science was advanced enough for us to believe that we could make a breakthrough, and where we had enough knowledge of the disease to have some idea about how to arrest it. It is hard to tell at the very early stages whether a project will succeed. In order to focus, you have to let go of some projects that look very attractive: you can't do everything at once.

David Whitwam, CEO of Whirlpool, explicitly discussed changes in the manager's role in terms that reproduce the image of Athena springing from Zeus's head (Maruca 1994: 139):

> According to the old paradigm of hierarchy and discipline, it wasn't [the] subordinate's place to question [the chairman's] decisions. Employees today question and challenge all the time. They don't accept things at face value. As a result, a contemporary CEO has to convince employees why transformation is necessary.

Whitwam declared that the power plays typical of Zeus are passé. Today, "just power" is not enough to be a good chairman. According to Whitwam, today's chairperson has to use rational argumentation to convince employees of the necessity of the task: "We need their heads thinking as well as their hands working" (Maruca 1994: 140). Whitwam's remarks suggest that he himself made a transition from the Zeus-like all-controlling style of leadership to Athena's rational powers of persuasion. Notice, too, the lack of any reference to employees' hearts (i.e., their emotions).

Whitwam's interview ends with a note that explains the transition from Zeus to Athena in an interesting way. Whitwam seems to say, do not focus on past glories (as an old warrior would), but look to the future with Athena-like wisdom and strategic vision (Maruca 1994: 145):

> As we look to the future, perhaps the greatest trap will be our own successes. Success has a way of drawing attention away from the present and future and onto the

past. The history of business is littered with companies that were short-term successes. Complacency should have no part in any organization. It is the responsibility of leaders to manage against it.

Here, Whitwam seems to argue that Zeus's delight in power and success is danger-ous, it can damage the organization. Therefore an Athena-like strategic focus on long-term planning for the future is a better approach. However, leaders have a responsibility – to manage against all odds – an idea related to Zeus's penchant for controlling fate. Thus it appears that Whitwam still has within him a bit of Zeus, hence our classification of him as a mixed god (we will present Whitwam as Zeus in the next section of this chapter).

Monsanto's Robert B. Shapiro is another manifestation of Athena. To the emotionally charged issue about environmental sustainability, Shapiro responds with rational analysis (Magretta 1997: 80):

Today there are about 5.8 billion people in the world. About 1.5 billion of them live in conditions of abject poverty – a subsistence life that simply can't be roman-ticized as some form of simpler, preindustrial lifestyle. These people spend their days trying to get food and firewood so they can make it to the next day. As many as 800 million people are so severely malnourished that they can neither work nor participate in family life. That's where we are today. And, as far as I know, no demographer questions that the world population will just about double by sometime around 2030.

Without radical change, the kind of world implied by those numbers is unthinkable. It's a world of mass migrations and environmental degradation on an unimaginable scale. At best, it means the preservation of a few islands of privilege and prosperity in a sea of misery and violence.

Shapiro explicitly attacked "soft" approaches that are "grounded in emotion or ethics" claiming instead that "sustainable development involves cold, rational business logic" (Magretta 1997: 81). While others may see sustainability as an ethical issue, Athena-Shapiro addresses it as a source of strategic advantage for Monsanto (Magretta 1997: 81):

Our nation's economic system evolved in an era of cheap energy and careless waste disposal, when limits seemed irrelevant. None of us today, whether we're managing a house or running a business, is living in a sustainable way. It's not a question of good guys and bad guys. There is no point in saying, If only those bad guys would go out of business, then the world would be fine. The whole system has to change; there's a huge opportunity for reinvention.

We're entering a time of perhaps unprecedented discontinuity. Businesses grounded in the old model will become obsolete and die. At Monsanto, we're trying to invent some new businesses around the concept of environmental sustainability. We may not yet know exactly what those businesses will look like, but we're willing to place some bets because the world cannot avoid needing sustainability in the long run.

Athena-Shapiro used his Olympic vantage point to provide this overview of technology as a potential solution to the need for sustainable systems that can feed the world's population (1997: 83–4):

> I am not one of those techno-utopians who just assume that technology is going to take care of everyone. But I don't see an alternative to giving it our best shot.
>
> Business leaders tend to trust technology and markets and to be optimistic about the natural unfolding of events. But at a visceral level, people know we are headed for trouble and would love to find a way to do something about it. The market is going to want sustainable systems, and if Monsanto provides them, we will do quite well for ourselves and our shareowners. Sustainable development is going to be one of the organizing principles around which Monsanto and a lot of other institutions will probably define themselves in the years to come.

He then told a story about how he approached solving the "world's problem" at Monsanto with strategic thinking. But notice how this rational thinker employs an improvisational approach and creates a happening (Magretta 1997: 84–5; see Chapter 3 for discussion of this type of drama):

> We have to reduce – and ultimately eliminate – the negative impacts we have on the world. There is no argument on that subject. But even if Monsanto reached its goal of zero impact next Tuesday, that wouldn't solve the world's problem. Several years ago, I sensed that there was something more required of us than doing no harm, but I couldn't articulate what that was.
>
> So I did what you always do, I got some smart people together – a group of about 25 critical thinkers, some of the company's up-and-coming leaders – and sent them off to think about it. We selected a good cross-section – some business-unit leaders, a couple from the management board, and people from planning, manufacturing, policy, and safety and health. And we brought in some non-traditional outsiders to challenge our underlying assumptions about the world. My request to this group was, "Go off, think about what's happening to the world, and come back with some recommendations about what it means for Monsanto. Do we have a role to play? If so, what is it?"

The happening produced an opportunity for Athena-Shapiro to experience the emotional side of his organization and this seemed to profoundly alter his management philosophy:

> That off-site meeting in 1994 led to an emerging insight that we couldn't ignore the changing global environmental conditions. The focus around sustainable development became obvious. I should have been able to come up with that in about 15 minutes. But it took a group of very good people quite a while to think it through, to determine what was real and what was just puff, to understand the data, and to convince themselves that this wasn't a fluffy issue – and that we ought to be engaged in it.
>
> People came away from that meeting emotionally fired up. It wasn't just a matter of Okay, you threw me an interesting business problem, I have done the analysis, here

is the answer, and now can I go back to work. People came away saying, "Damn it, we've got to get going on this. This is important." When some of your best people care intensely, their excitement is contagious.

So now we have a bunch of folks engaged, recognizing that we have no idea where we're going to end up. No one – not the most sophisticated thinker in the world – can describe a sustainable world with 10 billion to 12 billion people, living in conditions that aren't disgusting and morally impermissible. But can't sit around waiting for the finished blueprint. We have to start moving in directions that make us less unsustainable.

There's a quote of Peter Drucker's – which I will mangle here – to the effect that at some point strategy has to degenerate into work. At Monsanto, there was a flurry of E-mail around the world, and in a matter of four months a group of about 80 coalesced. Some were chosen, many others just heard about the project and volunteered. They met for the first time in October 1995 and decided to organize into seven teams: three focused on developing tools to help us make better decisions, three focused externally on meeting world needs, and one focused on education and communication.

But the urge to be rational is strong in Shapiro. He ultimately returned to analysis and rationality to explain his position:

We realized that many of the things we were already doing were part of a sustainability strategy even if we didn't call it that. We'd been working on pollution and investing in biotechnology for years before we thought about the concept of sustainability. As we made more progress in pollution prevention, it became easier for everyone to grasp how pollution – or waste – actually represents a resource that's lost. When you translate that understanding into how you run a business, it leads to cost reduction. You can ask, did we do it because it reduces our costs or because of sustainability? That would be hard to answer because optimizing resources has become part of the way we think. But having the sustainability framework has made a difference, especially in how we weigh new business opportunities.

Still, Shapiro learned what motivates people and his reasoning now includes consideration of their emotional and spiritual aspects (Magretta 1997: 85–7):

People in large numbers won't give their all for protracted periods of time – with a cost in their overall lives – for an abstraction called a corporation or an idea called profit. People can give only to people. They can give to their coworkers if they believe that they're engaged together in an enterprise of some importance. They can give to society, which is just another way of saying they can give to their children. They can give if they believe that their work is in some way integrated into a whole life.

Historically, there has been a bifurcation between who we are and the work we do, as if who we are is outside our work. That's unhealthy, and most people yearn to integrate their two sides. Because of Monsanto's history as a chemical company, we have a lot of employees – good people – with a recurrent experience like this: their kids or their neighbors' kids or somebody at a cocktail party asks them what kind of work they do and then reacts in a disapproving way because of what they think we

are at Monsanto. And that hurts. People don't want to be made to feel ashamed of what they do.

I don't mean to disparage economic motives – they're obviously important. But working on sustainability offers a huge hope for healing the rift between our economic activity and our total human activity. Instead of seeing the two in Marxist opposition, we see them as the same thing. Economics is part of human activity.

He then contrasts the Athenian approach of strategy and control with his vision of a more emotionally charged organization (Magretta 1997: 87):

Part of the design and structure of any successful institution is going to be giving people permission to select tasks and goals that they care about. Those tasks have to pass some kind of economic screen, but much of what people care about will pass because economic gain comes from meeting people's needs. That's what economies are based on.

The people who have been working on sustainability here have done an incredible job, not because there has been one presiding genius who has organized it all and told them what to do but because they want to get it done. They care intensely about it and they organize themselves to do it.

I don't mean to romanticize it, but, by and large, self-regulating systems are probably going to be more productive than those based primarily on control loops. There are some institutions that for a short period can succeed as a reflection of the will and ego of a single person. But they're unlikely to survive unless other people resonate with what that person represents.

We're going to have to figure out how to organize people in ways that enable them to coordinate their activities without wasteful and intrusive systems of control and without too much predefinition of what a job is. My own view is that as long as you have a concept called a job, you're asking people to perform to a set of expectations that someone else created. People give more if they can figure out how to control themselves, how to regulate themselves, how to contribute what they can contribute out of their own authentic abilities and beliefs, not out of somebody else's predetermination of what they're going to do all day.

But at the end of the interview Shapiro once again reverted to his Athena-like rational nature by insisting on a system of rational controls to monitor progress (Magretta 1997: 87):

For something at this early level of exploration, you probably want to rely for at least a year on a subjective sense of momentum. People usually know when they're going someplace, when they're making progress. There's a pace to it that says, yes, we're on the right track. After that, I would like to see some quantitative goals with some dates and very macro budgets. As the teams begin to come to some conclusions, we will be able to ignite the next phase of setting some specific targets.

Shapiro's interview shows us the emotional challenges faced by Athena-like managers as well as the rewards of overcoming the negative aspects of their character.

## Demeter, goddess of growth and renewal

Demeter, the daughter of Rhea and Cronus and sister to Zeus, was the goddess of agriculture, fertility, and growth. Her symbol is corn. In Greek mythology she was also the archetypal mother figure. In one story, thought to have been told only among the priests and priestesses of the Mysteries of Eleusis, Demeter took a Cretan youth as her lover and gave birth to Ploutos (a name that means wealth) whereupon a manifold harvest was brought forth. In a better-known story Demeter was depicted as the alter ego of her mother Rhea who wed Zeus and bore Persephone. Thus it was said that when Rhea became Demeter and gave birth to Persephone, she bore herself anew, hence Demeter's association with rebirth and renewal.

Later, Zeus gave Persephone in marriage to his brother Hades, ruler of the Underworld. When Persephone was abducted by Hades, Demeter grieved for her so intensely that the fields over which she held dominion refused to bear fruit, animals languished and all life on earth was threatened. To settle the matter, Zeus made a compromise between Hades and Demeter according to which Persephone would spend part of the year in the Underworld as Hades' queen, and the other part on Olympus with her mother. Thereafter, whenever her daughter returned to the dark kingdom of her husband, Demeter would grieve and humans suffered. Her moods are reflected in the changes of the seasons and in the cyclical fertility of the fields.

Demeter is responsible for the bounty of the earth and her virtues include maternal care, fertility, growth, and renewal. Growth and renewal are of particular interest in tales concerning the leadership of contemporary businesses. Demeter's capacity to create wealth is also telling and is a gift she shares with Hermes who bears the staff of wealth given to him by Apollo. Demeter is environmentally conscious but will fight for her offspring, perhaps to the point of endangering the earth. This paradoxical situation places CEOs who invoke her character in the precarious position of promoting environmental responsibility, except when the company's survival is at stake. Thus Demeter takes a local perspective born of her protective maternal instincts, and so you should expect a CEO who appears as Demeter to protect the child that is his or her company even when it means the earth suffers as a result. Demeter appeared in the interviews we read almost as often as Athena and, contrary to stereotypes of business leadership, her maternal management style was more common in the *HBR* interviews than was the paternalism of Zeus. In the interviews with CEOs who appeared as Demeter you can hear concern for the countries and communities where the company does its work, and for the employees who do that work.

Demeter lives in Arnold Hiatt's story of revival and restoration at Stride Rite (Stone 1992). His interviewer introduced him by remarking on his Demeterian ability to nurture growth, create wealth and provide for renewal in an industry (footwear) not known as a fertile field for US companies (Stone 1992: 95):

> At a time when most shoe companies have had difficulty operating profitably, Stride
> Rite has consistently come up with outstanding financial results. Since 1985, earnings

have risen every year, with net sales more than doubling to $574 million in 1991 and return on equity climbing to 31.3%. Much of that growth reflects the performance of Keds, which Stride Rite bought from Uniroyal and repositioned as a classic, reviving both the brand's identity and its market share.

Hiatt then began his interview with a typically Demetrian emphasis on conservatism and devotion to traditional values (Stone 1992: 96):

> . . . we see ourselves as a very traditional company. We are not in the fashion business, and we're not interested in setting trends. Our strength lies in building on classics, on knowing who we are. That is how we've succeeded as a company. And that same quality lies behind the social programs and policies we've introduced over the years. They are conservative in the best sense of the word because they restore something that was in danger of being lost – extended families, a healthy work environment. Moreover, they reflect the same values and business principles that have driven Stride Rite's evolution and growth as a company.

Hiatt is a person who is able to see poverty outside the window and "make the connection" – try to do something about it, but he does so in a way that makes sense for the company and its business. We repeat a portion of our only purely romantic story from Chapter 2, about opening the first corporate day-care center in the United States, because it so clearly shows Hiatt's maternal character in his concern for the children growing up in the neighborhood surrounding the old Stride Rite factory (Stone 1992: 96):

> It didn't take a great deal of imagination to make the connections. We were in the children's shoe business. We were in a decaying neighborhood surrounded by children in need. We had resources available in the form of empty manufacturing space. And we had a perfect model in the federal government's Head Start program. That's how the center got started.

Alain Gomez of Thomson is another modern expression of Demeter. In Demetrian fashion he chooses an organic metaphor to present his organization (McCormick & Stone 1990: 130):

> An organization is neither an island nor inert. It is a living system interrelated to a set of wider systems.

Gomez is the only one among the interviewed CEOs who openly expressed his love for the people working in his company: "Timing, intuition, is something the people at TCE are very good at and one of the things I love them for" (McCormick & Stone 1990: 130). He avoids the language of competition, favoring expressions of concern, care and nurturing. Like a good mother, Gomez is proud of the people working for him, glad to see how different they are:

> Our multiculturalism – and our ability to nurture it, develop it, and thrive on it. Culturally, the United States and Europe are melting pots. That is an asset, not a liability.

Compaq's CEO, Rod Canion, is Demeter-like as well. The title of his interview suggests his maternal values (Webber 1990): "Consensus, continuity, and common sense." Canion uses medical, as well as horticultural metaphors throughout an interview in which people are seen as important for the company. Just as Demeter wanted to keep Persephone with her on Olympus, Canion worried about retaining his employees which he claimed the company does with its supportive culture (Webber 1990: 116):

> It's not pay or stock or anything else that keeps people. People stay when they enjoy what they do. People stay when they fit the culture, when they are working in a supportive, helpful environment.

At Compaq people are encouraged to grow personally and mature through consensus management. Canion explained that once the company used management to make the "really tough, critical, long-term decisions," but now management caring "permeates the company" (Webber 1990: 117). Canion does not believe in speed and aggressiveness (Webber 1990: 120):

> When you seem to be moving slowly, if you're taking careful steps that turn out to be right, you get where you want to go faster than by speeding and making mistakes that slow you down or permanently derail you.

Canion believes in taking a commonsense approach to managing in a "fast changing business". However, that means qualitative thinking more than anything else, as numbers can be wrong, "those aren't magic numbers that we have to do whatever it takes to hit" (Webber 1990: 121). Quality is the top priority but in Demeter-Canion's view, quality is about people who care enough to do a good job (Webber 1990: 122):

> Quality isn't whether or not your products work. Quality is how people do their jobs . . . Every piece of the company is important.

It is the whole that should be in harmony, and if it is, quality will happen as a by-product of well being and development. The notion of quality as a quantity that has to be measured is alien to the way this modern Demeter thinks, as is the idea that quality of work can be induced by a motivating set of rewards.

## Old Favorites: Zeus, Ares and Hephaestus

In Greek mythology Zeus, Hestia, Demeter, Hera, Poseiden and Hades were the children of Cronus and Rhea, while Zeus fathered Hermes, Athena, Ares, Apollo, Artemis and Hephaestus, to name only a few of his many children. This kinship structure indicates that many of the gods revered by the ancient Greeks owed

allegiance to Zeus, not only by virtue of his superior power, but also by his patronage. This may explain why Zeus often tempered the use of his otherwise absolute power with paternalism. The fact that Zeus is not as popular in the current *HBR* pantheon as are Demeter, Hermes and Athena, presents us with an interesting puzzle and some potential insight into the changing character of leadership and managerial culture in our times.

In spite of his association with supreme power, Zeus was a relatively minor player in the *HBR* pantheon from 1989–98, as were Hephaestus (the technician) and Ares (the fierce competitor). This is surprising because Zeus, Ares and Hephaestus fit modern stereotypes of business leaders as powerful strategists, warlords and craftsmen who forge the tools and win the battles of economic competition. Yet these three gods appeared only three times each in the interviews we read and then not always in their pure form (three were present only in combination with another god). This indicates to us that Zeus, Ares and Hephaestus may have been losing their popularity to Hermes, Athena and Demeter during the last decade of the twentieth century.

The earlier popularity of Zeus, Ares and Hephaestus is suggested by the existence of the stereotype of the all-powerful business leader and the fact that these gods were still active in 9 of the 30 interviews we read. Nonetheless the greater presence of Hermes, Athena and Demeter points to significant change in managerial culture and its preference for the particular forms of leadership these gods portray. To us, Zeus, Ares and Hephaestus represent a power-wielding, control-oriented, and engineering-dominated era of business leadership that is giving way to the more communicative, dignified and rejuvenating era represented by the current in-crowd of Hermes, Athena and Demeter. What is perhaps most revealing regarding our hypothesis of change is the observation that when Zeus, Ares and Hephaestus appeared in the interviews we read they frequently spoke of the need to hold their powers in check, or to share power with others.

## Zeus, the leader of the gods

Zeus, supreme ruler of the gods of his generation, was noted for his emphasis on justice but also for his intelligence, which he used to make certain he was not replaced by a usurper. Today's Zeuses clearly stand for global power; however, it is worth noticing that, within the interviews with CEOs who appeared as Zeus, power was more often shared than wielded unilaterally. When the role of the manager was discussed by CEOs who appeared as Zeus, he made it clear that managers should not be power-hungry. These CEOs reported believing that employees must be empowered (by a Zeus-like CEO, of course), and this elevates them to the position of co-Zeuses.

Before the birth of Zeus, his father Cronus was told by his parents (Cronus's father was Ouranos or Heaven, his mother was Earth) that he would father a son who would take his place as master of the gods. In fact, Cronus had usurped

Ouranos and so, fearing the births of his own children, devoured each of them as they were born. When Cronus's wife Rhea was pregnant with Zeus she formed a plan to protect him from his father and, upon his birth, hid him in a Cretan cave. She gave a stone wrapped in swaddling clothes to Cronus to fool him, and he devoured the stone instead of the child. Cronus immediately realized Rhea's trick and spent years searching for Zeus, but did not find him. When Zeus grew into a strong young god, he confronted his father and forced him to throw up all of his brothers and sisters, along with the stone. In another story Zeus used the stone to demarcate the Earth's center point.

In his fight for supremacy Zeus was aided by his brothers Poseidon and Hades. During the war with Cronus, Zeus freed the children of Ouranos whom Cronus had imprisoned within their mother Earth when he had taken power from Ouranos. In gratitude, these ancient beings fought on Zeus's side and gave him the weapons he was known for: thunder and lightning. After defeating Cronus, Poseidon and Hades acceded the role of master of the gods to Zeus and the three of them cast lots to see who would rule which part of the universe. Zeus got the sky, Poseidon the sea, Hades the underworld. Earth was shared between them and Mount Olympus became their common home.

Zeus fathered many of the gods over whom he ruled, sometimes mortals bore his children and sometimes goddesses. Zeus had the ability to change shapes and often seduced his paramours by disguising himself, for instance as a swan, a bull, a cuckoo, a serpent or a rain shower. As supreme ruler of the gods of Olympus, Zeus was quick to dispense justice, usually by striking his target with a thunderbolt, when he felt he had been disobeyed. On the other hand, he also spent enormous energy acting as arbiter and conciliator to the other gods. Zeus could be an egotistical and authoritarian ruler who feared being usurped and so maintained tight reign over other gods by imposing rules for them to follow and swiftly punishing those who disobeyed him. On the other hand, tempered by his paternalism and devotion to justice, Zeus often worked hard to keep the peace on Olympus by smoothing relations between the other gods and creating alliances among them. Zeus thus simultaneously represents the virtues of universal power, paternal care, and justice. Wielding so much power, however, leaves Zeus vulnerable to its abuse, and along with his quick temper and penchant for acting on whim, renders him unpredictable and at times intimidating. When combined with his fear of being usurped, Zeus can become a dangerous character. Thus he represents both the dark and the light sides of power.

Zeus's paternalistic side shows itself in the interview with Robert Haas of Levi Strauss. Haas even uses the term "paternalism" to characterize the company's approach, but then backs off this characterization, recognizing that paternalistic expressions of power are less acceptable now than they once were (Howard 1990: 134):

> Levi has always treated people fairly and cared about their welfare. The usual term is "paternalism." But it is more than paternalism, really – a genuine concern for people and a recognition that people make this business successful.

Nevertheless, what is excluded at the front door, is allowed in at the back in the sense that Haas continues to take care of his metaphoric family and their literal family responsibilities. Like Zeus, Haas is not sentimental, he wraps his paternalism in a blanket of modern rationality saying (Howard 1990: 138):

> in the new, more dynamic business environment, a company has to understand the relationship between work and family. It used to be that what happened to your employees when they went home at the end of the day was their business. But today that worker's sick child *is* your business, because if she's worrying about her child or calling in sick when she isn't – and probably feeling resentful because she's had to lie – she isn't going to be productive. By contrast, if employees aren't worrying about things outside the workplace, if they feel supported – not just financially but "psychically" – then they are going to be more responsive to the needs of customers and of the business.

In this passage the face of the manager supports the argument Haas makes for paternalism by making concern for employees seem a rational thing to do.

Haas directly discusses his own use of power and the modern executive's need to share power (Howard 1990: 135):

> I can speak from experience. It has been difficult for me to accept the fact that I don't have to be the smartest guy on the block – reading every memo and signing off on every decision. In reality, the more you establish parameters and encourage people to take initiatives within those boundaries, the more you multiply your own effectiveness by the effectiveness of other people.

As a reflexive Zeus, Haas acknowledged his difficulties sharing power rather than simply throwing thunderbolts when he said: "In many ways, it's a much tougher role because you can't rely on your title or unquestioning loyalty and obedience to get things done" (1990: 135). Nonetheless this paternal god feels his responsibility for those he rules and demonstrates how he has learned to use his almighty power to develop leadership potential in others as well as to help them to reconcile their differences (Howard 1990: 136):

> That doesn't mean abdication. Managers still have to make decisions, serve as counselors and coaches, be there when things get sticky, and help sort out all the tangles.

John Reed of Citicorp presents another version of Zeus. Reed, in stressing the global power of Citicorp throughout his interview, gave his company an elevated and superior position like that Olympus had for the Greeks: "Our uniform presence around the world . . . lets us do things no one else can do" (Tichy & Charan 1990: 138). In his interview Reed seems to rule the world from Mount Olympus (Tichy & Charan 1990: 138):

> To make it work, you need three things: a shared vision and a common vocabulary around the world, an organization that can translate global scale into local advantage,

and the capacity to transfer local innovations around the world . . . Globality is our most important advantage, even over the Swiss, who have been the world's best private bankers.

Reed's Zeus shows himself to be a just ruler when he claims to rule the universe by occupation, not destruction: "Global competition is about occupying space and positioning yourself wisely – not wiping out the other guy" (Tichy & Charan 1990: 136). It is worth noting that no other interviewee used the term power in as direct and positive a way as did Reed, who frequently asserted his power to deliver the wishes of his subjects (or, by implication, to withhold them): "You want a piece of a paper company in Chile? A gold mine in Zambia? We can do it" (1990: 139). Such talk is reminiscent of Zeus presenting gifts to other gods and to mortals. Yet the dark side of Zeus's fear of being usurped is evident when Reed says: "global scale also gives us staying power" (1990: 139).

Just as the powerful Zeus promoted alliances among the gods and taught them to work together, Reed recalls his efforts to inspire collaboration (Tichy & Charan 1990: 139):

> In the early days, a few of us were catalysts, flying all over the world and urging people to work together. You create the supply by showing people what has been done elsewhere. Exposing people to success gives them the courage and drive to persist.

Like Haas, Reed understands he must share his power with others, deifying them a bit in the process. He says success can and should be "transferred." The interview ends with the following fatherly pronouncement: "We have lots of work to do; we're building a global business" (1990: 144).

David Whitwam of Whirlpool appear as a mixture of Zeus and Athena. Like Haas and Reed, Whitwam's Zeusian character speaks of global power (Maruca 1994: 136):

> The only way to gain lasting competitive advantage is to leverage your capabilities around the world so that the company as a whole is greater than the sum of its parts. Being an international company – selling globally, having global brands or operations in different countries – isn't enough.

In Whitwam's opinion, most international companies are not truly global whereas Whirlpool is thanks to the power of its brand. In asserting Whirlpool's global dominance, Whitwam claims Zeusian mastery of the Earth (Maruca 1994: 137):

> [W]e've worked . . . hard at Whirlpool to define and communicate our vision, objectives, and the market philosophy that represents our unifying focus. Our vision is to be one company worldwide.

Like Reed, Whitwam used the term power in a positive way, describing the company's capabilities in the global market.

## *Ares, god of war*

Ares, the Greek god of war and victory, was highly aggressive. His passion for competition made the battleground his favorite realm. Ares' uncontrolled emotionality, particularly his unbridled joy in violence and cruelty, made this god relatively unpopular among the Greeks. However, he had a benevolent side that redeems him for modern times – he was the giver of youth and of the youthful ambition to win that is frequently exercised in athletic competition. We see the competitive nature of Ares in many modern business practices, some of which led to the corporate scandals that emerged at the end of the twentieth century, which may account for his being cast aside once again as the twenty-first century begins.

Ares was a lover of Aphrodite, who bore him several children including Harmonia (harmony), Phobos (fear) and Deimos (terror). Some say that he fathered Eros (love) as well, though others believe that Hephaestus, Aphrodite's husband, was the father of this child. Modern versions of Ares are known by their aggressiveness, competitiveness and focus on winning. The ability to foster love and harmony as well as fear and terror, give a good sense of the conflicting emotions that accompany Ares-inspired leaders in modern times. Among the CEOs interviewed by *HBR*, Ares most often expressed himself through his competitive nature. The CEOs who appeared in their interviews as Ares were concerned with fair play and spoke of competitors with respect, even though the metaphors and the language they used were decidedly more aggressive than those used by the other god types in the interviews.

In his interview, Carl Hahn of VW posed as competitive Ares with ambitions for global dominance. What distinguished Hahn's Ares from Zeus is that his ambitions were stated in aggressive and warlike images (Avishai 1991: 104):

> Some have called Europe of 1992 a potential fortress. I see Europe not as a fortress but as a platform for global competition . . . Our effort to expand is actually part of an even more ambitious effort to reorganize within the new European platform. We seek to turn Volkswagen AG into a "federated" European company: a true multinational emerging from the European theater, gaining the capacities to compete across the board worldwide.

The importance of winning, so characteristic of Ares, was clearly on Hahn's mind (Avishai 1991: 106):

> In retrospect, this imperative to globalize has been advantageous to us. We are number one in Europe. We are number one in Italy after the Italian companies, number one in France after the French companies. We were the first European carmaker to penetrate the U.S. market, where we were the number one importer for many years.

What emerges from Hahn's interview is the image of a global warlord systematically laying siege to more and more territory. In the economic war some battles are

lost, as, for example, for the US car market, but these are seen as only temporary setbacks offering lessons to be learned on the road to ultimate victory (Avishai 1991: 109):

> Our U.S. manufacturing venture proved to be quite problematic. Our basic mistake was to entrust the design adaptation of the Golf – you knew it as the Rabbit – to "American" thinking: too much attention to outward appearances, too little to engineering detail.
>
> We were right to set up an assembly plant in Westmoreland, Pennsylvania in 1976. We knew we had to manufacture in dollars. We had every hope of building toward a 5% share in the United States.
>
> But we were not true to our heritage. We gave American customers a car that had all the handling characteristics – one might say, the smell – of a U.S. car. We should have restricted ourselves to our traditional appeal, aiming at customers who were looking not for American style, but for a European feel.

While global expansion is a slow process, Hahn never loses sight of the territories VW has already conquered. Hahn stressed the importance of winning when he listed the spoils of VW's warfare (Avishai 1991: 106):

> Next to making profits, our mandate was to motorize our country and large parts of Europe, to provide employment for tens of thousands of people. Even today, we provide 20% of the employment in Lower Saxony and 50% of its exports.
>
> In retrospect, this imperative to globalize has been advantageous to us. We are number one in Europe. We are number one in Italy after the Italian companies, number one in France after the French companies. We were the first European carmaker to penetrate the U.S. market, where we were the number one importer for many years.
>
> Although we did not do well in the United States during the late 1980s – we are down to just 1.5% of the market – when you look at other markets where we go head to head with global competitors – Switzerland, or Norway, or whatever – we have hardly ever lost market share. We have more than held our own in Canada. We are number one by far in Mexico, as well as in Brazil. By investing in several ventures in China, where we have also become the number one car manufacturer, we have established an important starting position in Asia, which will help create more export possibilities for our European operations. We are also doing rather well in Japan: we are the number one importer there, though this still amounts to about 50,000 cars a year.

In spite of his claims to want to "pursue a vision of divisional autonomy" for VW, Audi, Seat and Skoda, control is maintained at the top:

> The management board of Volkswagen Group is there to provide the leadership and coordination and to allocate the funds.

Ares was never afraid to tangle with other powerful gods. Likewise, Hahn faces fierce competition from Japan. Hahn says that VW must "grapple" with the

achievements of the Japanese (Avishai 1991: 106). He never underestimates VW's competitors and speaks about them with great respect, as all accomplished warriors do. Every competitor is a potential challenger – Ares will engage in competition with anyone who wants to try their powers, even mortals are worthy adversaries. In that, Ares is a democratic god who appreciates courageous opponents. Similarly, the employees are offered considerable freedom (codetermination) so long as they, too, are concerned about winning. Thus Ares sees all significant achievement as occurring on the battlefield.

Paul Cook combines Hermes and Ares. For Cook, innovation is a competitive undertaking: "You won't get innovation without pressure" (Taylor 1990: 98). He spoke of "winners and losers," placed great emphasis on success and stated that "the Japanese are eating us alive" (Taylor 1990: 99). He stressed the importance of "management by walking around", a more active form of leadership than that associated with the Athena-inspired "strategic thinker". The following quote by Cook invokes the youthful character of Ares and underscores his Ares-inspired obsession with achievement (Taylor 1990: 100):

> So the most important thing we do is build an organization – a culture, if you'll pardon the word – that encourages teamwork, that encourages fun and excitement, that encourages everyone to do things differently and better – and that acknowledges and rewards the people who excel.

Cook bases rewards on performance and makes his employees compete for them which, he admitted, causes "some unhappiness . . . but it also creates drive" (Taylor 1990: 101). He acknowledged that sometimes it is important to engage directly in battle, and spoke about taking strategic losses (Taylor 1990: 105):

> We had to do an aggressive selling job – and take a short-term financial hit – to persuade customers to adopt the new product.

He spoke of other, more difficult battles: "Innovation is a global game. You have to fight foreign competition before it starts" (Taylor 1990: 106). Nonetheless, Cook stressed that, like an experienced warrior, he will avoid battle when it is unnecessary. However, he justified this attitude in a warrior-like way by saying that it is "the toughest game to play."

Another example of the myth of Ares is given in the interview with Lawrence A. Bossidy of Allied Signal who presented an aggressive, even brutal, root metaphor (Tichy & Charan 1995: 70):

> I believe in the "burning platform" theory of change. When the roustabouts are standing on the offshore oil rig and the foreman yells, "Jump into the water," not only won't they jump but they also won't feel too kindly toward the foreman. There may be sharks in the water. They'll jump only when they themselves see the flames shooting up from the platform.

The leader's job is to help everyone see that the platform is burning, whether the flames are apparent or not. The process of change begins when people decide to take the flames seriously and manage by fact, and that means a brutal understanding of reality.

Ares' brutality appears again when Bossidy says (Tichy & Charan 1995: 70):

Let me explain it another way. We made a major commitment to use total quality as the vehicle to drive change. Everybody in the world has TQ or something like it. I want Allied Signal to be the people who do it, not the people who talk about it. TQ does not replace goals; it's the vehicle to facilitate progress toward your goals. Think about it. Anybody who makes his numbers and says, "I don't need TQ," has to walk the plank or change. Some people have changed, and some are gone.

He stated (Tichy & Charan 1995: 71):

Besides values, you have to have clear goals. People have to know where they're going. What is victory? Where do you want to be? Every year, we set three goals that we put in front of everybody. It creates focus.

Bossidy often spoke about the need for dealing honestly with tough questions and staying focused on results. He honors his competitors, pointing to their superior results and believing that the comparison will challenge his people to try to outdo them. Bossidy is competitive and projects his desire to win onto his employees (Tichy & Charan 1995: 71):

I think you don't change a culture. I think you coach people to win. Basically, people want to be successful.

In his opinion, "one of the worst things we do in corporate America is not tell people what we think of them" (Tichy & Charan 1995: 75). Employee appraisals should reflect the person's individual performance within the competitive context of business.

Bossidy, like Haas, realizes that his Ares needs to be contained. He says (Tichy & Charan 1995: 72):

The day when you could yell and scream and beat people into good performance is over. Today you have to appeal to them by helping them see how they can get from here to there, by establishing some credibility, and by giving them some reason and some help to get there.

and that (Tichy & Charan 1995: 76):

Today's corporation is a far cry from the old authoritarian vertical hierarchy I grew up in. The cross-functional ties among individuals and groups are increasingly important.

They're channels of activity and communication. The traditional bases of managerial authority are eroding. In the past, we used to reward the lone rangers in the corner offices because their achievements were brilliant even though their behavior was destructive. That day is gone. We need people who are better at persuading than at barking orders, who know how to coach and build consensus. Today, managers add value by brokering with people, not by presiding over empires.

Yet Bossidy is willing to make bold moves on the battlefield (Tichy & Charan 1995: 74):

I don't want to have to come back a year from now and restructure all over again. If we're going to take a charge, I want to take a big one.

And he quotes the old warlord, Teddy Roosevelt, as saying "The best executive is the one who has sense enough to pick good men to do what he wants done, and self-restraint enough to keep from meddling with them while they do it" (Tichy & Charan 1995: 77).

## Hephaestus, god of craftsmanship

Hephaestus, son of Zeus and Hera, was the god of fire and the smithy and was the only Greek god who worked. He was not very godlike, nor particularly virtuous for that matter, except in regard to creating perfect things. He was a divine craftsman who built palaces for the gods and supplied Zeus with thunderbolts. His gift was the craft of metalwork and with it he learned to make impenetrable armor, beautiful jewelry and magical objects that could move by themselves. He married Aphrodite, and when she was unfaithful to him with Ares, Hephaestus trapped the two of them in his bed using a set of magical chains that bound the lovers while they slept.

Hephaestus was cast out of Olympus twice. The first time occurred right after his birth. His mother Hera, disgusted by his hideously deformed legs, threw the imperfect god out of Olympus. Knowing he lacked the glamour of the other gods, Hephaestus concentrated on his craft (most of the time). The second time Hephaestus was cast out of Olympus it was for interfering in a quarrel between his parents. Zeus cast him onto the Greek island of Lemnos, which afterwards was known for producing fine metalwork.

Hephaestus's virtues are his craft and perfectionism. Modern day Hephaestuses concentrate on product and the techniques they use to perfect it, and are not concerned to bring glamour to their companies. Their limitations are those of the technician, namely not looking beyond technical achievements. A potential vice of the Hephaestus-inspired CEO is jealousy of others' gifts or achievements. The CEOs who appeared as Hephaestus in the *HBR* interviews we read were unconcerned with colorful narration and avoided personification, concentrating entirely on the products and technical aspects of their company and its management.

Robert F. McDermott of USAA portrays all the characteristics associated with Hephaestus, his interview shows no signs of the heroic or charismatic virtues seen in the interviews with CEOs who portrayed other gods. The language McDermott used is casual, pragmatic, down-to-earth and he rarely spoke of himself. Instead he focused full attention on the skills and techniques of providing good service. For example, he stated in the beginning of his interview (Teal 1991: 118):

> The mission and corporate culture of this company are, in one word, service. As a company objective, service comes ahead of either profits or growth.

To the question of the interviewer: "Is it really that simple?" McDermott answered that it is not – "it's service to a particular community of customers and members, because our niche in the market is very important to us" (Teal 1991: 118). Service is a complex matter that demands perfectionism. However, McDermott cannot retain the requisite knowledge for perfect service-giving for himself. Like Hephaestus, who taught his craft to the people of Lemnos, McDermott shares his knowledge and skills with USAA's employees (Teal 1991: 120):

> I can't sit here at this level and dream up ways of improving service. It's got to come from the people on the front line.

"Enriching the jobs" is another important theme in McDermott's interview and he uses the terms "learning" and "training" extensively. Another way of gaining skills is experience – through having employees work in "lots of different jobs and divisions" (Teal 1991: 120). McDermott says that jobs should be interesting, but also efficient: "People don't want to spend their lives doing effortless, pointless work" (Teal 1991: 123). He often referred to the military, where he worked before being appointed to his current position, but it is not the aggressive, competitive dimension of military service that McDermott emphasized; it is the morale of his employees that concerned him and he associated this with the quality of work life at USAA (Teal 1991: 123):

> At USAA, that [morale] includes the fitness centers and the softball diamonds and the cafeterias as well as good salaries and benefits, a clean, cheerful place to work, and 52 four-day workweeks every year. It also includes the dress code and high expectations. We give a lot, and we demand a lot. But most of all, the quality of work life here is a matter of our service orientation.

Not only was McDermott interested in the quality of jobs and work life at his company, but in the quality of the people employed, whom he described as well-educated, affluent, honest and honorable. But above all reigns the crafting of technology. The skills associated with the company's technology are not simply applied technical rationality, they are learned and the technology itself is constantly replenished by their learning, hence crafting is involved (Teal 1991: 126):

The systems we're developing are transparent. You can ask them why, and they'll explain the rules and show you why they did what they did. What's more, if you find a new rule, you can add it to the sequence. So both the operator and the system can learn.

Two other interviews are devoid of colorful metaphors and vivid narratives, and contain statements characteristic of Hephaestus: the interview with Tom Chapman of Greater Southeast Community Hospital (Nichols 1992) and the interview with Sir Colin Marshall from BA (Prokesch 1995). In spite of their nods to Demetrian virtues of locality (community) and care, the overall tone in these interviews is distinctively one of pride in skills and exactness of delivery.

Like Hephaestus, Greater Southeast Community Hospital's Tom Chapman left Olympus to serve on an earthly island – a community hospital. Although he app-renticed at a hospital in Boston that served the socially privileged, Chapman chose to work at Greater Southeast, looking after the health of many underprivileged people. At first blush, Chapman thus seems to be a pure expression of Demeter, and indeed he spoke of community and care-giving incessantly. However, once we realized that Chapman's job as CEO of a hospital was to oversee care-giving, we looked more closely at the godlike nature of his expressions and found Hephaestus a better match for Chapman's style, which is an unglamorous one of perfecting every aspect of the technical side of his business. For example, he speaks about a hospital pro-gram for feeding the elderly that Demeter would describe using more motherly tones (Nichols 1992: 93):

> At first, a lot of people around here doubted whether employees would choose to spend their lunch hours doing extra work. But we've found that clerical employees, who are detached from the caring mission of the hospital, like being involved in this nursing activity. They find it fulfilling. From the hospital's perspective, the program saves both time and money. We don't have to pay a highly trained nurse to perform a routine feeding, and we don't have lengthened stays brought on by infections resulting from the feeding tubes [that they would be using without hand feeding]. The patients also benefit physically and mentally from the added nutrition and from the extra social contact.

While Chapman speaks of extraordinary humanistic acts of others, he does so with his eyes trained on the cost-benefit ratio the hospital realizes through their actions. There is much other evidence of Hephaestus-inspired technical focus and the gift of perfection in Chapman's interview, but the most telling quote is one in which Chapman explained his leadership ambition in relation to the humanitarian pur-pose of his not-for-profit hospital (Nichols 1992: 91):

> There is a right reason and a real reason to do everything. The right reason to provide preventive care is to keep people healthy. The real reason Southeast provides preventive care is because it is more cost-effective to treat patients this way than it is to wait until they have had a stroke. The hospital's entire blood pressure program

costs, at a maximum, $20,000 to $30,000 a year to administer. It is probably the lowest cost health prevention program available. If you contrast that with the $30,000 it can routinely cost to treat just one stroke victim, you can see where the savings come from. Yet the government will not reimburse us for these prevention programs. And the more aggressively and efficiently we pursue these efforts, the more we slowly shrink our market share. That's the great irony: we need to keep the occupancy rate of the hospital up because that is how we fund all of our outreach programs. Yet the goal of these outreach programs is to keep people out of the hospital. So we're stuck.

Even though Chapman clearly understands the larger view, he remains focused on technically perfecting this organization.

Like Hephaestus, British Airway's Sir Colin Marshall wants to perfect customer service within the airline industry and in his interview with *HBR* he speaks of little except technical matters relating to the crafting of superior service for BA's customers. He stated (Prokesch 1995: 103): "Anyone can fly airplanes, but few organizations can excel in serving people." Marshall emphasized the craft-like character of BA's service effort when he stated (Prokesch 1995: 104): "We want [our customers] to know that we carry millions but to feel that our individual interactions with them weren't mass produced." His attention to detail and exacting standards are illustrated by BA's approach to marketing which Marshall claimed are more sophisticated than other airlines' (Prokesch 1995: 105):

First, we extensively and continuously study the market to pinpoint the segments that offer the possibility of generating a higher profit margin – segments such as business women, unaccompanied minors, and consultants – and identify those people among our customers. Then we create extensive lifestyle profiles of each customer, which we use both to increase ticket purchases and to sell other products and services. In addition to tracking how recently and how frequently customers have flown with us for business and for leisure, we track their broader purchasing behavior, lifestyles, their ability to influence other people's purchasing decisions, and their value needs. But identifying such customers is only half the battle. Learning from them so you can design and improve services that they will highly value over time is the other half. That's where we think we especially excel.

Hephaestus' perfectionism shows in Marshall's strategy for "orchestrating service" and his goal for making customer service at BA "seamless" (Prokesch 1995: 104):

Arranging all the elements of our service so that they collectively generate a particular experience. We try to think about what kind of impression or feeling each interaction between the company and our customer will generate.

For Marshall, where customer service is concerned, no detail goes unnoticed. He created a special unit within BA whose sole responsibility it is to represent the

customer's point of view in collecting data on service performance and feeding it back to management and operating units. Christopher Swan who heads the market-place performance unit explained (Prokesch 1995: 109):

> We look at everything down to when and whether the flight attendants served the packets of peanuts . . . It may seem small, but each customer comes away with an extremely personalized view of how a company served him. If a customer happens to be a peanut buff, the worst thing that can happen on a short domestic flight is for that person not to be offered a packet of peanuts. He'll remember that we didn't give him a packet while our competitors did.

## Rare and Absent Gods

We found it interesting to see which of the Greek gods rarely or never asserted themselves in the interviews. The rare gods (those mentioned only once or twice in the ten-year period of interviews we read) included Apollo, Persephone, Hades and Heracles. Persephone, the goddess who lived half her life in the darkness of the Underworld where she reigned as Hades' queen, and the other half in the splendid light of Olympus, was personified by the CEO of the only Mexican company represented in the interviews we read. This interview presents a double reality: on the one hand, the traditional Mexican world, depicted by the CEO as dark, and on the other, the new American free market, depicted as light. Raymond Smith, CEO of Bell Atlantic, was portrayed as Hades who delivers rewards and punishments – it is not well known today, but Hades had a generous side to him and liked to distribute riches to the deserving at appropriate times.

As for Apollo, the god of medicine, music and poetry, intellectualism probably renders him less appropriate for the role of a modern CEO than the other gods mentioned, although he does appear in two interviews in a secondary role, linked either to Hermes or Hephaestus. Apollo defeated the dragon Python to become master of Delphi and thus the god of prophecy. One could argue that prophecy does have a role to play in business leadership, though not one given much attention in the interviews we read. For example, Sir Colin Marshall's brief reference to BA's alliance with USAir sounds remarkably like a consultation with an oracle (Prokesch 1995: 102–3):

> We've conducted extensive research with USAir and have very strong indications that many people in the United States are willing to pay a premium not to be treated like cattle. . . . We think we – through USAir – could revolutionize the U.S. airline industry and create an entirely new section of the industry.

Similarly, Paul Allaire of Xerox sounded like a prophet when he proclaimed that: "In the future, Xerox won't just sell copiers. It will sell innovative approaches for performing work and for enhancing productivity" (Howard 1992: 109). In retrospect

(the interview was conducted in 1992), Allaire turned out to be correct about this as well as other prophecies such as (Howard 1992: 109):

> Our competitors are multiplying. Some of our Japanese rivals like Canon will certainly come along with us in this new digital world. But we will also be competing with companies that are now in the printing business or in the computer systems business. Increasingly, we are moving into the more complex business environment that a lot of computer companies already find themselves in – where we will compete against companies in some situations and cooperate with them in others.

Both Marshall and Allaire claimed to be using technical tools of prediction rather than divine inspiration. It remains to be seen whether rational prediction has eclipsed the gift of prophecy for all time.

Heracles was the greatest of the mythological heroes and a demi-god. From early childhood he accomplished many brave and extraordinary deeds. He is particularly famous for twelve tasks he carried out for Eurystes. Having successfully accomplished these, and other feats, he was elevated to Mount Olympus as an immortal god. Heracles appeared only twice in the interviews we read where the CEOs of Softbank and Eni narrated the various quests and trials that they passed against all odds on their journeys to becoming successful business leaders. Heracles is interesting in that the two CEOs who closely fit his character are entrepreneurs. Perhaps this indicates that the entrepreneur is a seeker after the status of godlike business leader, whereas CEOs of established firms (vs. the entrepreneurial founders of their companies) laid claim to their Olympic stature by virtue of professional appointment, a sort of birthright.

The interview with Softbank's CEO, Masayoshi Son, is an account of various quests and trials that Son successfully passed against all odds, almost miraculously. Like Heracles, Son's personal story is one of impossible quests (Webber 1992: 100):

> I went to the United States when I was 16 years old. I told my family I wanted to go, and everyone started crying, especially my mother. How come you're leaving our family and going all the way to the United States? She said, it's a bunch of barbarians who live in that country.

That was only the beginning – instead of staying in the US, Masayoshi Son decided to move to Japan after having completed his studies (Webber 1992: 101):

> I thought about [staying in the US]. In fact, a number of things argued in favor of staying in the United States. Many of my friends said I would be crazy to leave because I would have to start my business all over again in Japan. I already had a company established, and it would be much easier to keep doing that.

Moving to Japan would mean facing many more obstacles, from cultural ("negative perception of the entrepreneur") to financial ("Japanese banks will not loan money to you because they are more conservative"). However, Son decided to move anyway,

because that was part of his long-term vision. Against all the odds, after a difficult beginning, even this quest proved successful.

Another CEO who took on Heracles' character is Eni's Franco Bernabè. Bernabè tells the story of the transformation of Eni, how the "new enterprise [rose] from its ashes" (Hill & Wetlaufer 1998: 83). The story is not simple and the change required doing the impossible under unfavorable and sometimes even hostile conditions with no predestined or foreseeable solutions. Outside the company, unpredictability and ambivalence raged, and in the turmoil Bernabè transformed the company, making it modern and economically sound. He did that with the help of other people; however, the outside authorities were not always favorable (in the heroic sagas the gods were not always consistently loyal, either), but the main thing was not to listen to others too much, but rather to keep "an inner compass to indicate the way" (Hill & Wetlaufer 1998: 92–3). The hero is a solitary person, and the road to Olympus is full of betrayals, traps, and dangers.

Notably absent gods in the *HBR* management pantheon include the relational Here, the family and tradition-oriented Hestia, and Aphrodite of the passionate feelings. Whereas maternal, nurturing feelings are acknowledged in modern business through the inclusion of Demeter, passion and tradition seem to be excluded. Perhaps the relational archetypes of Here and Hestia are too dependent to fit the "modern identity narrative," that organizational scholar Barbara Czarniawska-Joerges (1994: 197) claimed "aims to achieve an impression of individuality, that is, independence from other people's reactions". Carly Fiorina's emphasis on HP's innovative past might suggest her as a candidate for expressing Hestia's character, whereas the seductive and emotional management guru Tom Peters (Peters 1989; Peters & Waterman 1982) may be the best available example of Aphrodite. We would expect to find a relational Here-type CEO at the helm of a company like JP Morgan that emphasizes collaborative teamwork in an industry noted for its machismo, arrogance, and individualism. But we are left to speculate, as these gods did not appear in the *HBR* pantheon of business leaders during the last decade of the twentieth century.

Also missing are Poseidon, the violent god of the sea who symbolizes the instinctive sphere, and the delirious and mystical Dionysus, god of wine and the theater. The *HBR* interviews we read confirm Bowles's (1993) observation that the gods that represent darker and chaotic aspects of humanity seldom appear in official managerial discourse. This does not mean that they are absent from real organizational life, but only that they are not celebrated by *HBR*, a topic to which we will return in Chapter 5.

There is one more absent god, not associated with emotionality or irrationality and who is clearly virtuous – Artemis, the uncompromising, who protects wild animals. Her modern version might be the feminist and/or environmental activist. Surely, she is an important female god and also a vital model of leadership in modern managerial culture as she is an ecologically aware defender of corporate ethics. Anita Roddick of the Body Shop with her opposition to animal testing, comes to mind as a potential carrier of Artemis's mythic virtues, though she also

carries Artemis's devotion to the hunt in that she sometimes falls short of her promise to protect (e.g., animals used for testing by her suppliers, fair trade in all of the countries with which she does business).

## Mythologizing Yourself and Others

In the first European military schools founded in the eighteenth century, one of the key objectives of training programs was the spiritual development of future officers. Studying the lives and personalities of legendary commanders such as Julius Caesar, Alexander the Great or Napoleon was a focal exercise in these schools that featured analysis of the character, values and virtues of great leaders and their development in the students. Perhaps it is time to return to the design of these early leadership training programs in order to recover ethics for business education by examining the character, values, virtues and vices of those business leaders we consider to be most worthy of our esteem. This is the reason we have been treating CEOs as mythic heroes or gods in this chapter. Like mythical figures used in all cultures at all times, this chapter treated the CEOs as personifications of universal aspects of the human condition, as powerful symbols of life, fate, transcendence and revelation, but also of ordinary human foibles and problems. Thus the myths expressed in the *HBR* interviews supply members of managerial culture with symbolic means to develop and communicate essential attributes of their identity by providing role models for virtuous behavior. In addition, they provide us with the means to describe in some detail the complex and changing ethics of contemporary managerial culture.

Eliade (1932/1991) regarded myth as a story about events that took place "in the beginning," before history, or in sacred time. Sacred time is different from linear or profane time. It is recreated in myth by continually re-enacting old knowledge in the here and now via mythological consciousness. The time-frame of myth is different from our everyday experience of time – it is located beyond past, present, and future. When a myth is retold all instants collapse in a mystical eternity. For both the myth's narrator and listeners, profane time is symbolically abolished along with consciousness of the everyday life-world. Because it resides within a different domain of experience, the customary logic and criteria for truth and falsity cannot be used to evaluate myth. The truth of a myth can be proven only by our collective response to it, as Eliade (1932/1991) explained:

> The periodic recitation of the myths breaks through the barriers built up by profane existence. The myth continually reactualizes the Great Time, and in so doing raises the listener to a superhuman and supra-historical plane, which among other things, enables him to approach a Reality that is inaccessible at the level of profane, individual existence.

Myths reveal the faces of the artist and the priest because they are linked directly to values, emotions, and ethics as opposed to the technical rationality of the manager's

face. It goes without saying that only emotionally mature people make good business leaders. It is less obvious, however, that attainment of a certain level of artistic and ethical development comes through mythic consciousness. Our reading of the *HBR* interviews suggests that aesthetic development means the ability to generate and choose values and to stick with them in the course of taking action, even when the going gets tough. It is our view that managers need aesthetic qualifications every bit as much as they need analytical and technical skills. In our view, this is a substantial piece of what effective leadership is all about.

Reviewing the *HBR* pantheon of business leaders shown in Table 4.1 and considering the relative popularity of different gods expressed in the *HBR* interviews we read, it would appear that late twentieth-century managerial culture exhibited a morality that was primarily based on the virtues of communication and rational strategy, and values for growth and renewal. This morality made secondary appeal to the virtues of global vision and influence tempered by a value for democratic power sharing (at least within the firm), competitiveness and technical achievement. The virtue of creativity and values for paradox (e.g., both generosity and severity) and entrepreneurship were present as well, but received less attention during this period of business history. This complex of virtues and values played against the vices of dishonesty, lack of emotion, over-protection (in respect of both paternalism and maternalism), sacrifice of the earth to business survival, aggression and over-confidence in technical solutions to human problems. Thus the moral foundation of managerial culture depicted in the *HBR* interviews we read was neither simple nor purely virtuous. It nonetheless shows the power of mythic consciousness to reveal the ethics of managerial culture and thus to help us better understand the face of the priest in contemporary business leadership. Like real life priests, business ideals are rarely realized in full, though they remain worthy of pursuit and glorification. Acknowledging our failures to achieve them is a healthy and necessary exercise on the road to self-purification.

Myths help you to develop the faces of the priest and the artist by promoting ethical and artistic virtues. Myths may be historically or factually false, but they are regarded by their believers as valid on the plane of eternal truth. Acceptance of myth requires an act of faith. According to Joseph Campbell (quoted in Bowles 1989), mythical consciousness grants self-knowledge by showing us who we are. Without myth, we would have no imagination for developing identity or culture or for avoiding the traps our humanity sets for us on the road to immortality.

## Find your god

Think about a person you admire, someone you consider a leader in your realm – an executive, manager or supervisor you have worked for, or a teacher, friend or family member who has influenced you. Find the Greek god you believe they embody, then write a mythic tale using their god and its stories as a template to give you a plot and ideas for describing their character and actions.

Next use the gods of Greek mythology or other characters of your liking (such as astrological signs, famous literary characters, cinematic roles, etc.) develop your own mythic character. Which god/character do you feel is expressing him or herself through you? For example, if you are using Greek mythology, your favorite god may be the nurturing Demeter, the rational Athena, Hermes the innovator, or Hermes the communicator. Be sure to consider the full pantheon in choosing your god model – which gods do you feel most attracted to? What gods do you most want to interact with? Which would you like to avoid?

Now place your mythic character into the frame of your life. How would your god act and react to the situations you encounter in your daily life? Translate some of your experiences into stories or plays that feature you acting out your god/character. Imagine that you have reached the height of your powers on this earth and tell the myth-inspired tale of the life that brought you to this moment. Weave into your tale ideas from Greek mythology about the god you feel is manifesting in you. For example, if Zeus is your model, tell how you earned your massive power and how you learned to handle it. How did you learn to manage the other gods? What conflicts did you resolve between them? How did you do it? Review the gifts of Zeus and relate them to your own abilities. Perhaps, like Zeus, you have the gift of disguising yourself to others. What disguises did you wear (were you the bull? the swan?), who was seduced by them, what progeny did your seductions bring forth? Be sure to describe your vices as well as your virtues, your defeats as well as your victories, and how you think and feel about them. Now, at the end of your reign, who will you bestow your gifts upon and why?

# 5

# Forming and Reforming the Institution of Management

In the Middle Ages of Europe, the power upheld by the sacred order of the Roman Catholic Vatican was transferred to kings and emperors via papal influence on their selection. The pope's power was believed to be God-given and so was considered to be both holy and essential to the successful reign of chosen leaders. We wondered if, in our times, the Harvard Business School plays a part similar to that of the Vatican in the Middle Ages; that is, acting as its agent, does *HBR* select the role models other members of managerial culture follow?

It seemed to us that, in the interviews with CEOs, *HBR* names the gods and goddesses of management and produces, disseminates and protects their mythology. Furthermore, the theories, concepts, ideas, stories and heroes selected by *HBR*'s editors for inclusion in their magazine provide key elements of modern management mythology that help to define the essence and the avant-garde of contemporary managerial culture. In these ways, *HBR* legitimates and condones the practices of a select few business leaders and thus gives substance and importance to the work CEOs do by shaping managerial culture to celebrate them as its gods and heroes. Furthermore, *HBR* offers aspiring members of managerial culture the knowledge they need to one day take the role of hero in the myths that will be retold by the next generation.

We argue that mythmaking requires both actors who are willing to perform the stories presented to them by mythological consciousness (the CEOs discussed in Chapter 4) *and* an institution to set the stage on which they act. Harvard Business School is the stage for the *HBR* interviews, but the staging is done by *HBR*'s editors in collaboration with the CEOs themselves. Through their interviews, the CEOs show the face of the priest as they carry sacred managerial knowledge from one generation of *HBR* readers to the next.

In this chapter we turn to the question of mythmaking and so depart from our approach in previous chapters. Here we present neither a collection of action stories and dramas told by the CEOs in their interviews (as we did in Chapters 2 and 3), nor of the mythical tales *HBR* presented as interviews (as we did in Chapter 4).

Instead we consider the role *HBR* plays as mythmaker. We do this by presenting our own interview conducted with *HBR*'s then editor-in-chief, Suzy Wetlaufer, who spoke with us about how she understood *HBR*'s interview process and the role the interviews play in shaping managerial culture. But first we describe the path of development managerial culture followed in the twentieth century, culminating in the institutionalization of the technical/rational face of business leadership.

## Managerial Culture and its Institutionalizing Force

In the middle of the twentieth century, James Burnham developed an influential theory that he propounded in his book *The Managerial Revolution* (1961). Having studied A.A. Berle's *Power Without Property* (1959), which described power distributions in American business, Burnham concluded that a new class of professional managers had appeared that was taking economic power out of the hands of company owners (capitalists) and claiming it as their own. At the time, this managerial revolution was generally seen as elitist in the sense that a small group of top managers would replace the small group of big capitalists who dominated the free enterprise system. In *The Power Elite*, C.W. Mills (1956) extended Burnham's ideas about the emergence of professional business management, suggesting that the new professionals and the old capitalists would combine to transform the power elite within American society. Concurrently, Yugoslav Marxist Milovan Djilas (1957) applied Burnham's ideas to communist societies in his book *The New Class*, in which he accused party aparatchiks, technocrats and managers of becoming the new class of exploiters.

American management pundit Peter Drucker (1993) recently reinterpreted Burnham's idea of a managerial revolution yet again, this time in a much more democratic (i.e., less elitist) way that he claimed is appropriate for post-capitalist societies. Drucker's re-interpretation involves four major points. First, contrary to Burnham's prediction, the number of people throughout the world performing managerial functions (e.g., allocating scarce resources in order to leverage their value; making financial decisions; leading, organizing and supervising the work of others) can be counted in the hundreds of millions, and this number is growing exponentially. Management is thus coming to dominate the role sets of the most active and creative parts of the world's population, including not only professional managers, but also entrepreneurs, public servants, activists, professionals and academics (not to mention artists and priests!).

Second, competitive forces increase the pace of change in the marketplace and thereby push companies to flatten their hierarchies in order to move fast and remain flexible. This implies decentralization and employee empowerment. Translated into social structure it means masses of people must perform managerial functions on either a permanent or an ad hoc basis. In front of our eyes, the bureaucratic pyramid, which once seemed invincible, is crumbling.

Third, behavioral and institutional patterns copied from the business world are being rapidly adopted by public administration, military and paramilitary organizations as well as healthcare, education, the media, art and religion. As this trend unfolds, the "managerial way" becomes increasingly the only socially acceptable way of acquiring and allocating scarce resources to achieve complex goals and to meet multiple stakeholder demands. As a consequence, almost everywhere, promotion means that people trained to be medical doctors, attorneys, civil and public servants, military officers, teachers, artists, priests and so on are at least partially and sometimes totally redefined as managers.

Fourth and finally, small firms, family-owned companies, farms and the like have to be run in a business fashion in order to meet the challenges of the marketplace. This means that even the entrepreneur and small businessperson must acquire and use managerial skills and techniques and adopt a managerial mindset. What is more, the differences between manager and entrepreneur blur, as millions of entrepreneurs become managers while managers, for their part, just as rapidly become entrepreneurs. For instance, moonlighting is becoming a way of life for university professors (acting as freelance consultants), plumbers (taking on extra jobs privately after normal working hours), public servants (teaching in universities), and even for the police (doing private security work alongside their police activities). Meanwhile, hundreds of millions of people actively invest in the stock market and thereby become business owners.

In contrast to Mills' notion of a power elite, Drucker's assertion of the rise and diffusion of managerial culture means both dispersion and concentration of economic power. On the one hand, hundreds of millions of people independently control vast financial and material assets. On the other hand, these resources can almost instantly be mobilized and focused through capital markets, networks, alliances, mergers, and acquisitions. In their masses, people are becoming independent economic agents selling their products, including their loyalty, to organizations.

To offer just one example, in France there were 650,000 managers employed by the private sector in the 1960s, but in 1998 this number had grown to over 2.5 million (Beverel 1998). This figure can be increased by at least an equal number of owner-managers of small businesses in different sectors of the economy, varying from plumbing to consulting, legal services, medicine, technical support and design. At least one million civil servants, police, military personnel, and employees of not-for-profit organizations were involved in the management of French organizations in 1998 as well. As a result the largest single group in the total French workforce in 1998 was managers.

Along with growth in their numbers, members of the managerial culture have been rapidly developing common characteristics that cross national boundaries such as educational backgrounds, skills and competencies, norms and values, life styles, behavioral patterns and rituals. They are, for the most part, English speaking; use similar cognitive structures, buzzwords and symbols; and can be considered one of the major forces behind the process of globalization. Paraphrasing Karl Marx's unfulfilled prophecy of a united proletariat one might say, with some irony, that it

is *managers* of all countries who are rapidly uniting. This process is reflected in the cosmopolitanism that contributes to the cohesiveness and further expansion of managerial culture.

Such a massive managerial culture has rather unusual characteristics. First, many people belong to it partially and temporarily – the university professor who is elected or appointed to be dean for a term, the priest selected to supervise the construction of a new church, the scientist asked to lead a research team through a particular project, the worker who is promoted to the job of foreman, all become managers. Some of them stay in that role, some quit, and some alternate between management and playing other roles. What is more, because of its partial and temporary nature, it is an open group. Masses of people get into and out of management on their way to social and economic advancement.

Second, managerial culture is immensely diversified not only geographically and ethnically (it covers the whole world) but also in terms of social and economic stratification. It includes barefoot street peddlers in Bangkok as well as the CEOs of Fortune 500 companies. All of these individuals consciously perform managerial functions and are subject to global and local market forces.

Third, because of the nature of market forces, managers have to develop both international (global) and local orientations (captured by the dictum "think global, act local" or by the hybrid "glocal"). The Internet and the spread of American-style management education only intensify pressures to adopt an international orientation. Then, under the increasing pressure of global competition, managers and entrepreneurs from all over the world use their common managerial skills, common language (business English) and common cognitive structures in order to secure their legitimacy (i.e., their right to control resources and use them to influence others). They find much of their legitimacy in the rapidly proliferating worldwide American model of management education.

In the United States alone, close to 250,000 people graduate from some kind of university level business management program every year and almost 70,000 are awarded MBA diplomas which generally are perceived to be passports to management careers and eventually to top leadership positions. Similar MBA programs are mushrooming all over the globe including the post-communist world. For example, over 150 institutions of higher education in Poland now offer programs in management.

Common educational backgrounds are one indicator of shared managerial culture. Education and the professional status it bestows enable managers to justify their power and privileges both to themselves and to others. One form this justification takes is the use of rankings and highly elaborate hierarchies of credentials certifying and legitimizing individuals, companies, and institutions. As Drucker explained in regard to credentialism (Harris 1993), although the managerial culture is unique in its scope and diversity, it still faces a need to justify its privileges. The institution of management shares this need for self-justification with comparable social groups that held power in the past, such as the European aristocracy during the Enlightenment, British and American industrialists following the industrial revolution, and the middle class of India after World War II.

Managerial culture provides a foundation for the diversified and inherently unstable group of people who struggle to identify themselves with others who have similar power and privilege and attempt to hold onto them. One of the important mechanisms for bringing this culture into being, celebrating its values, establishing its expectations, and keeping its members in contact with one another, is the institutionalizing force of management periodicals, most notable among these for the past 25 years or more, has been the *Harvard Business Review*. It is to the influence of *HBR* and its role in defining the criteria and expectations of management practice that we now turn our attention.

## Our Interview with *HBR*

[*SW*: Suzy Wetlaufer, former Editor-in-Chief, *Harvard Business Review*; *MJH*: Mary Jo Hatch, interviewer]

MJH:  Do you know *HBR*'s history of doing interviews with CEOs?

SW:   I don't know exactly when they started. *HBR* has always had a strong practitioner bent. And we have always wanted to have the voices of executives in our pages, because we are read primarily by senior and middle-to-senior level executives. And we thought that, along with presenting the best academic research and research that comes out of other forums, such as think tanks and consulting firms, that to have the voice and experience of a CEO was a really important part of the editorial mix.

So I don't know how many years ago exactly that the interview started. It certainly predates me, and I came eight years ago. Right now, we try to do five, six a year, we try to keep up with them, because, as I said, we just see the interview as a critical part of the mix of our content.

MJH:  We started our reading of the interviews with 1989 because that's when the Berlin Wall came down and Eastern European managers started to read *HBR*. During something like the first five years of the interviews we read, there's one every issue, five or six every year. Then it drops to only two or three a year.

SW:   Right.

MJH:  Now that you are moving to twelve issues a year I suppose it will change again.

SW:   Well, it would be wrong editorially, I believe, to try to have an interview in every single issue for a couple of reasons. One is, they take a lot of time and energy and thought. And second, I'm not sure that there are that many CEOs that we should be paying close attention to as examples of how to improve management. And so the general thought is, there was probably a time when it was appropriate for there to be an interview

in every issue – that was when we came out six times a year. Now that we're twelve times a year, we'll probably have four to eight interviews a year, if that many.

MJH:   Are the interviews relatively popular?

SW:    They're relatively popular. It's rare that they're the blockbuster of the issue – they usually fall in the middle of the pack, in terms of popularity with the readers.

MJH:   How do you decide whom to interview?

SW:    We're influenced by a bunch of factors. We want the interviews to pass the test that every other article in *HBR* does – that is, the interview has to have four elements that we look for in every article. One is robustness – meaning, does the content come from deep experience or research? With the interview, that would mean the CEOs we feature possess a track record that our readers would admire and respect, and indeed, want to emulate. The second criterion – or test – is for meaningfulness. Is the interview content relevant to our readers' experience? Will what the CEO has to say impact the way the reader does his work, thinks about his work now or tomorrow?

The third criterion for all articles, including the interview, is intellectual content. So, with the interview we ask, does this CEO have a theory of business? Does he or she have something to say that's a cogent, intellectual conceptualization of how they operate? Incidentally, we have certainly conducted interviews and later decided we could not run them because the CEO did not have a theory of business that was conceptualized in a way that would help our readers think about or run their businesses differently.

And, finally, there's the matter of engagement. We ask: will this CEO be engaging and interesting to our readers? Will they want to read this conversation from end to end?

So the interviews are selected looking at those four criteria. Now, it's important to note that when we interview CEOs, we don't go into the meeting to talk to them about everything under the sun. For example, we wanted very specifically to talk to Michael Dell about value chains and we wanted very specifically to talk to Michael Eisner about creativity in a commercial setting. What I'm saying, I suppose, it that sometimes CEOs are selected at the outset by the sheer fact that they're acknowledged to be experts in a certain area of management.

To be completely open about it, there is also an idiosyncratic nature to the selection process, because sometimes an editor is just simply fascinated by a topic area. For example, we have an editor who is just fascinated by venture capital and he pursued an interview with Vinod Khosla.

MJH:   Have you ever had a CEO turn you down?

SW:    Not flat out, no.

MJH:   It took a while to get Eisner.

*SW*:    Well, only because of his schedule. He was delighted to be in *HBR*.

*MJH*:   Oh, they must be flattered beyond belief.

*SW*:    I don't know about flattered, but Michael Eisner was certainly very eager to help and was extremely helpful, I met with him many times in the course of that interview. I don't think anyone we approached simply said flat no, not that I can think of, although there certainly may be cases that I do not know of.

*MJH*:   Have you tried for Bill Gates? That's a question I have heard people ask – why no Gates interview?

*SW*:    Bill Gates has written for *HBR* in the past. Have we tried to land an interview with Bill Gates? I don't recall. I don't think so. I do know that Bill Gates has received enormous media coverage recently, and when that is the case, we generally don't pursue an interview.

*MJH*:   Yeah. Well, he certainly is out there.

*SW*:    Yeah, he's out there, he's got his book and so forth. We want to make sure our interview sort of pushes the conversation forward, it's not just regurgitated content. That's very important to us.

*MJH*:   We were curious about the way that you prepare for an interview and how you prepare the CEO as well.

*SW*:    There's a significant amount of preparation that goes into these. The editor conducting the interview reads everything that's ever been written about the CEO. We talk to analysts who cover the company. I talked to many different analysts on the Street [Wall Street] that covered Disney, for instance. You talk to people who've worked with the CEO. You talk to people at the [Harvard Business] School that are experts on the CEO and the company. You just become an expert yourself in the industry and then you prepare questions. It can literally take months to prepare for these interviews.

As for process, we have a letter that we send to the CEOs we are about to interview that describes the nature of the interview. We inform them that *HBR* is not about news, we are not about "gotcha," we are not about uncovering deep, dark secrets – we are about your theory of business. We want to know why you have done what you have done because we want to present principles that our readers can apply to their own businesses. So we are interested in ideas. And so we prepare the CEOs that ideas are what we will hope to discuss with them.

Now, of course, that doesn't mean that they believe you. They often think it's just going to be like any other business magazine interview. That is, until they start experiencing it, until you go in and you start talking to them about ideas. And you don't ask them questions like, "why did you sell such-and-such?" and "Do you think that you got a good deal on that acquisition?" As soon as they realize that you're in there talking to them about management and their approach to business, they're pleasantly surprised. And then the CEOs – after the interview is

conducted – they see a draft of it. You really enter into partnership mode, because we have no desire whatsoever to surprise these CEOs. The *HBR* interview is intended to accurately and cogently reflect what the CEOs think and what they believe.

MJH: On the basis of my own experience of interviewing people, what surprised me the most about these interviews was how strongly their personal voices come through. Do you start with the transcript of the tape?

SW: Yes.

MJH: And then do you consciously try and preserve that pacing and that rhythm?

SW: Yes, absolutely, for a couple of different reasons. One is because it's the right thing to do – to be true to the transcript. Two, because with a lot of these CEOs, people know very well what they sound like. They're public; they're out there. I mean, people know how Michael Eisner talks, and we certainly didn't want people to read the interview and say, "Hey, where's Michael in this?" Finally, we leave the CEOs' voices in because they're often so colorful. I did an interview with Peter Brabeck of Nestle. It's very contentious – he's contentious. I didn't *have* to start the interview with him sort of snapping back at me. I asked him what's so good about something and he snapped back, what's so bad about it? – I forget the exact exchange – it was the right thing to do because that's the way he is.

Now, when I sent it back to him, I did say to him, please don't be put off by this, I want the published interview to reflect what our conversation sounded like. And he said okay.

MJH: Do other people from the company get involved in the editing process? Do they hand this responsibility off to their PR people or their communication experts?

SW: Oh, it depends on the CEO. Some do and some don't. I mean, Bernard Arnault of LVMH – nobody touched or looked at the interview but him. He owns the company, so that's part of it, I guess, but – we try very hard to keep it between *HBR* and the CEO.

MJH: Do you just do a one-shot interview as a starting process?

SW: As a starting process, but we typically tell them right up front – We will need to meet with you twice. Because you get the two-hour transcript back and then you think, oh, but this train of thought was so interesting, this was where we struck the really rich vein and we need to go back and reflect on that more and we need to ask more questions. And so there's a second interview, sometimes a third interview. Some of them are done on the phone, but you typically will have two big sessions.

MJH: And you typically visit them in their office?

SW: Yes.

MJH: So they're in their own territory?

SW: Yes.

*MJH*:  Has anything really surprising happened?

*SW*:  Well, there's always a surprise with every single interview.

*MJH*:  What are some of the big surprises you've had?

*SW*:  Well, how human they are, I guess. I mean, you go in and their reputations precede them and they're usually just very nice people. And I'm always delighted by how smart CEOs are. I think that in the popular press, they're depicted as sort of clever businessmen. But a lot of the CEOs that we profile have got incredible minds and are really intelligent. And so that doesn't shock me, but I'm delighted by it. Also, I think that sometimes we've been surprised by how accessible they are. That you call up, you send a letter and you get a fax the next day saying Yeah, we'd love to be interviewed by *HBR* and so forth. So that's always a happy surprise.

    I can't think of anything that should have knocked our shoes off. As I said, there's so much preparation that goes into these.

*MJH*:  Are all your editors involved in doing these interviews?

*SW*:  Pretty much – over time, they all do them. We actually like everyone to do them. I often say that the senior editors should be able to play every position on the field. And they should be able to do best practices, toolkits, feature articles and interviews, round tables.

*MJH*:  You mentioned that sometimes you'll go after a CEO because you think they can speak to a hot topic or a theme that you're interested in having in your magazine. But are there other ways that you define the themes? I know the titles often give away what the content of the article is going to be about and then you have the subhead –

*SW*:  Squib, is what we call the subhead.

*MJH*:  Squib, yeah. Do those emerge from the interview?

*SW*:  Yes. Our operating principle is that you go into the interview with a sense of what the theory of the piece will be. But you never know. I usually go into interviews with three or four big topic areas to discuss, and listen for which one or two pan out with the most content. For instance, with Peter Brabeck, I went in with three topic areas. One was globalization, being a global company. Another was R&D. And then the other was change and the nature of change and so forth. I told him, right at the beginning of the interview, these are the three things I'd like to talk to you about, let's see if we can cover them – and we did cover all of them. But the bulk of it was about change. Now, that having been said, I know that there are cases where you go in and the CEO surprises you by saying this is really where I am in my thinking about management.

*MJH*:  And you haven't anticipated it.

*SW*:  Yeah. Or you thought that it was going to be 20 percent and it becomes 80 percent.

*MJH*:  In the interviews themselves, when they're published, the text is marked off with the interviewer's questions. Are those the real questions that you

asked or do you have to rewrite them to fit the responses the interviewees provided?

SW:      Some of them are quite real and very direct and some of them are better-worded versions of what was actually asked.

MJH:   The flow is just amazing.

SW:      Yeah, the flow is nice, isn't it? We want the interviews to read like an article and we don't want them to read like a transcript, because if you published the raw transcript, everyone would fall asleep, because interviews have a lot of back and forth, like, Oh, are you comfortable in your chair? They're filled with shmush. And so we try to make the edited versions as much to the point as possible.

MJH:   And I suspect that you don't have to take – a lot of times there are unfinished sentences and things, but my sense is these interviews are awfully coherent and there isn't even that much editing. Probably a few ums and ahs and things that come out.

SW:      Well, you know, we do go back to the CEOs again and again and so they may have said something one way one time and then, if they look at it in print, they say, you know, I want to add this sentence or this idea is very cogent here and they're amplified and refined and so forth and so we're editing the final product together.

MJH:   When you do that, when you say you edit it together, do you do that over the phone?

SW:      Sometimes. I mean, they're moving targets, these guys. I remember sitting there in Fort Worth, Texas with Peter Brabeck, because I remember saying to his assistant, when is he in the United States next? I'd been to Switzerland twice or three times for that interview and then he was giving a speech in Fort Worth and I flew down there and we sat and talked in a restaurant. So it's a bit of both. Sometimes you go back and sit there in their office with them and sometimes you do it on the phone.

MJH:   But you literally go through the whole thing?

SW:      Line by line by line.

MJH:   That's how it's done. That's amazing.

SW:      Yes. It's fun. I do say, terribly fun.

MJH:   How many stages of this do you normally go through? Three or four or back and forth?

SW:      You know, it depends on the CEO. Jacques Nasser at Ford – I sent him the interview, he changed two words, it was over. With other CEOs, it's just a much more iterative process. So iterative that you can't count how many versions they did. And it's different with every CEO, it's different with each one. They all have different working styles.

MJH:   And most of them you say approve the final version themselves?

SW:      Absolutely.

MJH:   Do you let them see the finished version?

SW:      They see exactly what you would see as a regular *HBR* author.

*MJH*:   Would you tell about the assessment process that you use with your readers and how you get a feel for what's catching on? Do you do this assessment with the interviews as well as your other types of articles? Do you get much feedback?

*SW*:    Every issue of *HBR* is subject to reader research conducted by a professional firm. The interviews are part of that.

*MJH*:   And do readers sometimes suggest CEOs to you or themes that they'd like to hear covered?

*SW*:    They don't suggest CEOs, we've not had that experience, but occasionally they do suggest topics, and the range is wide. There's no general pattern. Like all publications, one thing we do look at is what articles our readers really like and that helps guide us in our acquisition strategy. Readers often react very positively to articles on decision-making, for instance. So we say, well, we will definitely keep our ears and eyes open for decision-making content.

*MJH*:   But that's pretty much a general level, so you just know what readers are responding to and if something comes up that fits the interview section, then you slot it there?

*SW*:    Yeah.

*MJH*:   The final set of questions I have goes back to sort of a broad, general idea – speaking as the editor-in-chief of *HBR* and on the grand scale of things, what do you think these interviews do for the field of management?

*SW*:    Let me think for a second. Well, they are both a mirror and a set of binoculars. In a way, they are a mirror to hold up to the world of management and they say here is a person who's doing what you're doing writ very large. Here's a person who is struggling with the same managerial challenges that you're struggling with and has had some measure of success with it or has got a new and interesting way of thinking about it. And in some ways, they are the mirror back to our readers of their hard challenges and their important work.

At the same time, some of the interviews are quite looking forward, saying you've not yet bumped into this problem or this person has a solution long before you even know the problem is occurring and there's a bit of a sort of saying, from where we sit, surveying the management landscape, this is a voice you should be listening to. And so they play both roles.

I do think that management is an intellectual endeavor and that it is built off of ideas and new ideas and what the interview says, not explicitly, but implicitly, is that senior level executives are intellectuals and have a theory of business that they do not go namby-pamby into that good night, that they are not reactive, that they actually are – excuse the word that is not really a word – proactive about how they approach business. And that ideologically, we think that's a good thing.

*MJH*:   And do you think that in your role you actually get to shape some of what managers think are important ideas?

*SW*:   Well – you know, this is a hard question for me to answer, because I don't want to – I would want to desperately avoid sounding as if we are arrogant in any way. I mean that's something that I abhor and I think we are, I hope, a clear and strong and valued voice in that we do try to help our readers think about what should be on their agendas. We really do want to do that, because we want the practice of management to improve. I mean, our aim is true, our goal is noble and we pride ourselves on stripping away the hype and the breathlessness around new ideas and saying here are the ideas that we think are worth being on the agenda.

So, inasmuch as the CEOs are part of our editorial mix and saying, Look, this is an important concept that this person is capturing in his or her work and ideology, then, yeah. We also hope that the CEOs are yet another way of reflecting back what are important editorial ideas right now.

I hope that answers your question.

*MJH*:   Well, it gives me something to work with. What do you see as your relationship to Harvard? I mean, this is an institution of enormous importance in the world.

*SW*:   I see our relationship much more with Harvard Business School, of which I'm a proud alumna. And I think that our relationship is quite clear, we're a wholly owned subsidiary of the Harvard Business School and they are the sole shareholder of this company. But the technicalities aside, we are editorially independent. And they do not drive or shape the editorial content of *HBR*.

Now, that having been said, brilliant work goes on at HBS and I am delighted to publish work that comes out of HBS. I also think brilliant work comes out of Sloan and brilliant work is going on at your institution and at Ivey and all sorts of places and so what we want to do is just find the very best ideas, wherever they come from. You know, they can come from a first-year doctoral student at INSEAD. We published that with great delight. So we just want very good ideas that are robust, meaningful, intellectual and engaging. We take them from wherever they may come.

Now, there is a branding issue, right, because the Harvard Business School has a great legacy and a great name and it stands for certain things. And we are proud of what it stands for and we like to be – we like to uphold that part of it. It stands for excellence, it stands for a deep belief in empirical research, it stands for – I mean, Harvard Business School has long been known to churn out practitioners, people who go out and practice business and we love that part of its legacy and we honor it.

So our relationship I think is one of deep respect. And yet at the same time, we are not Harvard Business School. We are an institution that is very lucky, we get the best of the school, but also are able to open our windows, really, to every, every place that's got good ideas. And we've published in the past year Mark Morris, Harold Bloom, Bill Parcells. And these people are not associated with the school in any way, shape or form and yet they have important things to say to managers, in our opinion.

*MJH*: I think that's right. Now I would like to test out an idea with you. My co-authors are from Poland and, for them, Catholicism is a very special thing. During the period when they were living under Communist rule, the Catholic Church was an institution that protected them in thousands of ways, so they have a very special affinity for this religion.

In any case, my two colleagues have been playing – and they got me to do it – playing with the metaphor of religion. Now, there's a very close affinity between aesthetics and spirituality and so the title of the book has become *Managers, Artists, Priests*.

*SW*: That's interesting, yeah.

*MJH*: During our development of these ideas, at one point, we did an elaboration of a Catholic metaphor. The market as, you know, God. And as we played with the metaphor further, we came up with the idea that the role Harvard plays is very close to that of the Vatican. That if business is a modern religion, Harvard would be the Vatican and the interviews with CEOs are very similar to the encyclicals of the Pope. How does that strike you?

*SW*: It strikes me as – on one level, it strikes me as completely outrageous, because it's just – it assumes that there's just much more sort of logic to it than there is. I mean, I think that – there is a heavy idiosyncratic nature to which CEOs we include in *HBR*. As I said, I like fashion and that's what got me interested in pursuing an interview with Arnault at LVMH. Of course, it ended up that Bernard Arnault had very fascinating things to say. But we did not choose him in the first place because he seemed Pope-like to us. And that's just one example. We chose Tom Siebel because one of the editors saw him at a conference and he struck her as really counter-cultural – not a leader of business, but an anti-leader. My point is, there is a lot less premeditation to interviews than you think.

*MJH*: We don't really know what those cardinals do when they pick the next Pope.

*SW*: I guess not. Perhaps they're all just sitting around in a meeting, and one of them says something like, "Hey, what about that guy from Poland? He seems cool." But let me push you a bit. I think that the place that I would start would be asking you, what makes you think Harvard is like the Vatican? I have been associated with Harvard my whole life.

I went there as an undergraduate and then I went there to business school and after my years at Bain, I came back here. And when people have this sort of gasp factor around Harvard, my theory is, man, they must have never visited the place. Harvard is just a bunch of human beings. And some of them are funny and some of them are smart and some of them are less funny and some of them are less smart. I mean, in general, the quality of people at Harvard is very high and everybody's very intelligent and so forth, but Harvard is not Oz. I have said to people repeatedly, much to their chagrin, that everybody who works for Harvard should go see this absolutely ding-dong movie called *Legally Blond*. I brought my children to see it – it's about a frothy young California girl who ends up getting into Harvard Law School in the most ridiculous way possible. In any case, the movie depicts how the rest of the world sees Harvard. It depicts a place where everyone is uptight and arrogant. They present this huge monolith – for instance, the movie constantly refers to Harvard Law School as Harvard. That's not how it works. Here at Harvard, it's each tub on its own bottom. It's a collection of nation states, not a nation.

So I know that the popular culture depicts Harvard as one big, single-minded institution. But my sense is that Harvard is filled with human beings who are idiosyncratic and varied and, frankly, very rarely in agreement with each other about anything.

So there's something pretty about the metaphor you're describing, but I don't know how close it is to reality – it's too neat.

MJH:    Of course, like any metaphor, it has its limits. It gives you a little bit of insight, though as you say, not enough. But what we want to use it for is to talk about the importance of inspiration in management and that this is what we see the future direction of management holding, that managers are going to become more inspirational characters. That's why we use the role of the priest as a metaphoric way of talking about what they do.

SW:    Yeah, certainly they have become more and more icons. In the past twenty years, you've just seen the rise of the CEO as an icon tremendously in American society.

MJH:    And you can't avoid playing into that. I mean, frankly, I don't know how you would.

SW:    Well, we try to avoid it as much as possible but we are fully aware of it. Each spring we have the *HBR* list of breakthrough ideas and one of the ideas this year is called the return of the everyday leader. And, in fact, we have this sense that, right now, with a bunch of different articles that we've run, that there's a sense that people are hoping to step back from the canonization of CEOs to say, really, powerful leaders exist everywhere in organizations. Some managers really should be canonized. But, really, the trend has been, over the past twenty years, to canonize CEOs.

And I think that the dot.com boom really exacerbated it, because we had all the 20-year-old billionaires whose faces would appear on magazines and their impudent, irrelevant drivel was turned into scripture. Thank God that stopped.

MJH:   Indeed! Suzy, thank you so much for your time.

## *HBR*'s Role in Managerial Culture

According to Suzy Wetlaufer, *HBR*'s role in managerial culture is, at least in part, intended. *HBR* aims to improve the practice of management in several ways: (1) mirror the challenges managers face in running their businesses; (2) present the ideas, principles and theories of successful managers; and (3) strip away the "hype and breathlessness" around new ideas. In short, according to Wetlaufer, the interviews try to articulate the interviewees' theories of the business. That substantive ideas are sought out is confirmed by the criteria applied to an interview before it is published; to be publishable the interview must be robust, meaningful, have intellectual content, and be engaging for the reader.

Along with the expected criteria of business success or expertise in an area of management, discussion of the selection of CEOs to be interviewed revealed several idiosyncratic sources of influence. These include the suggestions of HBS faculty, editorial interest in certain topics, and the personal interests and ideas of the interviewed CEOs. Though *HBR* editors do extensive research before conducting their interviews, and go into them with a sense of the topics the CEO knows best, occasionally a CEO will take an interview in an unexpected direction. At other times strong reader preferences for a topic or an editor's instincts will produce a desire to interview a particular CEO or lead an interview in a particular direction.

In addition to idiosyncratic factors introduced by editors and interviewees, Wetlaufer emphasized the influence generated by collaboration that occurs between the selected CEO and the interview editor, and the level of detail in which both parties become involved in the co-editing process. Thus, what emerged from the interview is a picture of *HBR* helping its chosen CEOs to provide important and useful information desired by fellow managers. Though Wetlaufer confirmed that the choice of whom to interview is under the control of *HBR*'s editorial team, and that interview content is shaped by the research that *HBR* staff members feed to editors prior to conducting interviews, the CEOs themselves are active creators of the product produced.

In regard to our equation of Harvard and the Vatican, Wetlaufer candidly told us that, at least from her perspective within *HBR* (a wholly owned subsidiary of Harvard Business School), Harvard is a federation of loosely coupled educational centers. Her description suggested that the mythic Harvard portrayed in films like *Legally Blond*, is actually non-existent. In Wetlaufer's words "Harvard is just a bunch of human beings." So, if Harvard is akin to the Vatican in its ability to influence

business leadership, it is so without laying claim to such powers. But then, the Vatican does not openly admit to its influence, even though most people clearly see it.

Finally, Wetlaufer revealed the return of the everyday leader as an emerging theme for the editors of *HBR* during the coming months or even years. Her comments suggest to us that the 1990s were myth-inflated due to the celebrity given to CEOs during that period. Although we agree with Wetlaufer's view that making CEOs (particularly young, unproven ones) into celebrities has not been a good idea, we do not believe that this implies that they will fade from public view anytime soon. Our claim is that all managers, and especially CEOs, will be the creators and carriers of new forms of culture in the twenty-first century. This implies that CEOs will continue to garner attention. What demands criticism, as Wetlaufer points out, is confusing them with rock stars or Hollywood celebrities. While they may share the spotlight with these cultural icons, the role of managers in global society is best carved from other stone.

To give CEOs the respect formerly granted to royalty and religious leaders places ethical demands on these executives as well as on their followers and their audiences. While some CEOs were presented with undeserved acclaim in the days leading up to the new millennium, and many heads were turned by all the attention, in the longer view what supports public interest in CEOs and managers is the leadership role they play in society. For better or worse, managers today are the men and women poised to carry democratic capitalism to every country on the globe. It is precisely the cultural influence of capitalism, not simply its political, economic and technical influence, that caused so much resistance to business to surface as we began the twenty-first century (e.g., the anti-globalization and anti-capitalism movements). The reach of managerial culture is greater than that of any colonial power exercised in the twentieth century and the risks are equally, if not more, threatening. Let us hope we learn to use the counterbalancing powers of democracy to reinforce the values of ethical responsibility and freedom among members of this emerging culture. It is our view, or at least our hope, that demanding creativity and ethics of business leaders will set the stage for our continued, if not renewed, existence in the years to come.

The institutionalizing force of business periodicals like *HBR* and educational establishments like the Harvard Business School allows them to shape ideas about what constitutes good management. In the twentieth century this influence was exercised in a way that favored the technical/rational face of the manager. However, as exceptionally influential segments of managerial culture, *HBR* and Harvard Business School have the power to shift expressions of value and expectations in such a way as to introduce the faces of the artist and priest. The interviews with CEOs published by *HBR* between 1989 and 1998 indicate just such a shift. And while Wetlaufer is no longer editor-in-chief of *HBR*, there are no indications as yet that inclusion of references to the aesthetic faces of business leadership was primarily the result of her leadership, or any part of the reason she left. Analysis of interviews with CEOs conducted after her replacement is appointed may shed more light on this question. Nonetheless, it is our conclusion that, during the last decade of the

twentieth century, *HBR* did indeed practice mythmaking in ways that deified the CEOs it interviewed, a conclusion with which Wetlaufer, then *HBR*'s editor-in-chief, concurred.

## Aesthetic Influences on the Institution of Management

In this book we have argued that management is a central institution of contemporary society and also that its proponents are members of the most important new culture to have emerged in modern times. Thus, *HBR* and the Harvard Business School do not operate alone to produce and protect the institution of management. They share influence with other management education establishments, the business media, think tanks, consultants, and members of the globalizing managerial culture.

Up to now, these influences have focused primarily on the technical and rational aspects of the practice of management, or what we have been referring to as the face of the manager. Yet, it is in the faces of the artist and the priest that one sees the difference between the manager and the fully developed business leader. A business leader draws on far more than technical proficiency to produce and articulate a creative and inspiring vision and see it through to success. It is our view that it is time to acknowledge all three of the faces of leadership and to reform the institution of management to reflect the presence of the artist and the priest alongside the manager.

Although it is likely that the aesthetic faces of the artist and priest have always been present in business, there has been a tendency to attribute their power to the face of the manager and this has led those well ensconced within the institution of management to downplay or ignore the aesthetic practices and values of business leadership to our collective detriment. When those who are responsible for socializing individuals to managerial culture focus solely or even predominantly on the face of the manager, they do a disservice to a world that depends upon the maturity and wisdom of its business leaders.

As the interview with Suzy Wetlaufer indicates, views similar to ours are held by some of those who wield considerable influence over the institution of management. In many corners of management education, in parts of the popular business press, among some consultants and management gurus, you will find discussion of the ideas, values and practices we have associated with the faces of the artist and priest. For example, Max De Pree, former CEO of Herman Miller, was one of the first to reflect on management aesthetics in his extremely popular books *Leadership Is an Art* (1989) and *Leadership Jazz* (1992). Management gurus such as Tom Peters and Warren Bennis soon followed, promoting similar aesthetically inspired approaches to leadership while, in the field of marketing, Bernd Schmitt and Alex Simonson touted *Marketing Aesthetics* (1997). With their discussion of post-heroic leadership in *Power Up* (1998), David Bradford and Alan Cohen anticipate the return to the everyday leader remarked upon by Suzy Wetlaufer.

In academic research, there have been several books on leadership and the aesthetic management of organizations including Antonio Strati's *Organization and Aesthetics* (1999) and Pierre Guillet de Monthoux's *The Art Firm: Aesthetic Management and Metaphysical Marketing from Wagner to Wilson* (2004). Joseph Pine and James Gilmore in *The Experience Economy* (1999) and Philip Mirvis, Karan Ayas and George Roth in *To the Desert and Back* (2003) explored corporate dramatization through examples of companies who use theater to do business. Charles Handy's *The Gods of Management* (1978) was an early and still influential book on the mythology of management.

## Distinguishing Manager, Artist and Priest

We recommend that you read some of the books mentioned above and use them to help you to recognize the faces of the artist and the priest in business. Use the many examples described in these books as data on which to hone your ability to see aesthetics at work by finding at least one example for each of the cells of Table 1.1 from Chapter 1. Then do your own study by hunting for more examples in your corner of the business world. Become a student of the artist and the priest. Write down the stories, dramas, and mythic expressions that you find around you.

The next step is to look for leaders who inspire you and interview them. Talk to them about their business and how they lead it. Ask them questions such as: What inspired you to become a leader? What do you think about and feel when you lead others? When are you most creative as a leader? What helps you to be creative? What interferes with your creativity? What are the leadership virtues to which you aspire? Have you yet achieved the full measure of these virtues? Where do you think you fall short and how do you hope to improve yourself? As they speak, ask them to draw examples from their own life. Listen to their stories attentively and write down their words. Then create a drama or myth using quotations from your interview as dialogue. Consider representing your interviewee as three different characters, one inspired by each of the three faces of leadership. How will you make clear distinctions between these characters? What will the manager, artist, and priest say to each other?

# 6

# The Business Leader
# as Artist and Priest

In his book *Cultivating Compassion* (2002), Buddhist scholar Jeffrey Hopkins describes in excruciating detail the proper technique for Buddhist meditation. No less than 10 pages are devoted to hints and warnings about such matters as posture, how to achieve it and when to abandon it; hand positions and their various effects on consciousness; the best pillows to use and how to arrange them under the buttocks; and so on. This attention to physical detail reflects the face of the manager because it involves perfecting the technical aspects of performing an ancient religious practice and because rationality is employed to explain how to achieve spiritualization.

A similar situation occurs in the realm of the artist. When artists gather to share their experience it is very often to technical matters that their conversation turns. For example, put a group of drummers together in a room and it will not be long before you hear them talking about the relative merits of different drum pedals. Or, if it is a group of painters, expect to hear more than you ever wanted to know about various colors. Artists and priests concern themselves with technical matters and apply rationality whenever they can to perfect their skills and improve their practices. Thus the realms of the manager, artist and priest are not strictly independent. Just as artists and priests use the technical/rational abilities of the manager, the manager needs the creativity of an artist and the inspiration of a priest to succeed as a business leader.

In previous chapters we provided numerous examples of the use of creativity and inspiration by business leaders and showed how a group of CEOs used storytelling, dramatizing, and mythmaking in the course of leading their businesses. In this chapter we summarize our thoughts about the faces of the artist and the priest in business leadership and suggest ways to align each of them with the face of the manager. It is not our belief that the manager's technical prowess and rationality should be abandoned to enthusiasm for stories, drama, and myth. Instead we believe that all three faces are required because the highest levels of business performance obtain only when technical rationality, creativity and inspiration are

**Figure 6.1** Successful business leaders are not only disciplined rational managers, they are also creative artists and inspired and inspirational priests who are fed by archetypes, symbols and myths that they access via mythological consciousness

combined (Figure 6.1 is our visual rendering of this idea). Thus, in this final chapter we intend to show you how the three faces of leadership can build upon one another's different virtues and abilities to create a leadership style appropriate to any of their realms.

Even though we argue that managers, artists, and priests can learn to use each other's gifts, we do not mean to call into question the value of keeping their realms separate. Each realm provides distinctive and much needed outcomes to the world: the realm of business pursues technical rationality to the heights of practical accomplishment, the realm of art provokes creativity to plumb the depths of human expression, and the spiritual realm seeks the ultimate perfection of human spirit. But at their foundations, where the basics for achieving their differently aimed ambitions are learned, lie a common pool of concerns with all three aspects of human existence. It is the recognition of the interdependence of technical rationality, creativity and inspiration that led to the thesis of this book, and now to its synthesizing conclusion.

## Business as Religion?

At times the realms of manager and priest become confounded leading some to ignore their seemingly obvious differences (e.g., the purposes of practical accomplishment versus spiritual perfection). Laurie Beth Jones' book *Jesus CEO* (1995) comes to mind for its direct application of the words of a spiritual leader to the leadership of business. You can find academic discussion of the ways that the sacred and the secular intersect in *Christ and Culture* written by the American Protestant theologian H. Richard Niebuhr.

Although it was never our intention to lead you into thinking that business is religion, it is possible to see business extending into the religious realm. Similar incursions between realms have taken place throughout history with those between religion and politics being well documented. For example, Queen Elizabeth I of England gained enormous political power by, among other things, symbolically replacing the Virgin Mary. While Elizabeth stopped short of declaring her own divinity, Lenin went so far as to ban all religions in the Soviet Union and its satellites, which paved the way for Stalin to develop a quasi-religious cult of Lenin worshipers, naming himself Lenin's only true disciple. Pictures of Lenin and Stalin replaced holy icons in Russian homes, and massive marches consisting of people carrying the portraits of these revolutionary leaders replaced religious processions.

Thus in both England and the Soviet Union politics made an incursion into religion where, for a time, it helped to develop political influence and legitimized the political order. However, the reverse effect was also observed. For example, when widespread religious and quasi-religious faith in Lenin was lost in the Soviet Union, the superpower of the Soviet state dissipated along with it. We make a parallel observation that, just as politics or religion invade the realm of business when a government focuses on increasing the efficiency of its educational organizations, or when churches use marketing research to maximize the reach of their message, business can extend into the realm of religion. But this is not an equation of the two. Instead we are suggesting that, through the cultivation of the face of the priest in business leadership, the purity of virtue and ethical values we admire in the priest archetype can be transferred to the realm of business where business leaders can enjoy inspiration and learn to inspire others. Similarly, cultivation of the face of the artist can welcome much needed creative courage and imagination into business practices.

## Using Faith to Redress Ethics in Business

Business scandals concerning management practices at Arthur Andersen and Enron in the US, in the Japanese banking sector, and at Parmalat in Italy have fanned the flames of discontent among many management critics who question the ethics of managerial culture and call for reforms in the institution of management. We are

convinced that the best way to address the problem of business ethics today is to balance the manager's technical/rational face with the face of the priest because aesthetic aspects of management can reclaim virtue and thereby offer ethical support to business leaders.

However, we must not forget that vice accompanies virtue. Focusing on aesthetics offers knowledge of the differences between virtue and vice and a profound sense of the significance and symbolism of the choices business leaders make, but it will not make the crucial decisions that determine ethical outcomes. Only business leaders themselves can do that, however, it is good to remember that they do it within a cultural context of influence and support created and maintained by the rest of us. It is ultimately we who uphold the institution of management and we have the capacity and responsibility to reform it as necessary. Like the priest, we must renew our courage and faith continuously.

But what is faith in a business context? It is faith in leadership and it is based in the purity of purpose that a leader represents. To create a faith-based organization, an explicit link between cultural beliefs and the institutional order (i.e., organizational hierarchy, rules, etc.) must be maintained. If this happens the organization will have aesthetic appeal, that is to say, there is a beauty to faith-based organizations that draws people together in *communitas*. Organizations that lack faith must rely solely upon authority to align their energies and coordinate their actions. The role of a business leader is, in part, to inspire faith in our organizations and sometimes this demands change.

The face of the priest inspires faith and motivates transformation, while the face of the artist provides the vision and creative courage to imagine change and present it seductively to others. But do not forget the importance of balance between all three faces of leadership. The seductive power of the artist and the inspirational appeal of the priest must be tempered by the discipline of the manager, otherwise practical outcomes will not result from the emotions and motivations stirred by the leader.[1]

## The Vision to Change: Creation, Inspiration, and Institutionalization

All businesses need creative and inspirational leaders in order to succeed. Without vision it is difficult for a leader to know the direction in which to apply his or her influence, and without creativity and inspiration it will be difficult to form this vision or to communicate its mobilizing force to other members of the organization. To be effective, visionary business leaders must first and foremost make contact

---

[1] The famous German sociologist Max Weber (b. 1864, d. 1920) discussed this principle in depth under the heading of the routinization of charisma (see Weber 1968/78). See also Mary Jo Hatch's (2000) article "The cultural dynamics of organizing and change" for discussion of Weber's ideas in relation to organizational culture change.

with the values shared by organizational members and other stakeholders. This is because it is employees and other stakeholders who realize the vision (or fail to do so) through their attitudes and behavior, and it is *their* values that determine whose influence they will accept and act upon. Furthermore, once vision is connected to accepted values it will guide organizational members and other stakeholders in performing their roles and developing commitment to them. It is a spiraling process: values encourage vision that calls forth behavior that expresses values that guide vision and so on.

It is not simple to connect vision to values in organizations because values layer one upon another, not necessarily in an orderly fashion, and because each person will relate to that web of values in their own way. It is the aesthetic appeal of a web of values and their association with a leader that accounts for that leader's power to attract individuals and influence their behavior, yet this appeal will be difficult to analyze and harder still to control. Nonetheless, when business leaders connect with the values of the sacred past of their organization, and of humanity in general, they infuse their vision with meaning that organizational members will grasp (see Figure 4.1). When they also harness their vision to the desires and expectations of the people who create and sustain the organization, motivation to accept and achieve their vision follows. The faces of the artist and the priest with their emphasis on stories, drama, and myths help leaders to make these essential connections.

However, do not expect creativity and inspiration to do all the work. A third ingredient, an aspect of the manager's face, is also necessary: institutionalization. Institutionalization refers to the embedding of behavior in day-to-day routine so that desired outcomes become more or less predictable. Just as creativity and inspiration depend on institutionalization to have lasting influence, institutionalization alone will not make a leader because all organizations must change to adapt to their environments. Institutionalization is more likely to block than to enable change.

Paradoxically, institutionalizing the behaviors needed to achieve a vision offers a leader the stability required to face future challenges while providing flexibility enough to change. This is because vision and its achievement inspire faith in leadership. It is to the leader that people turn when change is needed, and it is the leader who must courageously face the challenges and fears brought on by the need to change. This is where leaders must draw on their creativity and be open to inspiration, for where else will they come by the wisdom to lead? They need wisdom to choose between the elements of the institutional order: which shall be maintained and relied upon and which must be sacrificed to the quest for change?

Leaders change their companies *and* keep them the same, that is, they maintain some part of the core of their institutional identities even as they change other parts. This is how organizations manage to change and yet maintain their identity continuously over time.[2] Doing this with consciousness of the way their leadership

---

[2]  Pasquale Gagliardi discussed this paradox of organizational change in his 1986 article "The creation and change of organizational cultures: A conceptual framework".

reflects and connects to organizational and human history and culture will grant leaders the divine gift of vision. Thus creativity, inspiration, and institutionalization go hand in hand with the faces of the manager, artist, and priest to confront change and maintain identity.

## Aligning Manager, Artist and Priest

As Suzy Wetlaufer commented in her interview with us, the CEOs interviewed by *HBR* are unique individuals. Their differences can be seen in Table 6.1 that summarizes the material from the tables shown in Chapters 3, 4, and Appendix A. The variety of uses of story types, theater, and mythical god motifs shown in this table confirms this uniqueness in the realm of aesthetic consciousness. But such forms of analysis do not capture the CEO's ability to put these pieces together. In this final section of the chapter we will turn to the central message of this book – successful business leadership requires aligning the faces of manager, artist, and priest. It is to their alignment that we now turn our attention.

To think of yourself as an artist and a priest does not mean that you have to paint or preach. Your role is, after all, to lead a business. But the competences and power bases traditionally cultivated by artists and priests will be among those you will need to develop to reach your potential as a business leader. So watch your favorite artists and priests and learn from them what it means to be inspired to create or to create inspiration for others. You should also watch the artists and priests you do not like, learn from their mistakes and avoid their vices.

Your journey towards aligning the artist and priest with your managerial face should be fed by many sources. Concentrate on opening your mind to create readiness to accept inspiration and channel creativity. This can be done by reading books, watching films, attending theatrical performances and art exhibitions, listening to or playing music, dancing, painting, sculpting or drawing, and practicing the rituals of a spiritual path. The experiences you gain from these activities will provide symbols and myths you can incorporate into your stories or use to create drama or myth. Art and spiritual endeavor will inspire you to develop mythological consciousness that you can then tap when it is your turn to provoke and inspire others.

Above all, take time for reflection and personal assessment of yourself, your situation, the organization and environment you are working in, and the meaning of work in the context of life. This will nourish your artist and priest and give your manager's face a much-needed rest. The technical/rational face of the manager can make you an automaton, a workaholic who moves efficiently, yet mechanically, from one task to another, performing important and necessary deeds, but never withdrawing from the action to assess its course and realign with its purpose. You must learn to rotate your different faces, giving each some time in the sun. But do not favor one over the others, you must love them all equally.

**Table 6.1** Summary of story and theater types and mythological characters associated with the CEOs in the *HBR* interviews

| CEO, Company | Types of stories told | Types of drama used | Mythological character |
|---|---|---|---|
| George M.C. Fisher, Motorola | 3 epic<br>1 tragic<br>1 epic-tragic | Modern<br>Happening | Athena |
| Paul Cook, Raychem | 4 epic | Happening<br>Modern | Hermes<br>Ares |
| Alain Gomez, Thomson | 1 epic | Global<br>Modern<br>Happening | Demeter |
| Rod Canion, Compaq | 4 epic | Modern<br>Happening | Demeter |
| Robert Haas, Levi Strauss | 3 epic | Morality<br>Modern | Zeus |
| John Reed, Citicorp | 2 epic (1 quest) | Global<br>Modern | Zeus |
| Raymond Smith, Bell Atlantic | 3 epic<br>1 epic-tragic | Modern<br>Happening<br>Morality | Hades |
| Percy Barnevik, ABB | 3 epic | Global<br>Modern | Hermes |
| Carl Hahn, Volkswagen | 1 comic | Morality<br>Modern<br>Global | Ares |
| Robert McDermott, USAA | 4 epic<br>1 romantic | Morality<br>Modern | Hephaestus |
| Frederick Crawford, TRW | 7 epic (1 anti-epic)<br>1 tragic<br>1 comic<br>1 epic-comic | Modern<br>Morality | Hermes |
| Masayoshi Son, Softbank | 9 epic<br>1 epic-comic<br>1 epic-comic-tragic | Modern<br>Happening | Herakles |
| Arnold Hiatt, Stride Rite | 7 epic<br>1 tragic<br>1 romance<br>2 epic-tragic<br>1 epic-comic<br>1 epic-comic-romance | Morality<br>Happening | Demeter |
| Arden Sims, Globe Metallugical | 6 epic (1 saga) | Happening<br>Modern | Hermes |

**Table 6.1** (*cont'd*)

| CEO, Company | Types of stories told | Types of drama used | Mythological character |
|---|---|---|---|
| Phil Knight, Nike | 5 epic<br>2 tragic<br>1 epic-tragic | Modern<br>Happening | Hermes |
| Paul Allaire, Xerox | 2 epic | Modern<br>Happening | Hermes<br>Apollo |
| Tom Chapman, Greater Southeast | 1 epic<br>2 epic-romantic | Morality<br>Modern | Hephaestus |
| Nicolas Hayek, SMH | 3 epic<br>1 tragic<br>1 epic-tragic | Morality<br>Modern | Demeter |
| Ernesto Martens, Vitro | 1 epic<br>1 tragic | Global<br>Modern | Hermes<br>Persephone |
| Ed McCracken, Silicon Graphics | 2 epic | Happening<br>Morality | Hermes |
| David Whitwam, Whirlpool | 1 epic | Global<br>Modern | Athena<br>Zeus |
| Roy Vagelos, Merck | 2 epic | Modern<br>Happening | Athena |
| Lawrence Bossidy, Allied Signal | 2 epic (1 quest) | Happening<br>Morality | Ares |
| John Sawhill, Nature Conservancy | 2 epic | Morality<br>Modern | Hermes<br>Demeter |
| Colin Marshall, British Airways | 2 epic | Modern<br>Happening<br>Global | Hephaestus<br>Apollo |
| Robert Shapiro, Monsanto | 1 epic | Happening<br>Global | Athena |
| John Browne, British Petroleum | 2 epic<br>1 epic-tragic | Modern<br>Happening<br>Global | Hermes<br>Athena |
| Krister Ahlström, Ahlström | 2 epic | Modern<br>Happening<br>Morality | Athena |
| Michael Dell, Dell Computer | 2 epic | Happening<br>Modern | Hermes |
| Franco Bernabè, Eni | 1 epic (a saga)<br>1 epic-tragic | Morality | Herakles |

In order to encourage you to reflect and make personal assessment part of your life, we suggest a final exercise that starts with revisiting Table 1.1 one last time. It was our intention when we introduced this table in Chapter 1 to give you some definitions of the three faces of leadership. Having read chapters describing the aesthetic leadership practices of storytelling, dramatizing, and mythmaking, and having practiced these yourself, it is now time to align your manager's face with the face of the artist, and then with that of the priest.

We suggest you proceed as follows. First, purchase three loose-leaf binders and plenty of paper. Label one of them "The Manager," another "The Artist" and the last one "The Priest." Use your best penmanship and decorate as desired. Leave your marks on these books. Doodling is required.

Beginning with the "The Manager", reread the items listed in the cells of the manager's column of Table 1.1 and on separate sheets of paper describe explicit examples taken from your own experience to represent each of these topics in a personalized way. Make your descriptions rich with detail and find as many examples of each topic as you can. Here are some ideas to get you started. In writing entries for discipline, describe all the ways you have disciplined others or been disciplined yourself in your organization. What happened? Where did it take place? What rewards and punishments were involved, who got them and why? How did you feel? What was your reaction? How did others react? What lessons did you learn? Do not limit yourself to formal disciplinary actions taken, think of all the ways your behavior has been punished or rewarded, and how you have meted out punishments and rewards to others. Then think in terms of self-discipline, how you have used it or failed to do so, and how this has influenced your success as a leader or lack thereof.

The list of potential questions is endless. Do not feel you need to answer them all at one go. You may feel that you could continue this exercise forever, but at some point you will find that you have exhausted most of your ideas about this subject. It is then time to tackle the next item on the list: rationality. Continue down the list, writing detailed descriptions of your experiences until you have examined all the topics in the manager's column of Table 1.1. Do not be surprised if this first part of the exercise takes weeks or even months. There is no time limit, proceed at your own pace. Think of doing this in the Great Time.

As you amass more and more examples of the topics from the first three rows of the manager's column in Table 1.1, you will find yourself awash in paper. Buy, or better still, make divider sheets for your binder to organize your pages into sections for each topic (i.e., one each for discipline, rationality, organizing, controlling, etc.). Now read through all the examples you have written down and arrange them in the appropriate sections of your binder. This process will no doubt remind you of other examples you can add to your collection. Keep writing these down until you feel that you have a representative sample of your organizational life experience.

When you have a thick file in your "The Manager" binder, repeat the exercise by filling "The Artist" and "The Priest" binders with examples of your experiences related to the artist and priest columns of Table 1.1. Feel free to continue making

new entries in any or all sections of any of your binders for as long as you deem it useful, but do not become obsessed with this task. There is more.

Once you have a substantial body of description built up in the sections of your three binders, you can begin the work of aligning and integrating your faces. Take out "The Manager" binder and reread what you have written in one of the sections (discipline, rationality, etc.). Now, looking down the column in Table 1.1 that relates to *the artist* (not the manager this time), write about how you or your organization might have done the things that you described in your examples relating to the manager column in ways that better reflect the face of the artist. If you need inspiration, read from your Artist binder until your imagination is stimulated.

Next, follow a similar procedure using the face of the priest. Go back through the Manager binder one topic at a time considering how you might redo the things described there in a way that reveals the face of the priest. Only when you have done enough of these two exercises (applying the artist to the manager and applying the priest to the manager) to notice a significant change in your behavior, mood and effectiveness at work should you shift the direction of this exercise and consider how you could better reveal the face of the manager in the activities you have described in your artist and priest binders. The reason is that, as long as the manager is your primary face, it will be easy but inappropriate to let it continue to dominate the other two faces. If, however, you are an artist or a priest in your primary role as a leader, you will want to change the order described above, reserving your dominant face (either artist or priest) for last.

As a culminating step, write some stories, dramas or myths in which you tackle your most common or most important experiences again, only this time using the full force of all three of your leadership faces.

# Postscript

It has been our objective in writing this book to examine the principles and practices of some of the world's most admired CEOs, to invite you to hear their stories, experience their dramas, share their mythology, and above all to absorb the artistry and spirit of the managerial culture they symbolize. We hope by these efforts to have instilled both respect for and critical appreciation of the aesthetics of business leadership, its contemporary cultural influences, and its ancient origins. We further hope that, by following the suggestions for acquiring storytelling, dramatizing, and mythmaking skills and for developing, differentiating, and aligning the faces of the manager, artist, and priest, you will be propelled along your path towards effective business leadership. Godspeed.

# Appendix A

## List of Stories and Their Locations in the *HBR* Interviews

| Storyteller | Type | First line (page number from interview) |
|---|---|---|
| Fisher | Epic | We did a survey on customer visits a couple of years ago – who's been visiting whom, how good or bad we are at it. (108) |
| | Tragic | Motorola jumped way out in front on the car phone – so far out in front that there were pictures in magazines two or three years before the systems were actually available. (109) |
| | Epic-tragedy | In the early 1970s, when I was still at AT&T Bell Labs, we had a grand vision of picture-phones. (109) |
| | Epic | Take the radio data communications system we developed with IBM. We have an ongoing dialogue with IBM; I'm not even sure who came to whom on this project. (109) |
| | Epic | Sometimes top management has to take the lead to make it work. (111) |
| Cook | Epic | When we started the company, we didn't know what products we were going to make. (98) |
| | Epic | When we started Raychem, we began to learn what radiation chemistry could do. (98) |
| | Epic | About 25 years ago, we learned that the Naval Ordnance Laboratories were experimenting with metals that shrunk with incredibly high force when heated. (105) |
| | Epic | Wall Street does apply pressure; Raychem's market value dropped by 10% in one day last year when we reported disappointing quarterly results. (105–106) |

| Storyteller | Type | First line (page number from interview) |
|---|---|---|
| Gomez | Epic | Sometimes you can rejoin the first rank by being a shrewd follower. (130) |
| Canion | Epic | It's dissatisfaction, more than money, that leads people to leave. I learned that lesson early in my career. (116) |
| | Epic | Take our approach to the laptop market. The first time we looked at that market was back in 1984. (118) |
| | Epic | In the case of the laptop, all of the products that came out in the last part of 1989 demonstrated a set mentality. (119) |
| | Epic | At the beginning of 1983, we were just starting to ship our first product, and we needed to find a new vice president of sales. (119) |
| Haas | Epic | When I talk to employees about the development of the Aspirations Statement, I describe the stark terror I felt when I took over this company, just having turned 43 years old. (139) |
| | Epic | Dockers was like a new invention – a brand new segment in the casual pants market. (142) |
| | Epic | Two years ago, I gave a speech about the Aspirations at one of our worldwide management meetings. (144) |
| Reed | Epic | When Walt Wriston became chairman in 1970, we were the third largest bank in the United States after Chase Manhattan and Bank of America. (136) |
| | Epic quest | We started the consumer bank in 1974 on a blank sheet of paper. (138) |
| Smith | Epic | In the early 1980s, when we began to see real competition, Tom Bolger, my predecessor as CEO, and I agreed that we needed a new culture to support our business strategies. (121) |
| | Epic | As I traveled throughout our company before becoming CEO, I found that very few people |

| Storyteller | Type | First line (page number from interview) |
|---|---|---|
| | | really knew what we were trying to do as a company. (125) |
| | Epic-tragic | First of all, it was believed that the client service groups wouldn't work. In some quarters it was considered a dingbat idea that would go away. (127) |
| | Epic | The Champion program arose from one of our companies, Chesapeake & Potomac Telephone, and we spread it across the whole corporation in 1989. (127) |
| Barnevik | Epic | In 1986, Asea acquired Stromberg, the Finnish power and electrical products company. (98) |
| | Epic | When we decided on the merger between ASEA and Brown Boveri, we had no choice but to do it secretly and to do it quickly, with our eyes open about discovering skeletons in the closet. (100) |
| | Epic | Brown Boveri had operated in Germany for almost 90 years. (101) |
| Hahn | Comic | Our van business was born, for example, when a Dutchman told us how nice it would be if our indestructible, indefatigable vehicle had a box on the top of it so that he could transport eggs around Holland. (106) |
| McDermott | Romance | Whenever a war starts, most insurance companies are quick to invoke the war clause in their life insurance policies so they won't have to pay off on people killed in combat. (118) |
| | Epic | When I arrived here in 1968, I had six months to look around before I took over as CEO. (119) |
| | Epic | When I took over, I promised everyone change. (120) |
| | Epic | When I was 12 years old, my father took me to visit West Point, and on the way we drove across bear Mountain Bridge. (123) |
| | Epic | We had two pieces of electronic hardware back then, and we chose people to operate it on the basis of their high-school math grades. (125) |

| Storyteller | Type | First line (page number from interview) |
| --- | --- | --- |
| Crawford | Epic | I also gained a lesson in the economics of employment that year. (116) |
| | Epic | When I took over our Detroit plant, it was having a terrible time coming out of the recession after World War I. (116) |
| | Comic | There was a machine in the plant that was water-cooled. (117) |
| | Tragedy | About a month later, another worker came to see me with a tie-rod end (a steering part made by Steel products) and a blueprint. (117) |
| | Epic | One time Packard called me on a Friday afternoon, said it had a rush order to build some cars by Tuesday, and could we get them parts by Sunday night. (117) |
| | Epic | During the 1930s, Frances Perkins (Franklin D. Roosevelt's Secretary of Labor) wrote me a letter saying that the Congress of Industrial Organizations had presented cards showing that it had signed up over half the employees at one of our plants. (120) |
| | Anti-epic | Another time, during the war, Frank Graham, head of the War Labor Board, summoned me to Washington. (120) |
| | Epic | When Henry Ford started making real money from the Model T, he didn't raise wages right away. (121) |
| | Epic-comedy | A few years ago on a street in Cleveland, I ran into a woman who had worked for us during the war. (122) |
| | Epic | Before I became president, the owners of the company were primarily interested in enriching themselves. (122) |
| | Epic | Let me tell you a story about Sloan and how he really operated. (125) |
| Masayoshi Son | Epic | When I first started the company, I only had two part-time workers and a small office. (93) |
| | Epic | I started Softbank in 1981, a year and a half after I came back from the United States, after graduating from Berkeley. (94) |

| Storyteller | Type | First line (page number from interview) |
| --- | --- | --- |
| | Epic-comic-tragedy | When Softbank was only two or three months old, I decided that I needed to show the end users and dealers what software was available in Japan. (95) |
| | Epic-comedy | Actually, one person did call me from Osaka a few weeks after the show. (97) |
| | Epic | One of the first things I did was to expand the choice of software that Joshin Denki had. (99) |
| | Epic | When I started the company, I used straight bank loans. (99) |
| | Epic | I started the publishing division six months after I started the company. (100) |
| | Epic | When I was a student at Berkeley, I started my first business and even hired some of the professors to help me. (100) |
| | Epic | I also had computer game projects when I was at Berkeley. (100) |
| | Epic | I went to the United States to study when I was 16 years old. (100) |
| | Epic | In the beginning, it was very hard for us to get the best employees. (102) |
| Hiatt | Romance | Stride Rite is widely known for opening the first corporate day-care center in the United States. (96) |
| | Epic | Some time back, Senator Ted Kennedy visited the day-care center here in Cambridge to find out what was on working mothers' minds. (96) |
| | Epic | Before I came to Stride Rite, I owned a small children's shoe company called Blue Star Shoes. (97) |
| | Epic | Actually, I didn't set out to run my own company as much as I ran away from a big one. (98) |
| | Tragedy | Blue Star's revenues had grown to about $2 million, and we were starting to gain recognition for producing quality shoes at a modest price. (99) |
| | Epic | I went to J.L. Hudson's Department Store in Detroit and called on Stanley Isherwood, the dean of children's shoe buyers. (99) |

| Storyteller | Type | First line (page number from interview) |
|---|---|---|
| | Epic-comedy | By the time I joined Stride Rite, producing shoes in Boston was clearly uneconomical. (100) |
| | Epic-tragedy | Stride Rite's head of sourcing and I first visited the company three years ago on a trip to look for a Thai supplier. (101) |
| | Epic | To Stride Rite dealers who had done business on Main Street for 20 years, the malls that opened in the early 1970s were an expensive and uninviting prospect. (102) |
| | Epic | When I started at Blue Star, return on investment was the one demand I couldn't meet. (103) |
| | Epic-comic-romance | At one time we used to have an annual lunch for all the Stride Rite scholars. (103) |
| | Epic-tragedy | Ten years ago, though, Keds was a hodgepodge. (103) |
| | Epic | Take one of the new shoes for little girls that will soon be going into the Stride Rite line. (104) |
| Sims | Epic | Frankly, we didn't even expect to apply [for the Baldrige Award]. (118) |
| | Epic | To understand how Globe came to quality, you have to first understand where the company was when I joined it in 1984. (119) |
| | Epic | The first thing we did was give all the plant's employees, union and salaried workers, six hours of training in basic statistical process control, control charts, how to use a calculator, those sorts of things. (121) |
| | Epic | One of the first companies we worked with on quality was Ford. (121) |
| | Epic-saga | . . . in 1986, I started Globe's customer-visit program for our Beverly plant employees to drive home the importance of quality and consistency. (121) |
| | Epic | Back in 1988, Bob Jenkins, Globe's vice president of sales and marketing, made several trips to Japan to visit the big four ferroalloy makers. (128) |

| Storyteller | Type | First line (page number from interview) |
|---|---|---|
| Knight | Epic | Bill Bowerman, my former track coach at The University of Oregon and cofounder of the company that became Nike, had always customized off-the-shelf shoes for his runners. (92) |
| | Tragedy | We went into casual shoes in the early 1980s when we saw that the running shoe business, which was about one-third of our revenues at the time, was slowing down. (92) |
| | Tragedy | By the mid-1980s, the financial signals were coming through loud and clear. (92) |
| | Epic-tragedy | In the early days, when we were just a running shoe company and almost all our employees were runners, we understood the consumer very well. (93) |
| | Epic | Knowing what happened in casual shoes, you probably wouldn't think we'd have anything to do with dress shoes. (98) |
| | Epic | When people talk about Nike, the TV ads are practically all they want to talk about, but we became a billion dollar company without television. (98) |
| | Epic | The Hare Jordan, Air Jordan commercial that aired during the 1992 Super Bowl represented a big risk from both a financial and a marketing standpoint. (99) |
| | Epic | Three or four years ago we were recruiting two very exciting college basketball players, but before we signed them we checked with our network of college coaches. (101) |
| Allaire | Epic | Recently I was in Austin, Texas to make a call on a customer who until then had not wanted to have anything to do with us. (109) |
| | Epic | My favorite example comes from the management team that designed our new architecture. (118) |
| Chapman | Epic-romance | For instance, there is a senior citizen apartment complex right across the street from the hospital. (92) |

| Storyteller | Type | First line (page number from interview) |
|---|---|---|
|  | Epic-romance | If you can't find more financially attractive patients, you have to find more attractive and cost-efficient ways to treat the patients you have. (93) |
|  | Epic | We recently had an elderly patient who refused to eat. (94) |
| Hayek | Epic | Not so long ago, I was in the United States for a meeting with the CEO of one of your big companies. (100) |
|  | Epic-tragedy | The two companies that became SMH were the flagships of the Swiss industry. (101) |
|  | Epic-comedy | We built a giant Swatch. (103) |
|  | Epic | Let me give another example – our "Swatch the World" celebration in Zermatt last fall. (103) |
|  | Tragedy | Omega is one of the Swiss watch industry's great brands. (105) |
|  | Epic | One day, for example, I was seated with an entrepreneur from Hong Kong who sold finished watches. (107) |
| Martens | Tragedy | U.S. glass producers are huge compared with Mexican producers, and they were intent on keeping imports out of their market. (165) |
|  | Epic | I can remember a group of us standing on the 54th floor of the World Trade Center at 6:00 A.M. on the morning we were going to launch our bid. (166) |
| McCracken | Epic | About three years ago, when I was visiting Nissan, I asked a senior manager in the engineering organization what we could do to serve the company's needs better. (139) |
|  | Epic | In the mid-1980s, Kurt came up with a new graphics design that violated one of the fundamental design principles in the company. (144) |
| Whitwam | Epic | When we sat down to plan our future in 1987, it was the first time Whirlpool had every asked itself what kind of company it wanted to become in the next decade or the next century. (137) |

| Storyteller | Type | First line (page number from interview) |
| --- | --- | --- |
| Vagelos | Epic | Early on, I was working with the endocrinology group, which had a number of projects in progress. (108) |
| | Epic | Using the information that Medco had about diabetes, and with the cooperation of plan sponsors and the permission of patients, we set out to identify the progress of some 100,000 diabetics . . . (112) |
| Bossidy | Epic quest | In 1991, we were hemorrhaging cash. (70) |
| | Epic | I'll never forget one session in Phoenix with our field salespeople. (72) |
| Sawhill | Epic | In 1992, the Walt Disney company wanted to expand its operations in Orlando, Florida, to build its wild animal theme park. (115) |
| | Epic | The Georgia-Pacific Corporation wanted to consider how it might contribute to conservation but not give up all its rights to harvest timber in perpetuity on a particular piece of property. (115) |
| Marshall | Epic | An aircraft door was left open in a rainstorm before takeoff, and a passenger near the door unfortunately got showered. (109) |
| | Epic | I suppose my evangelistic determination to strive for customer-service excellence goes back to my career beginnings as a cadet purser with the former Orient Line shipping company. (111) |
| Shapiro | Epic | Several years ago, I sensed that there was something more required of us than doing no harm, but I couldn't articulate what that was. (84) |
| Browne | Epic | One case in point is how Schlumberger, the oil-field-services company, developed a special device for us called a logging tool. (155) |
| | Epic-tragedy | People often took an incremental or piecemeal approach to a project or an opportunity. (158) |
| | Epic | In the late 1980s, BPX was producing from onshore wells when we discovered that the field |

| Storyteller | Type | First line (page number from interview) |
|---|---|---|
|  |  | extended significantly offshore into Poole Harbor, an area of particular scientific interest and one of the most beautiful places in Europe. (160) |
| Ahlström | Epic | We asked one consulting firm to assess our situation. (115) |
|  | Epic | In 1995, with the help of Alden Lank and Fred Neubauer, two professors from IMD, and our personnel department, we inaugurated formal training aimed at family members in their twenties and thirties. (119) |
| Dell | Epic | As a small start-up, Dell couldn't afford to create every piece of the value chain. (74) |
|  | Epic | I was about to leave a meeting at Sony in Tokyo in January 1993 when someone ran up to me and said, "Oh, Mr. Dell, please wait one minute. I'm from Sony's power technology company. (83) |
| Bernabè | Epic-saga | I can look back now and see how important my training at Fiat was. (86) |
|  | Epic-tragic | . . . there were times of terrible stress. Perhaps the worst was when I was charged with taking a bribe. (85) |

# Appendix B
## List of CEO Interviews

Avishai, B. (1991) A European platform for global competition: An interview with VW's Carl Hahn. *Harvard Business Review* July–August: 103–13.

Avishai, B. and William, T. (1989) Customers drive a technology-driven company: An interview with George Fisher. *Harvard Business Review* November–December: 107–14.

Dyer, D. (1991) A voice of experience: An interview with TRW's Frederick C. Crawford. *Harvard Business Review* November–December: 115–26.

Hill, L. and Wetlaufer, S. (1998) Leadership when there is no one to ask: An interview with Eni's Franco Bernabè. *Harvard Business Review* July–August: 81–94.

Howard, A. and Magretta, J. (1995) Surviving success. An interview with the Nature Conservancy's John Sawhill. *Harvard Business Review* September–October: 108–19.

Howard, R. (1990) Values make the company: An interview with Robert Haas. *Harvard Business Review* September–October: 133–44.

Howard, R. (1992) The CEO as organizational architect: An interview with Xerox's Paul Allaire. *Harvard Business Review* September–October: 107–21.

Magretta, J. (1997) Growth through global sustainability: An interview with Monsanto's CEO, Robert B. Shapiro. *Harvard Business Review* January–February: 79–88.

Magretta, J. (1998a) The power of virtual integration: An interview with Dell Computer's Michael Dell. *Harvard Business Review* March–April: 73–84.

Magretta, J. (1998b) Governing the family-owned enterprise: An interview with Finland's Krister Ahlström. *Harvard Business Review* January–February: 113–23.

Maruca, R.F. (1994) The right way to go global: An interview with Whirlpool CEO David Whitwam. *Harvard Business Review* March–April: 135–45.

McCormick, J. and Stone, N. (1990) From national champion to global competitor: An interview with Thomson's Alain Gomez. *Harvard Business Review* May–June: 127–35.

Moss Kanter, E. (1991) Championing change: An interview with Bell Atlantic's CEO Raymond Smith. *Harvard Business Review* January–February: 119–30.

Nichols, N.A. (1992) Profits with a purpose: An interview with Tom Chapman. *Harvard Business Review* November–December: 87–95.

Nichols, N.A. (1993) From complacency to competitiveness: An interview with Vitro's Ernesto Martens. *Harvard Business Review* September–October: 163–71.

Nichols, N.A. (1994) Medicine, management, and mergers: An interview with Merck's P. Roy Vagelos. *Harvard Business Review* November–December: 105–14.

Prokesch, S.E. (1993) Mastering chaos at the high-tech frontier: An interview with Silicon Graphic's Ed McCracken. *Harvard Business Review* November–December: 135–44.

Prokesch, S.E. (1995) Competing on customer service: An interview with British Airway's Sir Colin Marshall. *Harvard Business Review* November–December: 101–12.

Prokesch, S.E. (1997) Unleashing the power of learning: An interview with British Petroleum's John Browne. *Harvard Business Review* September–October: 147–68.

Rayner, B. (1992) Trial-by-fire transformation: An interview with Globe Metallurgical's Arden C. Sims. *Harvard Business Review* May–June: 117–29.

Stone, N. (1992) Building corporate character: An interview with Stride Rite Chairman Arnold Hiatt. *Harvard Business Review* March–April: 95–104.

Taylor, W. (1990) The business of innovation: An interview with Paul Cook. *Harvard Business Review* March–April: 97–106.

Taylor, W. (1991) The logic of global business: An interview with ABB's Percy Barnevik. *Harvard Business Review* March–April: 91–105.

Taylor, W. (1993) Message and muscle: An interview with Swatch Titan Nicolas Hayek. *Harvard Business Review* March–April: 99–110.

Teal, T. (1991) Service comes first: An interview with USAA's Robert F. McDermott. *Harvard Business Review* September–October: 117–27.

Tichy, N.M. and Charan, R. (1990) Citicorp faces the world: An interview with John Reed. *Harvard Business Review* November–December: 135–44.

Tichy, N.M. and Charan, R. (1995) The CEO as coach: An interview with AlliedSignal's Lawrence A. Bossidy. *Harvard Business Review* March–April: 69–78.

Webber, A.M. (1990) Consensus, continuity, and common sense: An interview with Compaq's Rod Canion. *Harvard Business Review* July–August: 115–22.

Webber, A.M. (1992) Japanese–style entrepreneurship: An interview with Softbank's CEO, Masayoshi Son. *Harvard Business Review* January–February: 93–103.

Willigan, G.E. (1992) High-performance marketing: An interview with Nike's Phil Knight. *Harvard Business Review* July–August: 91–100.

# Bibliography

Aristotle (1996) *Poetics*. London: Penguin.

Avishai, B. (1991) A European platform for global competition: An interview with VW's Carl Hahn. *Harvard Business Review* July–August: 103–13.

Avishai, B. and William, T. (1989) Cus tomers drive a technology-driven company: An interview with George Fisher. *Harvard Business Review* November–December: 107–14.

Becker, H. (1982) *Art Worlds*. Berkeley: University of California Press.

Berle, A.A. (1959) *Power without Property: A New Development in American Political Economy*. New York: Harcourt, Brace.

Bettelheim, B. (1976) *The Uses of Enchantment*. New York: Vintage Books.

Beverel, P. (1998) Radioscopie du malaise des cadres. *Le Monde*, September 23.

Boje, D.M. (1991) The storytelling organization. *Administrative Science Quarterly* 36: 106–26.

Boje, D. and Dennehy, R. (1993) *Managing in the Postmodern World*. Dubuque, IA: Kendall/Hunt.

Bowles, M.L. (1989) Myth, meaning and work organization. *Organization Studies* 10(3): 405–21.

Bowles, M.L. (1993) The gods and goddesses: Personifying social life in the age of organization. *Organization Studies* 14(3): 395–418.

Bradford, D.L. and Cohen, A.R. (1998) *Power Up: Transforming Organizations through Shared Leadership*. San Francisco: Jossey-Bass.

Bruner, J. (1986) *Actual Minds, Possible Worlds*. Cambridge, MA: Harvard University Press.

Bruner, J. (1990) *Acts of Meaning*. Cambridge, MA: Harvard University Press.

Bruner, J. (1996) The narrative construal of reality. In J. Bruner, *The Culture of Education*: 130–49. Cambridge, MA: Harvard University Press.

Burke, K. (1969) *A Grammar of Motives*. Berkeley: University of California Press.

Burnham, J. (1961) *The Managerial Revolution*. New York: John Day.

Campbell, J. (1975) Folkloristic commentary. In P. Colum (ed.), *The Complete Grimm's Fairy Tales*. London: Routledge.

Campbell, J. (1976) *The Masks of God, Vol. 4: Creative Mythology*. Penguin: Harmondsworth.

Campbell, J. with Moyers, B. (1988) *The Power of Myth*. New York: Doubleday.

Cassady, M. (1997) *Theatre: An Introduction*. Lincolnwood IL: NTC Publishing Group.

Cassirer, E. (1946) *Language and Myth* (trans. S. Langer). New York: Dover.

Czarniawska, B. and Joerges, B. (1996) Travels of ideas. In B. Czarniawska and G. Sevon (eds.), *Translating Organizational Change*: 13–48. Berlin: de Gruyter.

Czarniawska-Joerges, B. (1994) Narratives of individual and organizational identities. In S. Deetz (ed.), *Communication Yearbook* 17: 193–221. Newbury Park: Sage.

De Mello, A. (2004) *Spiritwalk: Resources for Awakening*. Retrieved on February 6, 2004 from: www.spiritwalk.org/demello.htm

De Pree, M. (1989) *Leadership Is an Art*. New York: Dell.

De Pree, M. (1992) *Leadership Jazz*. New York: Currency Doubleday.

Djilas, M. (1957) *The New Class*. New York: Frederick A. Praeger.

Drucker, P. (1993) *Post-capitalist Society*. Oxford: Butterworth Heinemann.

Dyer, D. (1991) A voice of experience: An interview with TRW's Frederick C. Crawford. *Harvard Business Review* November–December: 115–26.

Eliade, M. (1932/1991) *Images and Symbols: Studies in Religious Symbolism*. Princeton: Princeton University Press.

Gabriel, Y. (2000) *Storytelling in Organizations: Facts, Fictions, and Fantasies*. Oxford: Oxford University Press.

Gagliardi, P. (1986) The creation and change of organizational cultures: A conceptual framework. *Organization Studies* 7: 117–34.

Gagliardi, P. (1996) Exploring the aesthetic side of organizational life. In S.R. Clegg, C. Hardy and W.R. Nord (eds.), *Handbook of Organization Studies*: 565–80. London: Sage.

Gardner, H. with Laskin, E. (1995) *Leading Minds: An Anatomy of Leadership*. New York: Basic Books.

Georges, R. (1969) Toward an understanding of story-telling events. *Journal of American Folklore*, 82: 314–28.

Georges, R. (1980) A folklorist's view of story-telling. *Humanities in Society* 3(4): 317–26.

Georges, R. (1981) Do narrators really digress? A reconsideration of "audience asides" in narrating. *Western Folklore* 40: 245–52.

Goffman, E. (1959) *The Presentation of Self in Everyday Life*. Garden City, NJ: Anchor Books.

Goffman, E. (1974) *Frame Analysis*. New York: Harper and Row.

Guillet de Monthoux, P. (2004) *The Art Firm: Aesthetic Management and Metaphysical Marketing, from Wagner to Wilson*. Stanford CA: Stanford University Press.

Handy, C.B. (1978) *The Gods of Management: How They Work and Why They Fail*. London: Souvenir Press.

Harris, G.T. (1993) The postcapitalist executive: An interview with Peter Drucker. *Harvard Business Review* May–June: 115–22.

Hatch, M.J. (2000) The cultural dynamics of organizing and change. In N. Ashkanasy, C. Wilderom and M. Peterson (eds.), *Handbook of Organizational Culture and Climate*: 245–60. Thousand Oaks, CA: Sage.

Herskovits, M.J. (1956) *Man and his Works*. New York: Alfred A. Knopf.

Hill, L. and Wetlaufer, S. (1998) Leadership when there is no one to ask: An interview with Eni's Franco Bernabè. *Harvard Business Review* July–August: 81–94.

Hopfl, H. (1995) Performance and customer service: The cultivation of contempt. *Studies in Cultures Organizations and Societies* 1(1): 47–62.

Hopfl, H. (1996) Authority and pursuit of order in organizational performance. *Studies in Cultures Organizations and Societies* 2(1): 67–80.

Hopkins, J. (2002) *Cultivating Compassion: A Buddhist Perspective*. New York: Broadway Books.

Howard, A. and Magretta, J. (1995) Surviving success: An interview with the Nature Conservancy's John Sawhill. *Harvard Business Review* September–October: 108–19.

Howard, R. (1990) Values make the company: An interview with Robert Haas. *Harvard Business Review* September–October: 133–44.

Howard, R. (1992) The CEO as organizational architect: An interview with Xerox's Paul Allaire. *Harvard Business Review* September–October: 107–21.

Hummel, R.P. (1992) Stories managers tell. *Public Administration Review* 51: 31–41.

Joncs, L.B. (1995) *Jesus CEO: Using Ancient Wisdom for Visionary Leadership.* New York: Hyperion.

Jung, C.G. (1964) *Man and his Symbols*, Garden City, NY: Doubleday.

Jung, C.G. (1968) *The Archetypes and the Collective Unconscious*, Vol. 9. London: Routledge and Kegan Paul.

Jung, C.G. (1969) *The Structure and Dynamics of the Psyche*, Vol. 8. London: Routledge and Kegan Paul.

Jung, C.G. (1971/81) *Archetypy i symbole: Pisma wybrane (Archetypes and Symbols: Selected Works).* Warszawa: Czytelnik.

Jung, C.G. (1974) *Dreams.* New York: MJF Books.

Kearney, R. (2002) *On Stories.* London: Routledge.

Kempiński, A.M. (1993) *Słownik mitologii ludów indoeuropejskich.* Poznań: SAWW.

Kirk, G.S. (1970) *Myth: Its Meaning and Functions in Ancient and Other Cultures.* London: Cambridge University Press.

Kołakowski, L. (1967) *Kultura i fetysze (Culture and Fetishes).* Warszawa: PWN.

Kołakowski, L. (1984) Czy diabel może być zbawiony i 27 innych kazan. (Can the devil be saved? And 27 other sermons) Londyn: Aneks.

Kostera, M. (1995) The modern crusade: Missionaries of management come to Eastern Europe. *Management Learning* 26(3): 331–52.

Kostera, M. and Koźmiński, A.K. (1995) Four theaters: Norms and values in management. *Polish Sociological Review* 3(111): 263–74.

Kostera, M. and Koźmiński, A.K. (2001) Four theaters: Moral discourses in Polish management. *Management Learning* 32(3): 321–44.

Koźmiński, A.K. (1999) Kultura menedżerska (Managerial culture). In: J. Kozielecki (ed.), *Humanistyka przełomu wieków (Humanities at the Turn of Century)*: 317–35. Warszawa: Żak.

Levi Strauss, C. (1978) *Myth and Meaning.* New York: Schocken Books.

Lewis-Williams, D. (2002) *The Mind in the Cave.* London: Thames & Hudson.

MacIntyre, A.C. (1984) *After Virtue: A Study in Moral Theory.* Notre Dame, IN: Notre Dame University Press.

Magretta, J. (1997) Growth through global sustainability: An interview with Monsanto's CEO, Robert B. Shapiro. *Harvard Business Review* January–February: 79–88.

Magretta, J. (1998a) The power of virtual integration: An interview with Dell Computer's Michael Dell. *Harvard Business Review* March–April: 73–84.

Magretta, J. (1998b) Governing the family-owned enterprise: An interview with Finland's Krister Ahlström. *Harvard Business Review* January–February: 113–23.

Mangham, I.L. (1987) Introduction: Offending the audience. In: I.L. Mangham (ed.), *Organization Analysis and Development: A Social Construction of Organizational Behavior.* Chichester: Wiley and Sons.

Mangham, I.L. (1998) Emotional discourse in organizations. In: D. Grant, T. Keenoy, C. Oswick (eds.), *Discourse and Organization.* London: Sage.

Mangham, I.L. and Overington, M.A. (1987) *Organizations as Theater: Social Psychology and Dramatic Performance*. Chichester: Wiley.

Martin, J. (1982) Stories and scripts in organizational settings. In A. Hastorf and A. Isen (eds.), *Cognitive and Social Psychology*: 255–305. London: Routledge.

Maruca, R.F. (1994) The right way to go global: An interview with Whirlpool CEO David Whitwam. *Harvard Business Review* March–April: 135–45.

McCormick, J. and Stone, N. (1990) From national champion to global competitor: An interview with Thomson's Alain Gomez. *Harvard Business Review* May–June: 127–35.

Mills, C.W. (1956) *The Power Elite*. Oxford: Oxford University Press.

Mirvis, P.H., Ayas, K. and Roth, G. (2003) *To the Desert and Back: The Story of the Most Dramatic Business Transformation on Record*. San Francisco: Jossey-Bass.

Moreno, A. (1970) *Jung, Gods and Modern Man*. London: Sheldon.

Moss Kanter, E. (1991) Championing change: An interview with Bell Atlantic's CEO Raymond Smith. *Harvard Business Review* January–February: 119–30.

Naumann, F.M. (1999) *Marcel Duchamp: The Art of Making Art in the Age of Mechanical Reproduction*. Ghent, Amsterdam: Ludion Press (distributed in the USA by Harry N. Abrams Publishers, New York).

Nichols, N.A. (1992) Profits with a purpose: An interview with Tom Chapman. *Harvard Business Review* November–December: 87–95.

Nichols, N.A. (1993) From complacency to competitiveness: An interview with Vitro's Ernesto Martens. *Harvard Business Review* September–October: 163–71.

Nichols, N.A. (1994) Medicine, management, and mergers: An interview with Merck's P. Roy Vagelos. *Harvard Business Review* November–December: 105–14.

Niebuhr, H.R. (1951) *Christ and Culture*. New York: Harper.

Osinski, Z. (1998) *Jerzy Grotowski: Zródla, inspiracje, konteksty (Jerzy Grotowski: Sources, inspirations, contexts)* Gdansk: Slowo-Obraz-Terytoria.

Peters, T. (1989) *Thriving on Chaos*. London: Macmillan.

Peters, T. and Waterman, R. (1982) *In Search of Excellence*. New York: Harper & Row.

Pine, B.J. and Gilmore, J.H. (1999) *The Experience Economy*. Cambridge, MA: Harvard Business School Press.

Prokesch, S.E. (1993) Mastering chaos at the high-tech frontier: An interview with Silicon Graphic's Ed McCracken. *Harvard Business Review* November–December: 135–44.

Prokesch, S.E. (1995) Competing on customer service: An interview with British Airway's Sir Colin Marshall. *Harvard Business Review* November–December: 101–12.

Prokesch, S.E. (1997) Unleashing the power of learning: An interview with British Petroleum's John Browne. *Harvard Business Review* September–October: 147–68.

Rayner, B. (1992) Trial-by-fire transformation: An interview with Globe Metallurgical's Arden C. Sims. *Harvard Business Review* May–June: 117–29.

Schmitt, B. and Simonson, A. (1997) *Marketing Aesthetics: The Strategic Management of Brands, Identity and Image*. New York: Free Press.

Schütz, A. (1982) *Life Forms and Meaning Structure*. London: Routledge and Kegan Paul.

Shenhav, Y. (1999) *Manufacturing Rationality: The Engineering Foundations of the Managerial Revolution*. Oxford: Oxford University Press.

Sievers, B. (1994) *Work, Death, and Life Itself: Essays on Management and Organization*. Berlin-New York: Walter de Gruyter.

Smith, A. (1937) *An Inquiry into the Nature and Causes of the Wealth of Nations*. New York: Modern Library (originally published in 1776).

Stone, N. (1992) Building corporate character: An interview with Stride Rite Chairman Arnold Hiatt. *Harvard Business Review* March–April: 95–104.

Strati, A. (1992) Aesthetic understanding of organizational life. *The Academy of Management Review* 17(3): 568–81.

Strati, A. (1999) *Organization and Aesthetics*. London: Sage.

Strenski, I. (1992) *Malinowski and the Work of Myth*. Princeton: Princeton University Press.

Taylor, W. (1990) The business of innovation: An interview with Paul Cook. *Harvard Business Review* March–April: 97–106.

Taylor, W. (1991) The logic of global business: An interview with ABB's Percy Barnevik. *Harvard Business Review* March–April: 91–105.

Taylor, W. (1993) Message and muscle: An interview with Swatch Titan Nicolas Hayek. *Harvard Business Review* March–April: 99–110.

Teal, T. (1991) Service comes first: An interview with USAA's Robert F. McDermott. *Harvard Business Review* September–October: 117–27.

Tichy, N.M. and Charan, R. (1990) Citicorp faces the world: An interview with John Reed. *Harvard Business Review* November–December: 135–44.

Tichy, N.M. and Charan, R. (1995) The CEO as coach: An interview with AlliedSignal's Lawrence A. Bossidy. *Harvard Business Review* March–April: 69–78.

Van Dijk, T.A. (1975) Action, action description, and narrative. *New Literary History* 6: 275–94.

Watson, T. (1994) *In Search of Management*. London: Routledge.

Webber, A.M. (1990) Consensus, continuity, and common sense: An interview with Compaq's Rod Canion. *Harvard Business Review* July–August: 115–22.

Webber, A.M. (1992) Japanese–style entrepreneurship: An interview with Softbank's CEO, Masayoshi Son. *Harvard Business Review* January–February: 93–103.

Weber, M. (1968/78) *Economy and Society* (edited by G. Roth and C. Wittich). Berkeley, CA: University of California Press.

White, D.A. (1996) 'It's working beautifully!' Philosophical reflections on aesthetics and organization theory. *Organization* 3: 195–208.

Willigan, G.E. (1992) High-performance marketing: An interview with Nike's Phil Knight. *Harvard Business Review* July–August: 91–100.

## Additional Reading and Resources

### *The aesthetics of management and managerial culture*

Furusten, S. (1995) *The Managerial Discourse: A Study of the Creation and Diffusion of Popular Management Knowledge*. Uppsala: Uppsala University.

Gagliardi, P. (1990) Artifacts as pathways and remains of organizational life. In P. Gagliardi (ed.), *Symbols and Artifacts: Views of the Corporate Landscape*: 3–38. New York: Aldine de Gruyter.

Linstead, S. and Hopfl, H. (eds.) (1999) *The Aesthetics of Organization*. London: Sage.

Sandelands, L.E., and Buckner, G.C. (1989) Of art and work: Aesthetic experience and the psychology of work feelings. *Research in Organizational Behavior* 11: 105–31.

Schein, E.H. (1992) *Organizational culture and leadership*, 2nd edn. San Francisco: Jossey-Bass.

## Storytelling

Czarniawska, B. (1997) *Narrating the Organization*. Chicago: University of Chicago.

Martin, J., Feldman, M., Hatch, M.J. and Sitkin, S. (1983) The uniqueness paradox in organizational stories. *Administrative Science Quarterly* 28: 438–53.

Polkinghorne, D. (1988) *Narrative Knowing and the Human Sciences*. Albany, NY: SUNY.

In addition to readings mentioned above and in the references for Chapter 2, the following films are recommended to aid the development of storytelling skills. They are not simply cinematic stories, which all films are, but they are films that are fundamentally *about* storytelling and/or storytellers or that show storytellers telling their stories:

*The Big Fish* – the story of a storyteller told by his son, brings up the issue of truth versus fiction in storytelling in an appreciative way.

*The Usual Suspects* – depicts the spinning of a tall tale by a criminal to his captor, brings up the issue of truth versus fiction in storytelling in a cautionary way.

*The Kiss of the Spider Woman* – two political prisoners use storytelling to while away their time in captivity.

*Smoke* – the final scene in this film depicts a story being told ("Auggie's Story") and shows both storyteller and listener. Over the final credits of the movie, the story is retold in a cinematic way (through pictures) rather than as face-to-face communication; the contrast makes the differences in form and effect clear.

## Drama and theatre

Burns E. (1972) *Theatricality: A Study of Convention in the Theater and in a Social Life*. London: Cox & Wyman.

Turner, V. (1982) *From Ritual to Theater: The Human Seriousness of Play*. New York: Performing Arts Journal Publication.

## Myth

Eliade, M. (1963) *Myth and Reality*. New York: Harper and Row.

Eliade, M. (1991) *Images and Symbols: Studies in Religious Symbolism*. Princeton: Princeton University Press.

Furusten, S. (1992) *Management Books – Guardians of the Myth of Leadership*. Uppsala: Uppsala University.

Kirby, M. (1995) Happenings. In M.R. Sanford (ed.), *Happenings and Other Acts*: 2–28. London, New York: Routledge.

Lefkowitz, M. (2003) *Greek Gods, Human Lives*. New Haven: Yale University Press.

Schmidt, J. (1992) *Słownik mitologii greckiej i rzymskiej (Dictionary of Greek and Roman Mythology)*. Warszawa: Książnica.

# Index

Note: "n" after a page number indicates the number of a note on that page.